BeachHunter's

FLORIDA GULF BEACHES

ACCESS GUIDE

Finding Your Paradise on Florida's Lower Gulf Coast

An Access Guide to Over 120 Gulf Coast Beaches
From Tarpon Springs to Marco Island.
Includes maps and photographs.

Second Edition

Revised and Updated

David McRee

Inquiries should be directed to David McRee by sending email to: beachhunter@beachhunter.net

Publisher: David B. McRee

All photos taken by the author, unless otherwise credited.

Cover design: Nathan McRee

Although the author has tried to make the information contained in this book as accurate as possible, he accepts no responsibility for any loss, injury or inconvenience sustained by any person using this book. Please use common sense when traveling and exploring Florida's beaches and islands.

ISBN-13: 978-1489589989

ISBN-10: 1489589988

This book is the map, not the territory. To really know the beauty of the beaches you must come and discover it for yourself. Maps become obsolete the moment after they are drawn; a tree falls, sand moves, buildings rise. This book reveals what I've discovered. It is only a map to help you make your own discoveries. What you discover will be yours to keep forever.

Since entrance and parking fees change regularly, if those details are important to you, check with the appropriate website, such as the Florida State Park's web site, or individual county or city web sites, which will contain up-to-date parking and entrance fee information for the various beaches.

Visit www.BeachHunter.net/updates to check for updates and error corrections.

Front cover photos: *Main photo, Longboat key; small photos left to right, Venice Pier, Little Gasparilla, Pass-a-Grille sunset, Naples Beach from the pier.*

Back cover photos: T*op to bottom, Anna Maria Island; Clearwater Beach; Caspersen Beach; St. Pete Beach; shells on Turner's Beach, Captiva; author with his kayak on Shell Key.*

A Few Words from the Author 1

Using This Book 2

The Sandy Beaches of the Gulf Coast 4

Gulf of Mexico Average Water Temperatures 5

Weather and Air Temperatures on the Lower Gulf Coast 5

BeachHunter's Recommended Beaches 8

South of Tampa Bay 8

Tampa Bay Area and North 8

Snorkeling 9

Shelling 9

People-Watching 10

Birding 10

Beach Camping 10

Nudism 10

Gay Beaches 11

Dog Friendly Beaches 11

Island Fishing Piers 12

Rock Jetties 12

Surfing on the Gulf Coast Peninsula 13

Top Surfing Spots 14

Surfing Near a Pier or Jetty 15

Wetsuits 15

Sharks 15

ADA Access 16

Beach Erosion and Accretion 18

Encountering Wildlife at the Beach 21

Dolphins 21

Manatees 21

Sea Turtles 21

Shorebirds 22

Beaches North of Tampa Bay 25

Anclote Key Preserve State Park 27

1: Anclote Key Beaches 28

Fred Howard Park 32

2: Fred Howard Park Beach 33

Sunset Beach Park 35

3: Sunset Beach Park Beaches 36

Honeymoon Island State Park 39

4: Causeway Beaches (free access) 41

5: Main Beach on Honeymoon Island 41

6: Dog Beach 42

7: Sand Spit Beach on Honeymoon Island 42

Caladesi Island 44

8: Caladesi Island State Park Beach 45

Clearwater Beach 48

9: Clearwater Beach and Pier 60 Fishing Pier 51

10: Mandalay Park 53

11: Kendall Street Access 54

12: Other Accesses 54

Sand Key 56

13: Sand Key Park Beaches 57

14: Bay Park on Sand Key 59

Belleair Beach and Belleair Shore 61

15: Belleair Beach Marina 62

16: Morgan Park 62

Indian Rocks Beach 63

17: Indian Rocks Beach Street-End Accesses 65

18: Indian Rocks Nature Preserve 66

19: Indian Rocks Beach Access (A Pinellas County Park) 66

Indian Shores 68

20: Tiki Gardens Access (A Pinellas County Park) 69

21: 190th Avenue Beach Access 70

22: 186th Avenue Beach Access 70

Redington Shores 71

23: Redington Shores Public Access 72

24: 178th Avenue Lot 73

25: The Long Pier 73

North Redington Beach 75

26: Public Walkways to Beach 76

Redington Beach 77

Madeira Beach 78

27: Archibald Memorial Beach Park 79

28: Madeira Beach Parking and Access (Pinellas County Park) 80

29: Tom and Kitty Stuart Park 80

30: Madeira Beach Street-End Accesses 81

31: John's Pass Beach 81

Treasure Island 83

32: Snowy Egret Parking Lot at Sunshine Beach 86

33: City of St. Pete Municipal Beach at Treasure Island 87

34: Treasure Island Beach Access (Pinellas County Park) 88

35: Sandpiper Parking Lot 90

36: Brown Pelican Parking Lot (Sunset Beach) 90

37: Ring-Billed Gull Parking Lot (Sunset Beach) 90

38: Tern Parking Lot Treasure Island Beach Center (Sunset Beach) 91

St. Pete Beach 93

39: Upham Beach 94

40: 51st Avenue Access 96

41: St. Pete Municipal Beach 96

42: Pass-A-Grille Beach 96

Shell Key Preserve 99

43: Shell Key Preserve 100

Fort Desoto County Park 102

44: East Beach 103

45: Bay Pier Beach and Dog Beach 105

46: Gulf Pier to North Beach 106

47: North Beach 107

Egmont Key State Park 109

48: Egmont Key Beaches 110

Skyway Bridge 112

49: Skyway Causeway Beaches 112

Beaches South of Tampa Bay 115

Anna Maria Island 117

50: Passage Key 119

51: Anna Maria Beach 121

52: Bayfront Park 122

53: Holmes Beach 123

54: Manatee County Public Beach 124

55: Palma Sola Causeway 124

City of Bradenton Beach 125

56: Cortez Beach 125

57: Coquina Beach 127

58: Leffis Key at Coquina Baywalk 128

Longboat Key 130

59: Whitney Beach and Beer Can Island (Greer Island) 132

60: Other Longboat Key Beaches 135

Lido Key 138

61: North Lido Beach 139

62: Lido Public Beach 141

63: Ted Sperling Park at South Lido Beach 142

Siesta Key 144

64: North Shell Road Access (Access #1) 147

Numbered Siesta Key Beach Accesses 147

65: Siesta Public Beach 149

66: Crescent Beach and Point-of-Rocks 151

67: Turtle Beach 152

Casey Key 155

68: Nokomis Beach 158

69: North Jetty Park 159

Venice 161

70: Venice Municipal Beach 162

71: South Jetty (Humphris Park) 164

72: Service Club Park 165

73: Venice Fishing Pier / Brohard Park 166

74: Maxine Barritt Park 167

75: Paw Park at Brohard Beach 167

76: South Brohard Park 168

77: Caspersen Beach Park 168

Manasota Key 172

78: Manasota Beach Park 174

79: Blind Pass Beach 177

80: Englewood Beach/ Chadwick Park 178

81: Stump Pass Beach State Park 179

Palm Island Archipelago 182

Knight Island (aka Palm Island) 184

82: Knight Island Beach Access Points 185

Thornton Key 186

Don Pedro Island 186

83: Don Pedro Island Beach Access 187

84: Don Pedro Island State Park 188

85: Little Gasparilla Island 189

Gasparilla Island 191

86: Street End Beach Parking 194

87: #1 Sandspur Beach, Gasparilla Island State Park 196

88: #2 Sea grape Parking Area, Gasparilla Island State Park 197

89: #3 Seawall Parking Area, Gasparilla Island State Park 197

90: Lighthouse Beach Park, Gasparilla Island State Park 198

La Costa Island 200

91: Beaches of La Costa Island 203

Sanibel and Captiva Islands 206

92: Sanibel Causeway Beaches 208

93: Lighthouse Park 210

94: Algiers Beach / Gulfside City Park 211

95: Tarpon Bay Road Access 211

96: Bowman's Beach 212

97: Turner's Beach and Blind Pass Beach 214

98: Captiva Island 215

Fort Myers Beach 217

99: Lynn Hall Memorial Park and Pelican Pier 220

100: Crescent Beach Family Park 221

101: Bowditch Point Park 221

102: Fort Myers Beach Accesses 223

103: Newton Park 225

104: Lover's Key State Park 225

105: Bonita Beach Dog Park (Lover's Key) 227

106: Big Hickory Island Preserve 227

107: Bunche Beach 229

Bonita Beach 231

108: Little Hickory Island Beach Park 232

109: Bonita Beach Accesses 233

110: Bonita Beach Park and Lely Barefoot Beach 234

111: Barefoot Beach Preserve (County Park) 235

Naples 237

112: Vanderbilt Beach County Access on Bluebill Avenue 238

113: Delnor Wiggins Pass State Park 240

114: Vanderbilt Beach County Park 241

115: Clam Pass County Park and Boardwalk 241

116: Gulfshore Boulevard Beach Access 244

117: Naples Municipal Beach (Park Shore area) 245

118: Lowdermilk Park Public Beach 245

119: Naples Municipal Beach (South of Lowdermilk Park) 246

Marco Island 248

120: Tigertail Park 251

121: South Marco Beach (Point Marco) 252

Beach Survival Tips 254

Red Tide 254

Water Quality 255

Strong Currents 255

Strong surf 256

Lightning 256

Sting Rays 256

Sharks 257

Sunburn and dehydration 258

Insects 259

Alcohol 259

Crime and personal safety 259

Jellyfish 260

Falling Coconuts (I swear I'm NOT making this up!) 260

Sea Lice 261

Quick Reference Guide 262

Very Quiet Beaches 262

Quiet Beaches 263

Residential Beaches 264

Congested / Public / Developed 265

Resort / Condominium Areas 266

Dog Beaches 267

The Author & the Book 268

Works Cited 269

A Few Words from the Author

Thank you for purchasing my book, now in its second edition. I believe it will provide you with accurate and useful information that you cannot get from other books currently on the market. This book will provide you with plenty of specific information about the beaches on the west coast of Florida, including many beaches that you would not otherwise know about. Our beaches have a lot to offer. I should know; I've been to them all. Not only are the beaches of Florida beautiful, they will provide you with a chance to explore and discover fascinating history, geography, extremely varied plant and animal life, and will give you the opportunity to visit places where nature is still in control. You will meet many interesting people because the Florida beaches and islands attract people from all over the world searching for a more relaxed and enjoyable lifestyle where the water is still clean enough to swim in, the weather is warm, and the sunsets and sunrises make everyone stop what they are doing to watch and contemplate.

All the beach communities are different. There is at least one you will visit that you will never be able to forget. I was born in Bradenton, Florida and have lived on the Florida west coast all my life, yet there are many beaches I'd never heard about, so I set out to discover them all. When my ancestors first came to Florida in the late 1800's, Florida was a much different place. From the time I was born, in the 1960's, the changes came more rapidly. Now there are some islands where you can hardly get to the beach for all the condominiums and commercial enterprises. But if you know where to go there is still plenty of natural beauty and solitude. So if you are looking for your special beach, this book is a really good place to start.

I take great pride in being an independent writer and publisher. Writers like me have complete control over their work thanks to computers and ever-improving print technology. We take credit for our successes and we take the blame for our mistakes and failures. My goal in writing this book is to provide useful information to people who want to know about the beaches of southwest and west central Florida. I believe this book is unique in what it offers. I hope it helps guide you on your next beach adventure.

I welcome your comments. Contact me by email at beachhunter@beachhunter.net. Please visit me on the web at BeachHunter.net for more information and to see photos of the beautiful beaches in this book, or visit my blog at BlogTheBeach.com.

Happy Beachhunting!

Using This Book

I've written this book for both visitors from other states or countries and for Florida residents who probably are not aware of the many different beaches along the lower west coast of Florida. It is quite time consuming to explore this area of the state, especially for people who work and have to travel on the weekends, or who have limited vacation time. Traffic can be very slow on the weekends and the best strategy for going to the beach is to get there before 10 am, find a parking spot, and stay put. Driving around in bumper to bumper traffic hunting for a parking spot is no fun, especially with a car full of kids. So, I've done most of the legwork for you.

I was born on the lower west coast of Florida and I've lived here all my life. In the course of writing this book I've discovered lots of beautiful spots I never knew existed. I've tried to write enough about each beach to help you decide if it's someplace you'd like to visit. I tell you how to get there (some of the best beaches are not indicated on any maps), where to park, and what the beach is like compared to other beaches. The beaches are numbered so the descriptions correspond to the numbered beaches on the maps and in the table of contents. A few of the beaches covered by this book are accessible only by boat or on foot.

You won't find much specific information about hotels, restaurants, or attractions in this book. The bookstores are already stocked full of those travel guides, as is the internet. This is a guide to the beaches. I decided to write about the beaches in this area because back in 1996, I couldn't find an accurate, detailed locator guide. Actually, I did find one, but it was so hopelessly out of date that it was almost useless. Beaches do change. So here it is, now revised and expanded in 2013, after many miles driven, many bridges crossed, and many wonderful days spent on the best beaches in the state.

I have sketched maps to go along with my descriptions of the beaches. These maps are only to give you an idea about which part of the coast various beaches are located. These maps are not drawn to scale and are not intended to be used for navigation. Please buy local street maps to refer to, or better yet, use a GPS and/or Google Maps. By using this book and printed or electronic street maps you should have no difficulty in finding any of the beaches described here. For your convenience, I have included latitude and longitude coordinates for each access in hemisphere decimal format. These coordinates came from Google Maps. You can type the coordinates into the Google Maps search bar and it will mark the location on the map. (Example: 28.1690, -82.8487). When doing so, be sure to type the minus sign in front of the longitude or you will end up in the wrong part of the world. Theoretically, you should be able to simply type those coordinates into your GPS to aid you in navigation, but accuracy is not guaranteed across devices. Please use common sense when using your GPS. Don't rely totally on it. I've made every effort to be as accurate as possible, but errors and typos happen and technology isn't perfect.

Most of the beaches on the Gulf coast are on "barrier islands." These are sandy islands that lie a short distance from the mainland and are reached by bridges which cross the shallow bays. The islands are generally elongated, narrow, and are in a north-south orientation. Narrow passes between the islands allow water to flow between the bays and the Gulf. All the islands have shallow, calm waters and clean sandy shores.

Because most Florida beaches are pure sand, they are subject to significant variation in width, depending on the weather and water currents. One strong winter cold front can remove 50 feet of beach overnight. Most beaches are renourished every few years to replace the sand that has been carried away by nature. Huge barges with noisy pumps and thousands of feet of huge rusty steel pipes pull sand from offshore onto the beach. Sometimes there is a lot of broken shell in this sand, so a natural sand beach is much nicer, but there are few of those remaining.

The beach parking situation is constantly changing. Streets where parking was once allowed, a few weeks later may no longer be open for beach parking. Hourly parking rates go up over time. As Florida's population increases, beach access will become more difficult, more expensive, and rules will become more and more restrictive in an effort to minimize the effects of increased visitors on an already largely overpopulated area. Fortunately there are still beaches in southwest Florida where access is easy, free, and uncrowded. This book tells you all about them.

The Sandy Beaches of the Gulf Coast

Each island, each beach in Florida has its own personality, given to it by its proximity to towns, its human population, its degree of development, its vegetation, its orientation to the prevailing winds and currents, and by the type of sand on its shores. There are basically three types of sand you will find on the lower Gulf coast: white sand, brown sand, and black sand.

The purest white quartz sand is found from the Pinellas County Beaches (St. Pete/Clearwater) south to about mid-Siesta Key, and also on Sanibel, Captiva, Cayo Costa, Fort Myers Beach and Marco Island. This is quartz sand that has washed down from the Appalachian Mountains. In many places the sand is almost pure white, like sugar. It is so clean that higher up on the beach where the sand is dry it sometimes squeaks when you walk on it, and it feels wonderful on bare feet. Since it is so white, it reflects the sun and doesn't get too hot even in midsummer. Also, since the grains are so fine, it packs hard near the water's edge and makes walking easy. In some places it is firm enough to ride a bike on. How does it compare to the pure white beaches of the Florida Panhandle? It is very similar. The main difference is that the quartz sand grains on the panhandle beaches are larger grains, giving a coarser feel to the sand.

Brown sand is found from the Turtle Beach area of Siesta Key to Casey Key. Grab a handful of this coarse sand and you'll find that there is a high content of polished, crushed shell mixed with the quartz crystals. This sand can be quite difficult to walk on down by the water's edge where it is wet. Your feet sink deeply into the sand and your calves will get a workout. Forget riding your bike on this sand.

Black or gray sand is found on the beaches of Venice, Englewood, and Palm Island, Florida. It is not black like the volcanic beaches of Hawaii, but the sand appears almost black in some spots because of all the dark fossilized material in it. Offshore from the Venice beaches are large fossil deposits, which constantly contribute their dark material to the beach. As you will read in the chapter on the beaches of Venice, the most popular fossil found here is the shark tooth. Though the sand on these beaches is not uniformly dark—some areas are a dark gray—much lighter colored sand may be placed over the gray or black sand during beach renourishment projects. This can make the shark teeth harder to find.

The three types of sand are not found exclusively at the beaches I have listed above. These are just the best representative beaches that come to mind. You will find the sand slightly different on each island. Important: Any sand that is not pure white gets very hot under the summer sun and will badly burn your feet. Always have shoes or sturdy sandals with you on the beach! Cheap flip-flops may not be good enough.

Gulf of Mexico Average Water Temperatures

Location	Jan	Feb	Mch	Apr	May	Jun	Jul	Aug	Sep	Oct	Nov	Dec
Key West	69	70	75	78	82	85	87	87	86	82	76	72
Naples	66	66	71	77	82	86	87	87	86	81	73	68
St. Petersburg	62	64	68	74	80	84	86	86	84	78	70	64
Cedar Key	58	60	66	73	80	84	86	86	83	76	66	60
Pensacola	56	58	63	71	78	84	85	86	82	74	65	58

Note: The above temperatures are "average" water temperatures as shown on the National Oceanic Data Center's website.

The temperatures you will encounter while swimming at the beach are often a few degrees warmer in the summer and a few degrees colder in the winter than the temperatures measured by the offshore buoys. This is because the shallow near-shore waters warm up and cool off more quickly than the deeper waters where the NODC's buoy data collection stations are located.

Weather and Air Temperatures on the Lower Gulf Coast

The "average" air temperatures one normally sees attributed to Florida are very misleading because the air temperature varies so much, so I won't list air temperature averages here. Generally, the further south along the Florida Gulf coast you go during the winter, the warmer the air temperature usually is. For instance, a cold day might bring a high of 51 degrees to St. Petersburg beaches, but a high of 61 degrees on Marco Island. Generally, the following information holds true on the lower Gulf coast of Florida:

December, January, February

Cool days and cooler nights. Daytime highs may range from 50 degrees Fahrenheit on a cold day, to the lower 70's on a warm day. Nighttime temperatures may dip into the upper 30's to low 40's along the beaches in the Tampa Bay area during the cold snaps, but generally upper 50's is more common. Further south, in the Naples/Marco Island area, the temperatures are usually 5 to 10 degrees warmer. Cold winds from the north can make an otherwise sunny 60 degree day seem a lot colder when you are exposed out on the beach. Warmer days during these months sometimes cause foggy conditions on the beach. It can seem like a beautiful beach day when you get in your car on the mainland, but when you arrive at the beach you may find it enveloped in a dreary fog. But as my northern friends often remind me, it's still better than a foot of snow.

March, April, May

The cold fronts are a lot less frequent beginning in March. By May they are weak and have the welcome effect of removing the humidity and creating a nice breeze for a few days. In my opinion, May is one of the most beautiful months to be in Florida. The water is at its clearest and has warmed up to a reasonable temperature somewhere above the 80 degree mark. By early April the daytime air temperatures are hitting the low 80's, while the nights dip comfortably into the low 70's. Spring bird migration brings plenty of bird species through the state, stopping to replenish their energy before continuing north to their nesting grounds. May begins sea turtle nesting season on our Gulf beaches. In April and May, manatees start to appear along the Gulf beaches as the water temperature increases.

June, July, August, September

During these months it's just dreadfully hot. Fortunately, the Gulf has a cooling effect during the day and keeps the beaches 4 or 5 degrees cooler than the cities and inland areas. You can count on 88 to 90 degrees during the heat of the day on the beach, while it may be 92 to 98 degrees in inland cities like Orlando. It is not unusual to experience a dead calm, especially during the morning hours, with the afternoons often enjoying a light sea breeze that often begins to stir around noon. At some point during the summer, usually by the 4th of July, the intense afternoon thunderstorms begin sweeping in from the east most every afternoon, causing daily lightning and heavy rains. Summer weather typically moves from east to west across the state. The afternoon storms can often cut short your day at the beach.

Sometimes the weather patterns change and the weather moves west to east for a week or so, causing morning showers along the coast, moving inland by noon. This weather pattern usually makes for a nice breezy afternoon on the beach and enough small surf for the kids to enjoy.

Hurricane season officially begins in June and continues through November. Generally, the greatest concern in Florida is during August, September, and perhaps early October. I've lived on the west coast of Florida my entire life and few are the times I felt endangered by a hurricane. Many people from the northern states or from other countries ask how we can feel safe living here with the fear of hurricanes. The answer is that most of us have little or no concern about hurricanes. If you live on the water, yes there is an elevated level of concern, and hurricane Charley showed us that even inland communities can be devastated by a really powerful storm. But very few hurricanes ever make a direct hit on the state. And when they do, we have several days warning so there is enough time to leave the state if you are really concerned. What we don't have to worry about in Florida are flash floods, earthquakes, killer tornadoes, ice storms or blizzards. The vast majority of hurricane threats turn out to be false alarms. If I were scheduling a trip to Florida I would be more likely to avoid August and September because of the heavy daily rains and lightning storms and the oppressive heat, rather than because of the danger of getting hit with a hurricane. Personally, I happen to like the rain, lightning, and heat, but then I'm not just here for a week or two trying to find the best weather possible. And, I have an air-conditioned house.

October, November, December

By October, the daily rains are over, the hurricane danger is diminished, and the scorching Florida sun has started to ease off a bit as it drops lower in the southern sky. October is my other favorite month in Florida (besides May). The daytime temperatures in October are still often in the upper 80's, but the humidity isn't as bad and the lightning is no longer such a threat. By November the cold fronts start coming through cooling things down a bit for a few days at a time, but generally there are still plenty of good beach days. December often sees some pretty chilly, windy weather and it can be harder to find a nice beach day, although in the most southern areas like Marco and Naples you are more likely to be laying out on the beach on a December day. Fall bird migration is in full swing during October, and Florida's islands and beaches are excellent places to spot some of our fall migrants as they stop to rest and feed.

That's a good summary of what you can expect, but keep in mind that it varies from year to year. I've seen frost in October, and I've enjoyed beautiful 82 degree days at the beach in December, January, and February. You just never know.

BeachHunter's Recommended Beaches

It's tough to recommend a single "best" beach, but I can pick out the beaches that keep calling me back again and again, year after year.

South of Tampa Bay

First, looking at the beaches south of Tampa Bay, without a doubt, **Siesta Key Public** Beach in Sarasota County is one of my all-time favorites. Yes it gets really crowded, and yes, parking can be difficult, but it is a very large beach. The sand is the finest, whitest sugar sand you will find anywhere and it slopes gently into clear, calm, very shallow waters. You can hang out with the crowd or walk up the beach and have plenty of space for yourself. It is the best beach for walking, running, bike riding, and just about anything else. **Caspersen Beach Park** in Venice is another favorite. It is a fairly quiet beach with a very natural shoreline. The dark sand beach and the native cabbage palms lining the shore as far south as the eye can see are the real Florida. Caspersen Beach has easy access, good parking, clean restrooms and a beautiful boardwalk along part of the beach. It's great for shelling, finding shark teeth, beachcombing in general, fishing, and when the water is calm and clear, snorkeling. On Sanibel Island **Bowman's Beach** is my favorite. Long and quiet with a trail through the pines along the beach, you can really relax here. **Naples Beach** is another favorite. With its lush graceful coconut palms and tropical beach landscape, Naples has the most tropical-looking beach on the Florida west coast. **Sand Dollar Island at Tigertail Beach** on Marco Island has a special charm that comes with being the southernmost significant stretch of beach on the west coast. It is one of the quietest beaches anywhere; no jets flying overhead; few noisy boats; just seabirds, a gentle breeze, and the sound of the warm tranquil Gulf waters lapping the flat sandy shoreline. Walk out on Sand Dollar Island on a weekday and you may find yourself alone without another person in sight. You'll feel like Robinson Crusoe.

Tampa Bay Area and North

My beach recommendations in the Tampa Bay area and northward begin with **Fort Desoto County Park,** a large island park in Tampa Bay. The beach between the Gulf pier and North Beach is huge and is part of the nature preserve. Even though it is enjoyed by many people, especially on the weekends, this beach maintains its feeling of tranquility and isolation from the city of St. Petersburg. To the north of Fort Desoto Park, **Pass-A-Grille Beach** is a long stretch of clean white beach with plenty of (metered) parking and plenty of room to find your spot. The water is shallow and great for swimming and the beach is great for walking a long distance. This is a beach you can play on all night if you like. Have dinner and drinks at one of the very good restaurants in this very small beach town and then take a sunset stroll. Further north, **Indian Rocks Beach** is a fine beach town without a lot of high-rise condominiums and has street-end beach accesses (most lack restroom facilities). Parking is free and access is easy to a fine residential neighborhood beach that does not suffer from heavy crowds. The County operated park at 17th Avenue is also a great beach if you want restroom facilities, but parking is not free. **Caladesi Island** off the coast of Dunedin is perhaps the finest beach in Pinellas County. It's a little trouble to get to; you have to drive to Honeymoon Island and pay for a ferry to take you on a 20 minute boat ride to Caladesi. From there you are on foot, and it is a large island park. But it is real Florida, much as the first settlers saw it, and the beach is first class, with no buildings or development of any kind. It is a special place. For a full-service beach, **Clearwater Beach's Pier 60** is hard to beat.

Snorkeling

You can snorkel off most any beach in Florida, but the southwest coast of Florida tends to have a fairly plain white sandy bottom. There's not a lot to look at, even when the water is clear. Snorkeling around rocks is often the most interesting. The water is usually at its clearest during the months of April, May, and June, but can be clear during other times of the year when we have several weeks of calm, dry weather. Wind and rain can reduce visibility underwater and long hours of sunlight during the summer can create high concentrations of plankton and algae in the water which reduces visibility. When snorkeling off the beach, the most interesting areas to concentrate on are the sandbar, which may have lots of sand dollars or conchs, and the plunge-step, which is that slight drop-off close to the beach. That's where you'll find the most shells, fossils, and on some beaches, shark teeth.

My favorite beach for snorkeling is **Crescent Beach** on Siesta Key. With its beautiful clear shallow water, and large, flat, submerged limestone rocks, Crescent beach attracts plenty of fish and creates a safe and inviting spot for excellent snorkeling for children and adults. **Caspersen Beach** has five rock reefs near the beach which make interesting snorkeling when the water is calm and clear. If you'd like to explore a shipwreck, **Bradenton Beach** has a 200 foot long molasses barge called the Regina that sank in the 1940's about 150 feet off the beach. It's in about 20 feet of water.

Shelling

The best beaches for **shelling** are generally found on **Sanibel Island**. The Blind Pass area between Sanibel and Captiva is particularly good. Be sure to visit the Shell Museum on Sanibel and consider attending the Sanibel Shell Show held in March by the Sanibel-Captiva Shell Club. The north end of **Bonita Beach** (Little Hickory Island) is a good shelling spot. Most beaches have a good selection of shells, particularly during the winter months. **Honeymoon Island** and **Caladesi Island** have some very nice shells to be found. On any island, one of the best places to look for shells is near a jetty. **Venice**, **Casey Key**, and **Manasota Key** are famous for the fossilized **shark teeth** that can be found rather easily on their beaches. Check out the Venice **Shark's Tooth Festival** now held in early April near the Venice Fishing Pier.

People-Watching

For people-watching, of course, go where the youthful crowds are: Clearwater Beach, Lido Beach, Siesta Key Public Beach, Fort Myers Beach, Vanderbilt Beach and the Naples area beaches.

Birding

For birding, Marco Island, Lover's Key, Sanibel Island, Cayo Costa Island, Fort Desoto Park, Caladesi Island, and Honeymoon Island are some of the best locations, any time of year, but especially during spring and fall migration. Spring and summer nesting season brings thousands of shorebirds together in concentrated locations on the beach to lay their eggs. They actually lay their eggs right in the sand. During nesting season, May through August, you may find portions of the beach roped off and marked with signs to keep people from trampling the eggs. Be sure to keep your distance from the nesting areas. If you cause the birds to fly, you are probably too close.

Beach Camping

There is limited camping on the southwestern Florida Gulf beaches. Fort Desoto County Park has an excellent camping facility and is the most easily accessible. Shell Key also permits overnight camping but is only accessible by boat and has no facilities whatsoever. Shell Key has an outstanding Gulf beach with a healthy dune system. It is a very remote beach with no lifeguards or rangers. Parts of the island are off limits as bird nesting areas. Shell Key is "primitive" camping. Cayo Costa State Park, also accessible only by private boat or ferry service, has tent camping and several rustic beach cabins for rent and has restrooms and showers. You will need advanced reservations for camping on Cayo Costa. Turtle Beach on Siesta Key has a small campground, and Ft. Myers Beach has the Red Coconut RV Resort which sits directly on the beach, however calling it "camping" is a stretch.

Nudism

There are no beaches on the lower Gulf Coast where nudism is legal. This doesn't mean it never happens, but it isn't legal. Those few who decide to risk baring it all are generally discreet. They choose a remote beach with few people and they take advantage of tall grasses and other foliage on the upper beach to remain out of view. Keep in mind that many beaches, especially state and county park beaches are routinely patrolled by lifeguards and/or law enforcement personnel riding all-terrain vehicles. If you choose to wear your birthday suit at the beach, be careful.

If you are looking for a specific type of beach experience, check my Quick Reference Guide near the back of the book. There I present a list of beaches classified into the following categories: Very quiet, Quiet, Residential, Congested/Public/Developed, and Resort or Condominium Areas.

Gay Beaches

There are a few beaches on the southwest and central Florida Gulf coast that attract gay visitors in larger numbers. Generally, they are Sunset Beach at the south end of Treasure Island, North Lido Beach in Sarasota, and Caspersen Beach Park in Venice.

Of course gay people are welcome on all Florida beaches, but those are the beaches in the area covered by this book where you'll often see as many or more gay couples on portions of the beach as you will heterosexual individuals and couples.

Dog Friendly Beaches

- Honeymoon Island's Dog Beach
- North Clearwater Beach
- Fort Desoto County Park Dog Beach and Park
- Paws Park at Brohard Park, Venice
- Don Pedro Island, and Little Gasparilla Island (both unofficially)
- Gasparilla Island (outside the state park)
- Sanibel Island
- Fort Myers Beach (Estero Island)
- Bonita Beach Dog Park on Lover's Key

Island Fishing Piers

- Pier 60, Clearwater Beach
- The Long Pier on Redington Beach
- Merry Pier, Pass-a-Grille Beach (Bay side)
- Gulf Pier, Fort Desoto Park
- Bay Pier, Fort Desoto Park
- Skyway Bridge Fishing Pier
- Rod & Reel Pier, Anna Maria (Bay side)
- Anna Maria City Pier (Bay side)
- Bradenton Beach Pier (Bay side)
- Venice Pier
- Sanibel Lighthouse Park (Bay side)
- Pelican Pier, Fort Myers Beach
- Naples Pier

Rock Jetties

The following structures are listed from north to south and are generally suited for fishing. A few rock structures not located at an inlet may be suitable for snorkeling during calm, clear water, as noted in the text of the book.

- Sand Key Park
- Madeira Beach at John's Pass
- Sunshine Beach at north tip of Treasure Island on John's Pass
- Sunset Beach at south tip of Treasure Island on Blind Pass
- Upham Beach at north tip of St. Pete Beach at Blind Pass
- Pass-a-Grille Jetty
- Longboat Pass at south end of Anna Maria, Coquina Beach
- Beer Can Island. Possible concrete or rock jetties or groin construction planned.
- Point-of-Rocks, mid-Siesta Key (not a jetty, but a large outcropping of flat limestone rocks)
- Venice Inlet. Jetties on both sides of the inlet (Casey Key and Venice)
- Caspersen Beach (lots of rocks on and off parts of the beach, but not actually a jetty)
- Captiva Island, north end at Redfish Pass
- Turner's Beach on the south end of Captiva at Blind Pass
- Doctor's Pass has a jetty on both sides of the inlet, Naples Beach
- South Marco Beach (small jetty and breakwater)

Surfing on the Gulf Coast Peninsula

If you are interested in surfing on the southwest Gulf Coast, the best time to come would be January through March, since that is when the cold fronts sweep across the state. Generally the wind picks up from the southwest in advance of the front and kicks up a choppy 2-4 foot swell with cloudy skies, and then as the front passes, the sky clears (usually) and the wind becomes westerly, then northwesterly. The best surf comes when the wind backs around to the northeast, usually the next day, and creates an offshore wind that creates cleaner, steeper-faced swells that are much more enjoyable than the blown-out chop from the day before. But sometimes by the time the wind turns to the northeast, there is not enough swell left to ride. That's surfing on the Gulf coast.

Surfing waves from a distant hurricane on the Florida Gulf coast.

July, August, and September is peak hurricane season. When there is a hurricane, a tropical storm or a strong low-pressure trough in the Gulf, excellent swells may suddenly make an appearance, sometimes for a few hours, sometimes for a few days. These are usually strong high-energy (for the Gulf) waves that are fun to ride. But they are very difficult to predict. So you almost have to keep your surfboard in your car and keep checking the surf several times a day to find the waves. Jobs and school can severely interfere with this approach to wave hunting. If you are serious about finding surf in Florida I would highly recommend a book by Amy Vansant called The Surfer's Guide to Florida. Parking and access information is seriously outdated, but the surf break location info is still relevant and detailed.

For Gulf coast surf info on the web and some outstanding Gulf coast surfing photos and videos, check out www.gulfster.com. For information on the location of specific surf spots on the Florida Gulf Coast, check out www.wannasurf.com. The information is quite good and specific.

Top Surfing Spots

Florida's Gulf of Mexico has a sand bottom. This means that there are very few distinctive surfing breaks. The surf is much the same everywhere. Good surf is more a function of whether the tide is high or low, incoming or outgoing; the wind speed and direction; the direction of the swell, and the orientation of the shoreline.

Longboarding at the Venice jetty.

Nevertheless, the waves are usually better for surfing next to a pier or jetty, or near some underwater feature, such as a sandbar that has a particular shape, however transitory.

Years ago I was not too interested in giving away the better surfing spots. But with today's internet and social media, they are all pretty much well-known and overcrowded and I don't recommend any of them for beginning surfers unless you are accompanied by more experienced friends who can teach you the ropes. Don't feel that you have to go to one of the top surfing spots to have a great surfing experience.

Here are the most consistently good surfing spots:

- Sand Key Park Jetty

- Sunset Beach (Treasure Island)

- Pass-a-Grille Jetty on a south or west swell.

- Anna Maria Island's Beach Street

- Cortez Beach Piers

- Nokomis Beach Jetty (North Jetty, Venice Inlet)

- Venice Beach Jetty (South Jetty, Venice Inlet)

Those are consistently the top spots, and the ones that get crowded first.

Surfing Near a Pier or Jetty

Generally, when the swell direction is from the southwest, the surf will be better on the north side of a jetty. When the swell is from the northwest, you'll look for better waves on the south side of the structure. Some jetties will perform quite well with most any swell direction. You just never know for sure what it's going to be like until you arrive.

An incoming tide will usually help boost the power of a swell. With a small swell, an outgoing and low tide can almost kill the swell, but you might see it pick back up as the next high tide approaches. On the other hand, a high tide might result in a mushy wave that can only be ridden with a longboard, whereas on a low tide it becomes steeper and easier to catch with a short board. Each break and each swell is different.

Wetsuits

My general rule is that when the water temperature dips below 70 degrees, it's time to bring out some type of wetsuit, depending on your personal needs. Above 70 degrees I might prefer to wear a wetsuit vest if the air is cool. The truth is that I've seen people surfing in 60 degree water without any type of wetsuit.

Sharks

Occasionally a surfer on the Gulf coast may see a shark. Once in a great while a surfer may get bumped by a shark in rough murky water. I cannot recall any surfer on the Gulf coast between Tarpon Springs and Marco Island ever being bitten by a shark in my lifetime. Use common sense and the risk is very small.

ADA Access

Getting to the beach can be quite a challenge for people with limitations on their mobility, but most of the beach towns in this book provide a way for physically challenged people to get onto the beach. I am not an expert on the Americans with Disabilities Act. Some beach facilities indicate that they are ADA compliant. Others, which may not technically be in compliance with the Act, may make some effort to accommodate individuals with mobility challenges. I have tried in this book to make general observations about accommodations that exist at each beach. Improvements and upgrades are being put in place regularly.

Beach wheelchair designed for soft sand.

What provisions are typically made for disabled access?

- "Handicap" parking spaces are located close to the beach, near a sidewalk. Most, but not all are paved surfaces.
- A sidewalk or other hard surface provides access to ramps of varying degrees of steepness which lead to restrooms, outdoor rinse-off showers, the snack bar, and ultimately to the sandy beach.
- Some public beaches and parks offer special beach wheelchairs free of charge. These chairs have large balloon tires and are made of strong saltwater-proof materials. Some can be wheeled into the shallow water on calm days. They are not self-propelled so they would require an able person to push the chair across the sand.
- A few beaches provide a special beach access surface, which is a thick, hard mat across the sand to provide some additional help for wheelchairs or strollers to get across the sand. Unfortunately the only mats I've seen so far don't get you anywhere near the water's edge. Look for improvements in the use of these mats in the future.

16

I have tried to make notations in this book regarding beaches that provide special access accommodations and those that provide beach wheelchairs. If you know that you will need special access or assistance, please call ahead and inquire. In most cases, the wheelchairs are in the custody of the lifeguards, the concession, or park rangers. Hours of availability may be limited. Florida state parks are particularly good about making arrangements for providing beach wheelchairs. Just call the park in advance of your visit and let them know of your needs.

The photos above and below illustrate a typical beach ramp for wheelchair/disabled access and the special beach access surface mat on the sandy beach.

Beach Erosion and Accretion

Photo: Storm surge eats away the dune on Pass-a-grille Beach.

A beach is a living thing. Erosion and accretion are natural processes, they are neither good nor bad, except as they affect your preferences. Erosion is when sand leaves the beach and goes somewhere else, making the beach narrower or steeper.

Accretion is when sand arrives at the beach from somewhere else and makes the beach wider. Some beaches are particularly vulnerable to erosion because of their proximity to nearby passes, currents, erosion control structures, or because of interference by humans. Other beaches accrete for the same reasons.

Upham Beach in Pinellas County has one of the most rapidly eroding shorelines in Florida. In contrast, beaches like Anclote Key and Keewaydin Island are actually growing naturally.

The beaches of Florida are monitored by state and local governments, and fresh sand is pumped through a large steel pipe onto the beach from dredges offshore when it is determined that the beach has become eroded to the point where it poses a danger to homes on the beach or when it interferes with tourism. When you go to a particular beach, it may be wide or narrow or somewhere in-between, depending on whether it is eroding or accreting and whether it has recently been artificially renourished.

The main effect you will experience from beach renourishment (other than noticing that you have to walk further to get to the water) relates to the color, feel, and composition of the sand. Renourished beaches are built up by bringing in sand from other submerged locations. Sometimes the sand might come from a nearby tidal delta in a pass. Other times the sand might come from further offshore. The new sand is likely to have broken shell in it, and perhaps finer silts. Unfortunately this new sand has a tendency to become hard-packed on the beach and can sometimes be uncomfortable to walk on with bare feet. In some cases the new sand is very pure and contains no shell. This creates an excellent beach. During renourishment, you'll often see large steel pipes on the beach, like the one pictured in the photo. A sand and water slurry is pumped from offshore through the pipes and is deposited on the beach.

Renourished beaches usually have to be "groomed" with a mechanical rake pulled behind a tractor. You'll often see these "beach rakes" driving up and down the beach. This grooming prevents the new sand from becoming hard packed. I suspect it also helps reduce no-see-um populations.

Photo: This is a mechanical beach rake pulled by a tractor.

Encountering Wildlife at the Beach

Most visitors to Florida's Gulf beaches enjoy looking for birds, dolphins, manatees, and sea turtles. There are a few things you need to know about seeing and interacting with the wildlife on our beaches.

Dolphins

Dolphins can be seen year-round on any beach. Most of the time they are a few hundred feet offshore, but sometimes they come in really close to shore to chase fish. It is exciting to see them work together to catch fish. For a closer look at dolphins it's a good idea to take one of the many near shore dolphin cruises. The boat captains know where to go to find the dolphins, and the dolphins know where to find the boats. They like playing in the boat's wake.

Manatees

Manatees (sea cows) are mainly seen during the warmer months when water temperatures are above 70 degrees. Late spring, summer, and early fall is when you are most likely to see manatees along the Gulf beaches, inlets, and back bays. Sometimes they come into really shallow water during mating season. During the winter months the manatees migrate up rivers to warmer waters found in Florida's springs, or in waters near power plant water discharges. By visiting those places it's easy to see a lot of manatees close-up. Please remember that it is against the law to chase a manatee, or to try to ride it. If the manatee comes to you, it's OK to gently touch it, but you should not pull on their flippers as they are easily damaged. These laws to protect our manatees are taken very seriously and they are strongly enforced. Most of the people in Florida are very protective of the manatees.

Sea Turtles

Sea turtles are not often seen by beach visitors although some of the turtles do live here year round. What most people see are the tracks in the sand left by the female sea turtles during nesting season. These tracks are sometimes referred to as a turtle crawl. From May through July the female turtles come up out of the water, usually at night or very early morning, dig a hole in the sand, lay about 100 eggs, then cover up the hole and crawl back to the water. Sometimes they come out of the water and go back without laying eggs. This is called a "false crawl." From July through October the baby turtles hatch underground and dig their way out, then head for the water. They swim several miles offshore, nonstop, where they hide in the Sargassum seaweed that forms large floating masses at the sea surface. This is where they rest and find food and cover. For many reasons, not all of them known to us, sea turtle populations are decreasing, so a lot of effort is being made to help them.

How to Help Sea Turtles

If you find hatchlings that are wandering away from the Gulf, take them to a dark area of the beach and put them down in the sand near the water. Let them walk to the water on their own. If they are not crawling strongly, you can place them in the shallow water and let them swim away. Be sure to notify Florida Fish and Wildlife at 1-888-404-FWCC. You may also try to call a local sea turtle organization for advice.

If they are in immediate danger, put them in a dry container and keep it in the shade until official help arrives. Do NOT put them in a container with water; they will use up all their energy trying to swim. Do not put them in an air conditioned space. Shade is fine.

Also, do not confuse a land tortoise with a sea turtle. Land tortoises cannot swim. If you put them in the water they will drown. A tortoise has feet with little claws. A sea turtle has flippers.

Shorebirds

Florida has many types of shore birds, from gulls and terns, to long-legged herons, to sandpipers and plovers, and more. Many of these birds travel thousands of miles over open oceans during spring and fall migration. Some are just stopping in Florida to refuel, so it's important to avoid disturbing them if possible. Please don't let your children chase the birds.

Some shorebirds nest right here in Florida, laying their eggs right on the beach in a colony of other nesting birds. One of the reasons dogs are not allowed on the beach is that the birds see them as predators. Their presence scares the birds, causing them to take flight and leave their eggs exposed to the sun and to other birds, raccoons, or crabs. In Florida we have volunteers called Shorebird Stewards who are specially trained to monitor bird nesting sites and to educate the public about the birds and why parts of the beach are off-limits to humans during nesting.

One of the biggest concerns we have is with birds that have gotten fishing line wrapped around some part of their body. This is an almost certain death sentence for the bird. When it flies to a roost to sleep at night, the line often becomes wrapped around a branch, tethering the bird to that branch until it dies. When fishing line gets wrapped around a bird's leg, it cuts off the circulation and the bird will lose the leg. It is not uncommon to see birds hopping around on one leg on the beach or on fishing piers.

If you hook a bird while fishing, you should gently reel the bird in. Carefully hold the bird to prevent its wings from flapping—protect your eyes from the bird's beak—and find where the hook is. If the bird is just hooked through the thin skin, you may be able to push the hook on through and pull it out of the bird and then cut the line. Don't try to back the hook out. If the bird has been hooked more seriously, it will need to be taken to a bird rescue facility where it can be surgically removed by wildlife veterinarians. A phone call to a nearby rescue facility will usually bring a volunteer out to pick up the bird. Some fishing piers have cages to put the bird in so you don't have to hold the bird until the volunteer arrives. Injured or tangled birds can be quite difficult to catch. The bird rescue volunteers have received special training on how to catch an injured bird in a way that is least likely to injure them further.

Here's a list of bird rescue organizations in southwest Florida:

St Petersburg / Clearwater

- Clearwater Audubon Society 727-798-2385
- St. Petersburg Audubon Society 727-526-3725
- Pinellas County SPCA 727-586-9591
- Guy Harvey Outpost, Tradewinds Resort 727-360-5551

Bradenton / Sarasota

- Wildlife Education & Rehabilitation Center 941-778-6324
- Save Our Seabirds 941-388-3010
- Wildlife Center of Venice, Florida (Day 941-484-9657) (Emergency 941-416-4967)

Sanibel Island – C.R.O.W. 239-472-3644

Naples

- Von Arx Wildlife Hospital at Conservancy of Southwest Florida 239-262-2273

If you can't find a rescue operation near you, call the Fish and Wildlife Conservation Commission's help line at 1-888-404-FWCC .

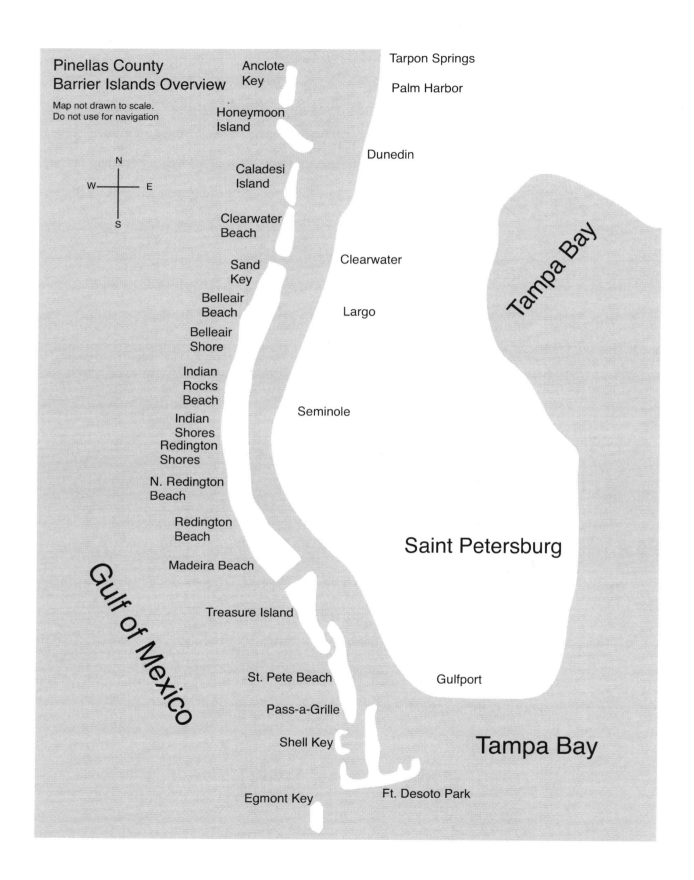

Pinellas County
Barrier Islands Overview

Map not drawn to scale.
Do not use for navigation

Tarpon Springs

Palm Harbor

Anclote Key

Honeymoon Island

Dunedin

Caladesi Island

Clearwater Beach

Clearwater

Sand Key

Largo

Belleair Beach

Belleair Shore

Indian Rocks Beach

Indian Shores

Seminole

Redington Shores

N. Redington Beach

Redington Beach

Madeira Beach

Treasure Island

Saint Petersburg

Gulf of Mexico

Tampa Bay

St. Pete Beach

Pass-a-Grille

Gulfport

Shell Key

Tampa Bay

Egmont Key

Ft. Desoto Park

Beaches North of Tampa Bay

(Pinellas County)

The Pinellas County Beaches extend along some 30 miles of barrier islands from Fort Desoto County Park at the mouth of Tampa Bay, northward to Anclote Key off the coast of Dunedin and Palm Harbor. With a few noteworthy exceptions, the Pinellas County barrier island beaches can be summarily described in one word—overbuilt. In fact, for much of the long drive over the islands it's sometimes hard to tell you're near the beach at all. On many stretches of Gulf Boulevard, the only clues that you are near the beaches are found in the names of businesses along the road, especially in the names of hotels, motels and condominiums. That, and people crossing the street everywhere in their bathing suits—let's not forget that.

Condominiums are an inescapable part of the beach landscape on the Pinellas beaches. All the beaches in Pinellas have them except for Fort Desoto, Shell Key, Pass-A-Grille, Caladesi Island State Park, most of Honeymoon Island, and Anclote Key.

Some people are not comfortable with too much nature. They like lots of amenities, lights at night, shops to browse in and bars to hop. If you are this type of person, you will probably find the St. Pete-Clearwater beaches to your liking since they have all the amenities you are accustomed to. Pinellas County beaches are an excellent choice for folks who like to have all the comforts of home practically within walking distance. On some beaches it's quite possible to take a taxi from the airport directly to your hotel and never need a car again during your entire vacation.

It's easy to see that years ago the islands had considerable charm with their tidy wooden beach cottages, a few choice fresh seafood restaurants, and plenty of greenery to give people room to stretch out and breathe. Most of these cottages are still here, although generally in a much renovated way. And more rentals have been built around, in-between, on top of, in front of, and behind what was already there in a way that suggests some sense of urgency to fill up every square inch of sand with rent-producing (and property tax revenue generating) buildings. All too commonly whatever greenery is left appears to have been an accident, with trees and bushes squeezed into whatever small nook and cranny they can find, much like tenacious weeds springing up through cracks in the sidewalk.

A few of the beach communities have maintained some sense of reasonable scale, and I'll point those out. On islands wide enough to accommodate communities on the east side of Gulf Blvd, the homes are spaced in a more normal fashion with lawns and nice trees, but you can't always see those areas from Gulf Blvd.

Major exceptions to the overdevelopment are Fort Desoto County Park, Caladesi Island State Park (accessible only by boat), and Honeymoon Island State Park, Shell Key, and Anclote Key. These are all preserves of remarkable tranquility and natural beauty, completely void of commercial enterprise. Pinellas County is to be commended for preserving and maintaining islands that let us see and enjoy what Florida was once like.

If you want to find some greenery and nature, any of the parks and preserves are within easy reach for a day-trip.

Despite the overdeveloped nature of most of the islands, the beaches themselves are very nice, and well cared for. Since the purpose of this book is to help you get to the beach, let's get right to it, starting with the northernmost beaches of Pinellas County and working our way south, towards Tampa Bay.

Mile Markers

Pinellas County Barrier Islands use the mile marker system to make it easier to find various locations. The markers are numbered 1 through 25 in half-mile increments. Mile marker #1 is in Pass-A-Grille. Mile marker #25 is in Clearwater Beach. I'll refer to mile markers where I think it will be helpful.

Anclote Key Preserve State Park

Nearest Mainland City: Tarpon Springs

GPS Coordinates: (28.1690, -82.8487)

Directions: Anclote Key is located in the Gulf of Mexico about 4 miles west of Tarpon Springs and is accessible only by boat. There are passenger ferries that operate out of the sponge docks in Tarpon Springs; however they only stop at Anclote Key for an hour or so—not enough time to enjoy a day at the beach. There are really only two ways to get to spend time on Anclote Key. The first is to buy or rent a motor boat, or make friends with someone who has a boat. The second is to paddle a kayak out to the island.

Pets: No dogs allowed on Anclote Key or Three Rooker Bar. Pets are currently allowed on North Anclote Bar but must be on a leash no longer than 6 feet and must stay out of posted areas.

Disabled Access: No special accommodations for the mobility challenged.

Restrooms: Composting toilets on Anclote Key at the picnic area not far from the lighthouse, and at the north end near the primitive camping area. Bring your own paper and hand sanitizer.

Food and Drink: None. Bring your own food and drink. Take all your trash with you off the island.

Alcohol: Not allowed.

Shelling: The taking of live shells or live sand dollars is prohibited.

Lifeguards: None.

Camping: Primitive camping is allowed on the north end of Anclote Key and on North Anclote Bar. You must notify the ranger that you will be camping on the island.

1: Anclote Key Beaches

Anclote Key is a barrier island in the Gulf of Mexico about 4 miles off the coast of the city of Dunedin, Florida. It is a State Park Preserve and can only be reached by boat. The island itself is about 4 miles long and barely 800 feet wide at its widest point. The eastern side of the island is mostly mangrove swamp. The middle inland portion of the island is forested with pine trees, cabbage palms and sea grape trees. The Gulf beach is what most people are interested in and runs the full length of the western side of the island.

In the early 1970's something interesting happened to Anclote Key: It started growing. Because of a mysterious die-off in sea grasses off the beach, sand that was once held in place by the lush underwater grasses became mobile and flowed to the north and south end of the island, adding nearly a mile of beaches to Anclote Key. The island is still growing (Clayton, 2012, pp. 42, 43).

There are two buildings on the island: the historic lighthouse—built in 1887 and restored to its former glory in 2003--and the full-time resident ranger's house. The lighthouse is generally open to the public only two days each year, courtesy of the nonprofit citizen's support group Friends of Anclote Key State Park. The days the lighthouse is open is announced in advanced via posting on the web site www.anclotecso.com.

Other than the Ranger's house and the lighthouse, Anclote Key is completely undeveloped. On a weekday you may find yourself completely alone on the four miles of sandy Gulf beach or on the trails. The beaches have a good selection of shells and flotsam since there is no beach rake to disturb what naturally washes up. The island is an excellent place for birding. In the early days deer used to be found on Anclote Key, but today the only mammal left on the island is the raccoon. Gopher tortoises and Box turtles live on the island as well. Mosquitoes are fierce after dark and can even be a nuisance during the daytime in the interior. Come prepared for mosquitoes and no-see-ums. If you're camping, make sure the netting on your tent is fine enough to block the tiny no-see-ums. I hear a citronella candle can help, but I would not rely solely on that.

Three other islands are included in Anclote Key Preserve. Slightly less than one mile to the north is North Anclote Bar, which has about 4500 feet of white sand beach on the Gulf. It's not much more than a sand bar with some grass and low beach plants covering a small portion of it.

South Anclote Bar is a hooked sand bar attached to the southern end of Anclote Key and is a favorite place for boaters to anchor. The passenger ferries from Tarpon Springs often pull up to the beach on South Anclote Bar to let passengers disembark and explore. It's a good place for shelling.

Photo: Visitors approaching the Anclote Key Lighthouse.

Three Rooker Island is between Anclote Key and Honeymoon Island. It began life as a sandbar in the 1960's and was then called Three Rooker Bar. Now it's big enough to be called an island. The northern half-mile of Three Rooker Island is cut off from the rest of the island by a narrow channel, so technically Three Rooker is actually two islands. There is no ferry to Three Rooker Island, so you'll need to have your own boat to get there. To access the island by kayak, the shortest route would be to paddle from Sunset Beach Park in Tarpon Springs. You could also paddle from Honeymoon Island State Park. Camping is not allowed on Three Rooker Island. Parts of the island may be off-limits to humans during spring and summer bird nesting season. Dogs are not allowed on the island.

Kayaking to Anclote Key is not too difficult. The water between the mainland and Anclote Key is generally very shallow. The shortest route is to launch from Fred Howard Park and paddle to the south end of Anclote Key, a distance of about 2.25 miles. It is an open water trip, so plan accordingly and take the weather forecast into account, especially the wind forecast. I would recommend making the trip on weekdays since boat traffic can be quite heavy on weekends and holidays. Dodging boats and hitting boat wake all day can be tiring. I would not recommend the trip for beginning kayakers, or those who don't have some experience in open water crossings. Kayakers should be prepared with the proper boat, paddling skills and equipment. Fred Howard Park closes at dusk, so you would need to plan to return before then.

One option is to launch from Anclote Gulf Park on the Anclote River. It's a 3.5 mile paddle to the north end of Anclote Key. This is probably the best option for kayak camping because it puts you closest to the camping area on the northern part of the island. Anclote Gulf Park has a pier that is open 24 hours and you can park your car overnight.

Another place to launch a kayak to southern Anclote Key is Sunset Park which is a short distance south of Fred Howard Park. It also allows overnight parking. Just be sure to let the Pinellas County Sheriff's Office know you are leaving your car there overnight (727-582-6200). The park gate closes at dark.

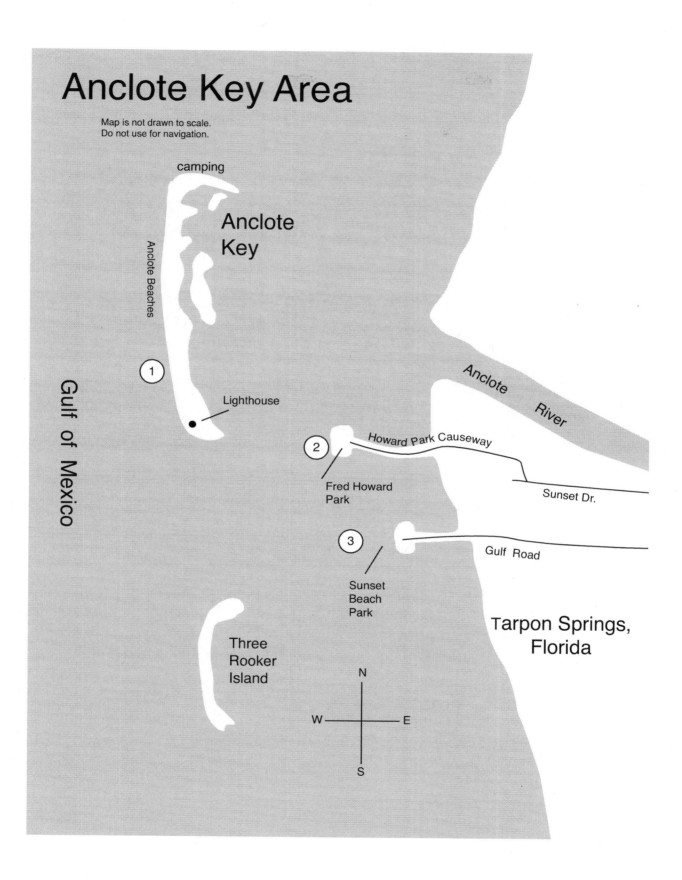

Anclote Key Area

Map is not drawn to scale.
Do not use for navigation.

camping

Anclote Key

Anclote Beaches

Gulf of Mexico

① Lighthouse

Anclote River

② Fred Howard Park

Howard Park Causeway

Sunset Dr.

③ Sunset Beach Park

Gulf Road

Three Rooker Island

Tarpon Springs, Florida

N
W — E
S

Fred Howard Park

Nearest Mainland City: Tarpon Springs

GPS coordinates: (28.15442, -82.80562)

Directions: 1700 Sunset Drive, Tarpon Springs, FL. Fred Howard Park is well off the beaten path. From US 19, take County Road 582 (E Tarpon Ave) west about one mile to S. Pinellas Avenue. Drive north on S. Pinellas and make a left on E/W Orange Street. Continue west on Orange Street, which merges into N. Spring Blvd. Follow N. Spring Blvd around the waterway and it becomes Riverside Drive. Follow the twists and turns of Riverside Drive all the way to Sunset Drive. Turn left (west) on Sunset Drive and follow it a half-mile to Howard Park Causeway. The causeway takes you through a large wooded park to the beach.

Pets: Pets are not allowed on the beach or in the beach parking lots.

Disabled Access: Restrooms are wheelchair accessible.

Restrooms: The beach and the park have restrooms.

Food and Drink: None. Bring your own food and drink. Glass containers are not allowed in the beach area. Grilling is not allowed in the beach area, but is allowed in the park.

Alcohol: Not allowed.

Shelling: Below average beach shelling, but there are plenty of live shells out on the mud and grass flats for the serious sheller. Be aware of Florida's rules on taking live shells.

Lifeguards: On duty 9 am to 5 pm daily from March to September.

Camping: Not available.

2: Fred Howard Park Beach

Fred Howard Park is a 155 acre wooded park with a causeway that reaches nearly one mile out into St. Joseph Sound to a man-made island with a man-made white sand beach. It is extremely popular, mainly I think because the area is not well served by major highways to the natural beaches of Clearwater and Dunedin. There is a daily entrance fee per car. As of this writing the fee is $5.00.

The 900 foot long crescent shaped white sand beach is framed by a rock jetty on either end. The shallow bay waters are more suited to wading than to swimming. The beach tends to have quite a few small rocks and broken shell near the water's edge and it collects a fair amount of manatee grass (a local seaweed). Half of the island is parking lot, the other half is beach. The only shade on the island is provided by some sabal palms between the parking lot and the beach.

Across the bay you can see Anclote Key. Fred Howard Park is a good place to launch a kayak to make the 2 mile paddle to Anclote Key. Just be sure you're back by sunset when the park closes.

Photo: Fred Howard Park beach, looking south.

Photo: Fred Howard Park Beach, looking northwest.

Looking north from Sunset Beach Park. Fred Howard Park can be seen in the distance.

Sunset Beach Park

Nearest Mainland City: Tarpon Springs

GPS coordinates: (28.144593, -82.790394)

Directions: 1800 Gulf Road, Tarpon Springs, FL. Sunset Beach Park is the little brother to Fred Howard Park. From US 19, take County Road 582 (E Tarpon Ave) west about one mile to S. Pinellas Avenue. Drive north on S. Pinellas and make a left on E/W Orange Street. Continue west on Orange Street, which merges into N. Spring Blvd. Follow N. Spring Blvd around the waterway and it becomes Riverside Drive. Follow the twists and turns of Riverside Drive all the way to Sunset Drive. Turn left (west) on Sunset Drive and follow it to N. Florida Avenue. Turn left (south) on N. Florida Avenue and proceed half-a-mile to Gulf Road. Turn right (west) on Gulf Road and proceed to the beach.

Pets: Pets are not allowed on the beach or in the beach parking lots.

Disabled Access: Based on my observations, I would not consider this to be a wheelchair or disabled-friendly park.

Restrooms: Yes.

Food and Drink: None. Bring your own food and drink.

Alcohol: Not allowed.

Shelling: Below average beach shelling, but there are plenty of live shells out on the mud and grass flats for the serious sheller. Be aware of Florida's rules on taking live shells.

Lifeguards: None.

Camping: Not available.

3: Sunset Beach Park Beaches

Sunset Beach Park is a manmade island located at the end of a short causeway and sits about 1400 feet out in St. Joseph Sound. It has 500 feet of more or less sandy beach on the shallow bay waters which are more suitable for wading than for swimming. The beach is typical of a bay beach: flat, hard-packed but slightly muddy with a smattering of small rocks and broken shell. It is a popular spot for windsurfing and kite-boarding. As of this writing entrance and parking are free. Park hours are 7:30 am till dusk.

Like its big brother Fred Howard Park, visible across the bay one mile to the northwest, this little island is half beach, half parking lot. It offers picnic tables, a volleyball net, a covered picnic pavilion overlooking the water, a boat ramp, and a covered pavilion where they hold concerts in the park monthly. Visit www.TarponSpringsMusic.com for the concert schedule.

The unpaved parking lot is not highly structured, so you could probably work a moderate sized motorhome in, especially if you arrive fairly early on a weekday. There are also roadside spots available on the approach to the park, close to the shady picnic area.

This park is a fairly good launch point for kayaks to make the trip to Anclote Key or Three-Rooker Island. Although the park closes at sunset, overnight parking is allowed. Just be sure to let the Pinellas County Sheriff's Office (727-582-6200) know you are camping on Anclote Key and are parking overnight at Sunset Beach Park.

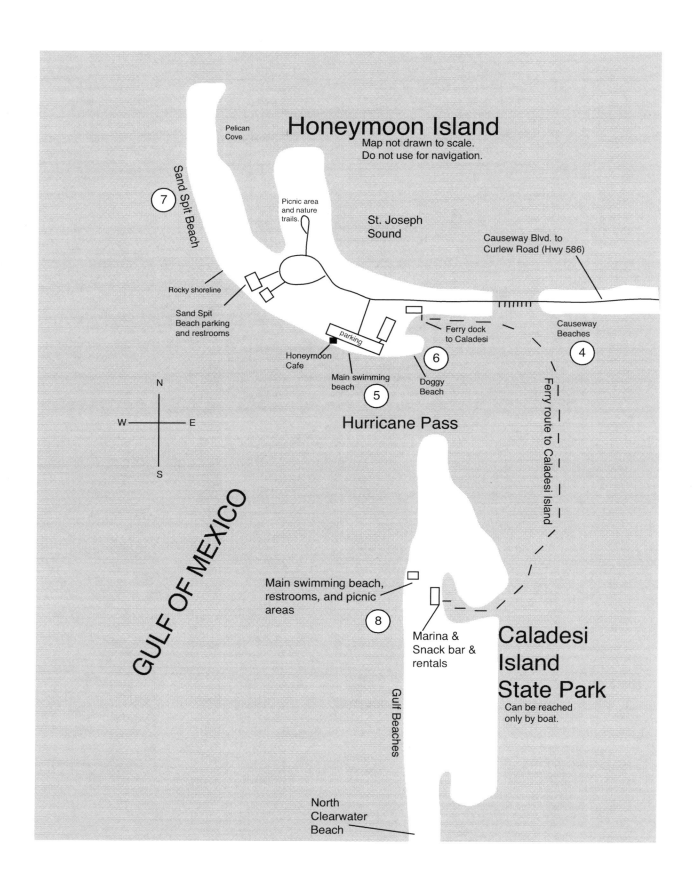

Honeymoon Island

Map not drawn to scale.
Do not use for navigation.

Pelican Cove

Sand Spit Beach

⑦

Picnic area and nature trails.

St. Joseph Sound

Causeway Blvd. to Curlew Road (Hwy 586)

Rocky shoreline

Sand Spit Beach parking and restrooms

parking

Honeymoon Cafe

Main swimming beach

⑤

Doggy Beach

⑥

Ferry dock to Caladesi

Causeway Beaches

④

N
W — E
S

Hurricane Pass

Ferry route to Caladesi Island

GULF OF MEXICO

Main swimming beach, restrooms, and picnic areas

⑧

Marina & Snack bar & rentals

Caladesi Island State Park

Can be reached only by boat.

Gulf Beaches

North Clearwater Beach

Honeymoon Island State Park

Nearest mainland city: Dunedin and Palm Harbor

Major access roads: Curlew Road (Highway 586)

Directions: #1 Causeway Blvd., Dunedin, FL. Take Curlew Road (Highway 586) west through Dunedin, continue over the bridge across St. Joseph Sound and you will arrive on Honeymoon Island. Entrance fee: The Florida State Park entry fee applies. Reduced fee for pedestrians and cyclists. The Park is open from 8am until sunset, 365 days a year.

GPS Coordinates: (28.06038, -82.81974)

Pets: Dogs are allowed in the park. Dogs are only allowed on the beach in the designated dog beach area at the southern end of the island. Service animals are allowed in all areas of the park.

Disabled Access: Concession buildings, restrooms and beach access boardwalks have wheelchair-friendly ramps. Beach wheelchairs are available upon request. Call the Ranger Station at 727-469-5942 for more info or to arrange assistance.

Restrooms: Clean, modern restrooms are located near the beach and parking areas.

Food and Drink: There are two food concessions at the main beach access: South Beach Pavilion and Café Honeymoon.

Alcohol: Not allowed on the beach.

Shelling: The taking of live shells or live sand dollars is prohibited.

Lifeguards: Seasonal, during posted hours.

Camping: None. In 2011, the state Department of Environmental Protection put forth a plan to bring in private contractors to build and operate a campground on Honeymoon Island as part of a plan to make the Florida State Park system more financially self-sufficient. After forceful opposition from the public and from local nonprofits concerned with preserving natural resources, the plan was scrapped.

Weddings: Honeymoon Island is one of the most popular beaches for weddings in the area. The South Beach Pavilion is built to accommodate wedding receptions.

Located at the west end of State Road 586 (Curlew Road) in Dunedin, this State Park attracts nearly 700,000 visitors each year. This is not surprising since it is easily accessible by car and is located adjacent to one of the most populated metropolitan areas in Florida. In the early 1800's the island was called Sand Island, then was changed to Hog Island by the late 1800's, named after a hog farm operation on the island. In 1921, a hurricane split the island, creating Hurricane Pass and Caladesi Island, which is to the south of Honeymoon Island. It was named Honeymoon Island in the 1940's when a vacation paradise for newlyweds was created. This lasted until World War II when it became a rest and relaxation haven for exhausted factory workers.

In 1964 Honeymoon Island was connected by bridge to the mainland. Over the years, several developers have owned the island and the east end of Honeymoon Island sports several condominiums.

By 1970, environmental impact studies halted development on the island and in 1974 the Department of Natural Resources acquired the remaining undeveloped parts of the island (nearly

3,000 acres, many of which are under water). The island was officially opened to the public as a state park in 1982.

Honeymoon Island State Park has an excellent nature center located near the park entrance which has educational exhibits and an elevated deck overlooking the bay that's great for bird watching. Bring your spotting scope or binoculars for the best bird viewing.

Also near the park entrance is the Caladesi Island Ferry dock and ticket office. This is where you can take the 20 minute passenger ferry ride to Caladesi Island State Park, just across Hurricane Pass.

4: Causeway Beaches (free access)

(GPS: 28.05579, -82.80680) Between the mainland and Honeymoon Island is a mile or so of beach along the causeway. The causeway has a paved bike path which is heavily used by walkers, runners, skaters, and bicyclists. Cars can pull off the road and park on the beach. Restrooms are provided and there is a concession that rents kayaks and catamarans. If you rent a kayak on the causeway, you can paddle to the northern tip of Caladesi Island in about 20 minutes. However, there are no restroom facilities at the north end of Caladesi and it is a further paddle to the Caladesi marina, food concession, and restrooms. It is possible to paddle from the causeway to enjoy the northern end of Caladesi Island, and then paddle a short distance across Hurricane Pass to Honeymoon Island to use the restroom facilities, buy refreshments and have lunch.

Access to the causeway is free. Sunbathers, fishermen, and kayakers get a lot of use from this beach. If you don't mind all the traffic zooming by on the causeway, it's not a bad beach. There are no lifeguards.

5: Main Beach on Honeymoon Island

(GPS: 28.05950, -82.82649) The most easily accessed beach on the island is Main Beach, which has a clearly marked entrance. A large parking lot and a system of boardwalks provide access to a nice white beach. There are two food concession buildings on Main Beach. The South Beach Pavilion is larger and has a large covered outdoor pavilion which is suitable for wedding receptions. Bicycles and beach equipment are available for rent. Lifeguards may be on duty during posted hours. The Honeymoon Café is a bit smaller, but also features a small, covered outdoor seating area. It also has a beach supply shop, clean restrooms, and a lifeguard is on duty during posted hours. Both buildings have a great view of Hurricane Pass and Caladesi Island, and a distant view of the tall resorts on Clearwater Beach.

6: Dog Beach

(GPS: 28.05687, -82.82301) Just to the south of Main Beach is a relatively narrow beach for dogs. It's right on Hurricane Pass and has a great view of the northern tip of Caladesi Island. Little plastic bags are provided for doggie-doo, and there is a rinse-off station for dogs. To get from the parking area to the dog beach requires an 800 foot hike through treeless sand trails. There is no shade on the beach and no drinking water on the beach, so be sure to bring some cool water for your dog to drink.

7: Sand Spit Beach on Honeymoon Island

(GPS: 28.06454, -82.83267) Drivable roads only provide access to about half of the island. The westernmost place you can drive to is the parking lot that provides access to a two mile sand spit beach which curves to the north. Clean restrooms are provided in the parking lot. Since most Florida beaches are pure sand, you may be surprised to find part of the beach here covered with rough limestone rocks. Walking on the beach requires sturdy shoes and some degree of care. However, after walking north for a few hundred yards, the rocks give way to a nice white sandy beach. The rocks are left over from an attempt to develop the island back in the 1960's.

Sand spit beach is an excellent place to find interesting shells, natural sponges and sea whips washed up on the beach. I would rate it the best shelling beach in the area. Care must be exercised when swimming on these beaches, as there are sometimes strong currents near the beach and there are no lifeguards. There are no restroom facilities or drinking fountains out on the long sand spit beach, and the area behind the small dunes is off limits because it has been deemed an environmentally sensitive area. There are no trees on the beach for shade, and no picnic tables. A few widely spaced benches perched at the edge of the dune provide a place to rest and contemplate the scenery. The sand is white and hard-packed, great for walking or running. A sand trail meanders through the grasses and small mangrove trees above the beach and comes in handy when the tide is high and where the beach is narrow. There are no buildings on this part of the island, and looking east provides a view of a virgin pine forest. Walk all the way to the north tip of Honeymoon Island and you'll have a nice view of Three Rooker Island half a mile away.

There are plenty of trails to hike on Honeymoon Island and opportunities for birding are excellent. The quiet, shallow backwaters of Honeymoon Island are off-limits to motorized boats, creating an excellent opportunity for kayakers to explore. For the more experienced kayaker, a paddle to Three Rooker Island, less than a mile off the northern tip of Honeymoon Island may be in order.

Photo: Top, concession. Bottom, rocky area on sand spit beach.

Photo: Caladesi Island State Park beach, looking north toward Honeymoon Island.

Caladesi Island

Nearest mainland cities: Dunedin and Palm Harbor

Major access roads: Curlew Road (Highway 586)

Directions: Take Curlew Road (Highway 586) west through Dunedin, continue over the bridge across St. Joseph Sound and you will arrive on Honeymoon Island. Take the passenger ferry to Caladesi Island.

Note: Refer to the map of Honeymoon Island, which also shows the beaches of Caladesi Island.

GPS Coordinates: Honeymoon Island Ferry Dock (28.06011, -82.81844). Caladesi Island Marina ferry dock (28.03188, -82.819367). Caladesi State Park southern boundary on the beach (28.0158, -82.8277) not exact.

Entrance fee: Fees are in place. Check the FloridaStateParks.org web site for current fee schedule. If you take the ferry from Honeymoon Island, the entrance fee is included in the ticket price.

Hours: 8 am to sunset.

Pets: Pets are allowed in the park, but not on the beach. Pets must be on a six foot hand held leash. Pets are not allowed on the ferry.

Disabled Access: ADA restroom facilities are available, and the boardwalk to the beach will accommodate a wheelchair. Beach wheelchairs are available upon request. For more information or to arrange assistance call the Ranger Station at 727-469-5918.

Restrooms: Yes. Clean, modern restrooms are located on the boardwalks to the beach.

Food and Drink: Hot food, drinks and limited beach supplies and souvenirs are sold at the marina.

Alcohol: Allowed in designated areas only. Not allowed out on the beach.

Shelling: The taking of live shells or live sand dollars is prohibited. Shelling is best in the winter months after the wind has been blowing onshore for several days.

Lifeguards: There is a lifeguard seasonally, as posted.

Camping: Camping is not allowed, however there is a marina with floating docks which allows boats to dock overnight for a fee. It has electric and water hookups. Three of the dockage sites are ADA accessible.

Weddings: Caladesi is a great place for a beach wedding. Check with the park concession for details, or consult with a local wedding planner.

8: Caladesi Island State Park Beach

Caladesi Island, also known as "Hog Island," is the home of Caladesi Island State Park. The island was once part of Honeymoon Island to the north until a hurricane in 1921 split the island in two. The island is accessible mainly by boat, either private boat or by the Caladesi Ferry Service departing from Honeymoon Island. Caladesi Island has 3 miles of absolutely beautiful Gulf beaches with shallow, clear, calm waters. The white sandy beaches are very wide and flat, sloping gently into the shallow Gulf waters. There are no buildings or development on the island other than the 108 slip marina and café and the main Gulf beach restroom facilities and boardwalk. The rest of the island is covered with mostly native vegetation. There are no paved roads on the island, and no cars other than the ranger's pickup truck and a few golf carts used by park personnel.

A 3-mile nature trail loop meanders through the southern half of the island, leading through a pine forest and oak hammock to a natural water hole. The water hole isn't much to look at and could more accurately be described as a mud hole, but it is the only reliable source of fresh water for the wildlife on the island. Kayaks can be rented at the café, with which you can explore a 3.25 mile kayak trail through the tall dense mangroves and grass flats. It's an excellent trail and I highly recommend it. It's sheltered from the wind and is also one of the coolest activities during the heat of the summer, since the mangrove trees meet over the top of the trail and provide shade.

A 25-foot high observation tower is planned for construction in 2014 on the island. Called the Caladesi Discovery Center, it will be built on the site of an old fire lookout tower that was torn down in the 1980's. The tower will be ADA accessible with an elevator. It will provide an excellent view of Caladesi and the surrounding islands.

Wildlife is abundant on Caladesi Island. I've seen wild turkeys, Great Horned owls, armadillos, raccoons, rabbits, hawks, and every imaginable type of bird here. Rattlesnakes are present.

The easiest way to get to Caladesi is to take the Caladesi Connection Ferry which departs daily from Honeymoon Island State Park. Generally, ferry leaves the marina hourly from 10 am to 5 pm, 7 days per week, though hours may vary seasonally. You have to buy a ticket to take the ferry, but children aged 4 to 12 have a reduced price and tickets are free for children under age 4. You have to enter Honeymoon Island State Park to board the ferry. This means you have to pay the park entrance fee as well as purchase the ferry ticket. The ferry allows visitors 4 hours on the island. This helps to prevent everyone from waiting till the end of the day to return and avoids overloading the ferry.

Another way to get to Caladesi is to rent a kayak from the vendor "Sail Honeymoon" on the causeway leading to Honeymoon Island. Visit sailhoneymoon.com for more information. From the causeway it's about three-quarters of a mile across a shallow bay and Hurricane Pass to paddle to Caladesi. This way you are not limited to 4 hours, but it's more expensive than the ferry, and more effort. Or of course if you have your own kayak you can either launch from the causeway or enter Honeymoon Island State Park and launch your kayak from Main Beach. From there it's a very short paddle across Hurricane Pass to Caladesi Island.

From Clearwater Beach, you can walk north along the beach to Caladesi Island. Dunedin Pass, which once separated Clearwater Beach from Caladesi, is filled with sand in a very permanent way since the passage of Hurricane Elena in 1985. From Pier 60 on Clearwater beach, it would be roughly a three mile walk to the southern portion of Caladesi Island.

The history of Caladesi Island is very interesting and is well documented by a woman who was born and raised on Caladesi. You will be drawn in by the story of Myrtle Scharrer Betz, who grew up as the only child on Caladesi Island, then called "Hog Island," or sometimes even "Sharrer's Island." She lived in a homestead there with her father, Henry Scharrer. Myrtle was born on Caladesi in 1895 during a winter storm so strong that it blew all the water out of the bay for three days. She was named after the wax myrtle plants common on the island. Myrtle tells the story of daily life on Caladesi Island in her book "Yesteryear I Lived in Paradise: The Story of Caladesi Island." It is not a long book, but reading it will greatly enhance your enjoyment and understanding of Caladesi Island and what life was like on Florida's barrier islands before electricity, roads and cars. The book is for sale in the park concession and can be found on the usual online book retail web sites.

The Caladesi Island passenger ferry is pictured above.

Photo: Clearwater beach looking north toward Pier 60.

Clearwater Beach

Nearest mainland city: Clearwater

Major access roads: Gulf-to-Bay (Highway 60)

Directions: 1 Causeway Blvd., Clearwater Beach, FL. <u>From Clearwater</u>, take Highway 60 west over the Clearwater Bridge and Clearwater Memorial Causeway to the barrier island of Clearwater Beach. When you get to the island you will encounter a roundabout instead of a traffic light. Follow the signs to beach parking at Clearwater Beach and Pier 60.

<u>From Sand Key</u>, follow Gulf Blvd. north over Clearwater Pass via the Sand Key Bridge. There is no toll. After crossing the bridge, turn left onto Gulfview Blvd.

Entrance fee: There is no entrance fee to any of the Clearwater beaches, but all parking is metered. Most meters accept debit or credit cards as well as coins and bills.

Hours: Varies according to location. Main beach parking closed from 1 am to 6 or 7 am every day, as posted.

Pets: Pets are not allowed on areas designated as public beaches (around Pier 60), but leashed dogs are allowed on the beaches north of Somerset Street.

Disabled Access: The beach and Pier 60 are ADA compliant. Special beach wheelchairs are available from the lifeguards.

Restrooms: Clean, modern restrooms are located throughout the Pier 60 area. Other street accesses do not provide restrooms.

Food and Drink: There are two beach concessions at Pier 60, and numerous restaurants within walking distance of Pier 60.

Alcohol: Not allowed out on the beach.

Shelling: Shelling is average. You'll find the most shells at low tide after a storm or strong winter cold front. Otherwise, shells are widely scattered.

Lifeguards: Pier 60 has excellent lifeguard coverage.

Camping: There are no opportunities for beach camping on Clearwater Beach.

Weddings: Clearwater Beach is a prime location for beach weddings. This beach has top quality hotels directly on the beach, plenty of excellent restaurants, a fair amount of shopping, and plenty to see and do.

The congested thoroughfares of Clearwater lead to the even more congested Clearwater Beach. A somewhat narrow, entirely upscale island between Sand Key and Caladesi Island, Clearwater Beach can be divided into two distinct districts: the commercial district south of Acacia Street, and the residential district north of Acacia Street, known as North Beach. Mandalay Avenue is the main through street that runs north and south from Highway 60 to the north tip of Clearwater Beach Island. From Highway 60 south to the Sand Key Bridge, the main through streets are Coronado Drive and South Gulfview Blvd. Clearwater has about 2.5 miles of beautiful white sandy beaches which are connected at the northern end to Caladesi Island, for a total of 5.5 miles of sandy beach. You can walk along the beach without obstruction from one end of the island to the other.

I think of the commercial district as "Orlando on the Beach." And if this is Orlando on the Beach, then Mandalay Avenue and Coronado Drive are the equivalents of Orlando's International Drive. Clearwater Beach doesn't have that artsy, eclectic, thrown-together "old Florida" look and feel of the Key West and Fort Myers Beach kind, peppered with dive-bars and hole-in-the-wall restaurants between avenues of wood-frame old Florida homes surrounded by rambling bougainvillea and graceful coconut palms. Instead, everything is fairly new and lacking in any historical authenticity. However, most people who come to Clearwater Beach are simply looking to have a good time and enjoy the beach. They aren't looking for Historic Old Florida. They want comfort, entertainment, good food and convenience. Clearwater Beach delivers. It's clean, slightly trendy, and has everything you need and more. And best of all, everything is within a five-minute walk from the beach.

Parking meters are big business here, as are beachfront restaurants, hotels, resorts, and tourist oriented shops. Clearwater Beach is heavily used, not only by tourists, but by the locals as well. And it attracts a much larger proportion of young adults than the average Gulf Coast beach community. By mid-morning, traffic is heavy, even during the off-season. Parking is easiest to find if you arrive before 11 am.

The southern end of Clearwater Beach forms a hook that creates shoreline overlooking Clearwater Pass. This section of the island is completely dominated by large hotel/resort/restaurant complexes. In fact, the "music" from one of the entertainment complexes can be heard all the way across the pass at Sand Key Park. A seagull-eye view of this tourist mega-complex can be had from the bridge over Clearwater Pass. Take a walk up on the bridge—it's a great place to take photos and is one of the highest bridges on the Gulf coast other than the Sunshine Skyway Bridge over Tampa

Bay. Marco Island and Estero Island far to the south also have tall bridges with commanding views of their islands.

Just north of the Public Beach is Mandalay Park at Rockaway Street. Mandalay Park has a metered parking lot on the beach with two on-the-beach restaurants, one at each end of the parking lot.

Continuing north on Mandalay Avenue, at Acacia Street, you come to another roundabout that marks the entrance to the North Beach Residential District. A helpful sign informs you that there are no hotels past this point. There are beach accesses north of Acacia, but for the exception of a handicap parking spot at the Bohenia Circle North access, they don't offer parking for cars. If you are on foot or riding your bike, there are several good public access points. There is nothing particularly remarkable about the North Beach area. There are some luxurious beach houses mixed in among the regular homes, including some of very interesting design. The plant life and landscaping is not particularly lush or scenic, nor is there anything of historical significance here. The beach is where the action is.

If you like action, a youthful crowd, cruising cars, beachside restaurant food, shopping, upscale beachfront monolithic hotels, and lots of lights at night, all mixed in with a beautiful white beach, you will love Clearwater Beach, the Gulf coast's little "Orlando on the Beach."

9: Clearwater Beach and Pier 60 Fishing Pier

(GPS: 27.97622, -82.82889). 1 Causeway Blvd., Clearwater, FL. This is an expansive beach facility built around a wide, flat, powdery white quartz sand beach. The water is tranquil and shallow and very swimmer friendly. Lifeguards are on duty during the day. Pier 60, a concrete fishing pier extending several hundred feet into the Gulf of Mexico offers a great view of the coastline and the water, as well as fishing 7 days per week, 24 hours per day, except Christmas Day. There is a full bait house on the pier that rents and sells fishing gear, live bait, snacks and drinks. You do not need a fishing license to fish from the pier.

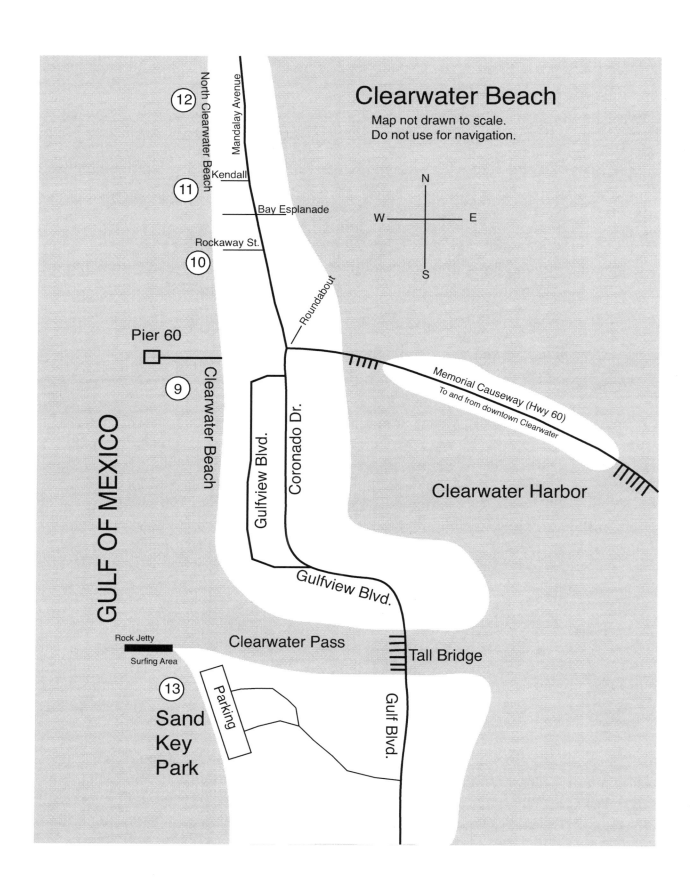

Clearwater Beach

Map not drawn to scale.
Do not use for navigation.

N
W   E
S

⑫

⑪

⑩

Pier 60

⑨

GULF OF MEXICO

North Clearwater Beach

Mandalay Avenue

Kendall

Bay Esplanade

Rockaway St.

Roundabout

Clearwater Beach

Gulfview Blvd.

Coronado Dr.

Gulfview Blvd.

Memorial Causeway (Hwy 60)
To and from downtown Clearwater

Clearwater Harbor

Rock Jetty

Surfing Area

Clearwater Pass

Tall Bridge

⑬

Sand
Key
Park

Parking

Gulf Blvd.

Sunsets at Pier 60 is a nightly event on and around the pier and the Pier 60 Pavilion, featuring artists, crafts persons selling handmade items, musicians, and buskers (street performers). This entertaining event takes place from 6pm to 10pm nightly. The pavilion often features live music. The beach has volleyball nets and beach umbrellas and chairs are available to rent. There are plenty of public restrooms and showers and there is a food concession and playground equipment for children. Across the street is Clearwater Harbor with sightseeing boats, a dinner cruise, and fishing charters leaving daily. I told you this is a busy place didn't I? If you get hungry or thirsty after hanging out at the beach, just walk across the street and you have your pick of restaurants and grilles.

Plenty of fairly expensive metered parking is provided in beachfront parking lots along Gulfview Blvd and at Pier 60. As of December 2012 the rate was $2.75 per hour or $16 for the day. The lot is closed from 1 am to 7 am. Metered parallel parking is available along Gulfview Blvd. as well. There is additional metered parking at the Marina on the bay side. Generally, the beachfront parking lots are the most expensive. Parking rates one block off the beach are cheaper.

Also, a few blocks north of Pier 60 and the roundabout, on the east side of Mandalay Avenue tucked between all the shops, are two metered public parking lots. One is just south of Papaya Street, the other is north of Papaya Street, next to the CVS Pharmacy. They are difficult to see, but they are there.

If you are staying in a local hotel and don't want to drive around, catch a ride on the Jolley Trolley which comes by every 20-30 minutes. The trolley serves routes along the Clearwater Beach, Sand Key, Island Estates, and downtown Clearwater. The main trolley station is located in the Memorial Civic Center at the main entrance to the beach. Visit www.thejolleytrolley.com for route information and services. It's very inexpensive.

10: Mandalay Park

(GPS: 27.98428, -82.82763) Located on the Gulf side of Mandalay Avenue between Rockaway Street and Bay Esplanade, about a half-mile north of Pier 60, Mandalay Park has a small grassy park with shade that serves to partially conceal a good sized paved parking lot that provides access to a very nice wide, white powdery beach. On either end of the parking lot are beachfront restaurants with indoor/outdoor seating. On the south end, the Rockaway Grill; on the north end, the Palm Pavilion Seaside Grill, both great spots to watch the sunset while sipping a frozen drink and munching a grouper sandwich. The park also has public restrooms. Parking is metered. Meters are enforced from 6am to 1am, 7 days per week. From 1am to 6am the lot is closed.

11: Kendall Street Access

(GPS: 27.986002, -82.827674) This access with parking is just a few blocks north of Mandalay Park on the Gulf side of Mandalay Avenue between Kendall and Avalon Streets. The lot overflows into an additional parking area north of Avalon. These lots have metered parking and are open from 8am to 10pm. They have no public restrooms or other amenities. However it is the same beautiful beach. Parking at this lot puts you at a small distance from the commotion of the Pier 60 area. You may find a few free parallel parking spaces on Kendall and on Avalon. There is also metered parallel parking along Mandalay Avenue, one block from the beach.

12: Other Accesses

There is metered parking at the Clearwater Beach Recreation Center on Bay Esplanade just north of Mandalay Park. It's on the east side of Mandalay and is quite a large lot. The meters are enforced varying hours based on the day of the week.

In the six-block area between Kendall Street and Acacia Street there is metered parking along Mandalay Avenue, as well as some metered and some free parking on some of the side streets (Heilwood, Glendale, Idlewild, Cambria, and Somerset). Each of the listed side streets dead-end at the beach and a path to the beach is provided.

North of Acacia Street, Mandalay Avenue is no longer the closest north-south road to the beach. Eldorado, one block west, most closely parallels the beach. From Mandalay, circle the roundabout on Acacia to get to Eldorado. There is no public beach parking north of Acacia Street, other than one handicap space at access#4 on Bohenia Circle North at Eldorado. If you are traveling on foot or by bike, any of the beach access trails north of Acacia can accommodate you, though there are no restroom facilities since they are mainly intended for area residents. The accesses consist of a bicycle rack, a wooden boardwalk and a sand trail between houses to the beach. The accesses are numbered and I list them here from north to south:

1. Juniper Street & Eldorado Ave
2. Laurel Street & Eldorado Ave
3. Gardenia Street & Eldorado Ave
4. Bohenia Circle N & Eldorado Ave (has one parking space for handicap decal)
5. Mango Street & Eldorado Ave
6. Bohenia Circle S & Eldorado Ave
7. This access is between Bohenia Cir S and Acacia on Eldorado

Leashed dogs are allowed on the beach in this area (north of Somerset Ave.); however they cannot be taken onto Caladesi Island State Park beach if you decide to walk that far.

Photo: North Clearwater Beach, looking toward Caladesi Island.

Juniper Street has the most northern public access trail to Clearwater Beach. The further north you walk the further back the houses are built from the beach. If you walk for about a mile and a half, you will find yourself on Caladesi Island, which is a state park. North Clearwater Beach is quiet and beautiful and has the shallow, calm waters typical of Clearwater Beach. There are, of course, no facilities, food, or beverages on these "private" beaches so you have to bring your own food and drink. At least bring water if you walk a long distance during the heat of the day. It gets really hot out here. And remember that even a "private" beach is open to the public below the high-tide line. The beach is public. Access may not be public, but the beach is...if you can get to it.

Clearwater Marine Aquarium

One thing you don't want to miss while you're in the area is the Clearwater Marine Aquarium (CMA), home of Winter the dolphin. This is a working marine animal hospital which takes in injured or stranded sea turtles and dolphins for treatment and rehabilitation. They've created some excellent educational exhibits for the public and will also take you on a tour of the hospital facilities. The CMA is located between the bridge and the island at 249 Windward Passage, Clearwater, FL. Visit their web site at SeeWinter.org.

Sand Key

Nearest mainland city: Clearwater, Largo

Major access roads: Gulf-to-Bay (Highway 60)

Directions: <u>From Clearwater</u>, take Highway 60 west over the Clearwater Bridge and Clearwater Memorial Causeway to the barrier island of Clearwater Beach. When you get to the island you will encounter a roundabout instead of a traffic light. Follow the signs to beach parking at Clearwater Beach and Pier 60. Continue past the Pier 60 entrance and follow either Gulfview Blvd or Coronado Drive south over the bridge across Clearwater Pass to Sand Key.

<u>From Largo</u>, take East Bay/West Bay (Highway 686/595) west over the Belleair Causeway. Turn right on Gulf Blvd and you will be on Sand Key. Drive north for 3 miles to Sand Key Park.

Entrance fee: There is no entrance fee to any of the Sand Key beaches, but most parking is metered. Most meters accept debit or credit cards as well as coins and bills.

Hours: Varies according to location.

Pets: Pets are not allowed on the beach, but Sand Key Park has a fenced dog park.

Disabled Access: Sand Key Park offers ADA access and special beach wheelchairs are available.

Restrooms: Clean, modern restrooms are located at Sand Key Park. Other street accesses do not provide restrooms.

Food and Drink: Sand Key Park offers drink vending machines.

Alcohol: Not allowed out on the beach.

Shelling: Shelling is average in most areas of Sand Key. You'll find the most shells at low tide after a storm or strong winter cold front. The best spot is usually at Sand Key Park near the jetty. Otherwise, shells are widely scattered.

Lifeguards: Sand Key Park has lifeguard coverage in season during posted hours.

Camping: There are no opportunities for beach camping on Sand Key.

Weddings: Sand Key is a prime location for beach weddings. Sand Key Park is very popular with weddings which generally must be coordinated with the park vendor.

Sand Key is a fourteen mile long barrier island immediately to the south of Clearwater Beach, right across Clearwater Pass. The island is home to the communities of Belleair Beach, Belleair Shore, Indian Rocks Beach, Indian Shores, Redington Shores, North Redington Beach, Redington Beach, and Madeira Beach. Each community has its own personality, and each offers varying degrees of beach access to the public, from no public access (Redington Beach), to the very generous access and free parking available in Indian Rocks Beach. When the name "Sand Key" is used, it generally refers to the end of the island just north of Belleair Beach. The majority of the Sand Key area was purchased by US Steel in the 1970's and is now home to some of the largest condominiums on the Gulf Coast. Thankfully, the northern tip of Sand Key is now owned by Pinellas County and is the home of Sand Key Park.

13: Sand Key Park Beaches

(GPS: 27.96109, -82.82960) This 95 acre Pinellas County Park is located at the north end of Sand Key at 1060 Gulf Blvd., Clearwater, FL. It is separated from Clearwater Beach by the very wide Clearwater Pass. After you've had enough of the sights and sounds of the heavily commercialized Clearwater Beach and would like to see some grass and trees and get a little peace and quiet, head south to Sand Key Park. In addition to a huge white sand beach on a shoreline without condominiums, there is a very large grassy park, some of which is shaded. The parking lot is one of the largest of any beach on the Gulf Coast. Parking is currently a flat daily fee of five dollars. Although I've not personally seen it filled up, I'm sure it is filled during the peak of the season. The park boasts of having more than one million visitors each year

Photo: Sand Key Park and jetty—the view from the Clearwater Pass Bridge.

The beach is soft white sand and its gentle curve extends nearly half-a-mile before the monstrous condominiums blot out the skyline. I have to say that the condominiums between Belleair Beach and Sand Key Park are the biggest, ugliest, most out-of-place edifices I could imagine. No, actually, I couldn't have even imagined it. Really, you have to see them with your own eyes. They are like a mountain range. Fortunately they are far enough from Sand Key Park that they don't overpower it.

The Park has two picnic shelters with grills, a playground, a fenced doggie park, picnic tables, and water fountains. The beach area has beach cabana rentals, beach chairs, 9 outdoor showers, and two bathhouses with changing stalls and restrooms. Pets must be on a leash. Nine boardwalks lead through the dune area to the beach. The beach is so wide that it is a fairly good walk to the water from the parking lot—about 700 feet on average.

Sand Key is a long island, extending as far as the eye can see to the south, but ending abruptly at Clearwater Pass to the north against the rock jetty. Surfing is allowed only very close to the jetty, but not on other areas of the beach. The Sand Key Park jetty is one of the most popular surfing spots in Pinellas County.

The negative aspects to Sand Key Park include the huge condominiums to the south of the park, which tend to detract from the scenic view, and the shape of the beach and position of the jetty tend to cause seaweed and flotsam to collect on the beach, particularly after a storm or cold front.

On the positive side, the parking and restroom facilities are excellent, the beach is wide and the sand is very good quality white quartz. Lifeguards are present 9 to 5 from March through September, or as otherwise posted, and beach equipment is available for rent, including kayaks. Also there are extensive grassy areas, a dog park, and picnic facilities, including two covered pavilions with tables. It's a fairly large park with a good beach. There are outdoor rinse-off showers and drink vending machines at each of the two beach facilities buildings and a beach vendor operates a café concession on Friday, Saturday, and Sunday.

14: Bay Park on Sand Key

(GPS: 27.94115, -82.83660) This small public park is located at 1551 Gulf Blvd across the street from the beach. As of this writing, parking is free. The park has tennis courts and a small playground, but I did not see restroom facilities. To get to the beach you have to walk across the street and proceed either north or south to either end of the Ultimar condominiums. There is a paved and fenced beach access trail at either end of the condominium buildings. The access entrances are difficult to see from the roadway because of the surrounding vegetation. These access points have no restrooms and no other facilities. The south access is about 500 feet from the parking lot. Then you have to walk another 300 feet to the beach. The north access is about 700 feet from the parking lot, and then you have to walk another 400 feet to the beach. The beach is wide and white, but is overwhelmed by the tall condominiums. Shelling is good, especially after a storm or cold front.

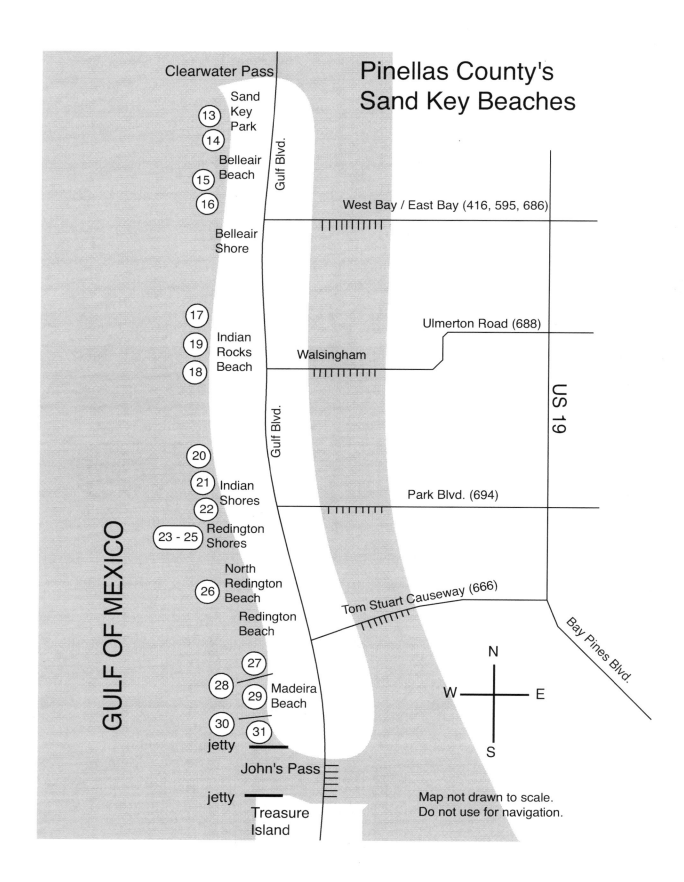

Pinellas County's
Sand Key Beaches

Clearwater Pass

Sand Key Park
13
14

Belleair Beach
15
16

Belleair Shore

17
19   Indian Rocks Beach
18

20
21   Indian Shores
22

23 - 25   Redington Shores

North Redington Beach
26

Redington Beach

27
28
29   Madeira Beach

30
31

jetty

John's Pass

jetty

Treasure Island

GULF OF MEXICO

Gulf Blvd.

West Bay / East Bay (416, 595, 686)

Ulmerton Road (688)

Walsingham

Gulf Blvd.

US 19

Park Blvd. (694)

Tom Stuart Causeway (666)

Bay Pines Blvd.

N
W   E
S

Map not drawn to scale.
Do not use for navigation.

Belleair Beach and Belleair Shore

Nearest mainland city: Largo

Major access roads: East Bay/West Bay (Highway 686/595)

Directions: From Largo, take East Bay/West Bay (Highway 686/595) west over the Belleair Causeway.

Entrance fee: There is no entrance fee to any of the Belleair Beach accesses, but all parking is metered. Most meters accept debit or credit cards as well as coins and bills.

Hours: Varies according to location.

Pets: Pets are not allowed on the beach.

Disabled Access: Morgan Street access is ADA compliant and includes a ramp to the beach.

Restrooms: Morgan Street access has restrooms.

Food and Drink: Bring your own.

Alcohol: Not allowed out on the beach.

Shelling: Shelling is average to good. You'll find the most shells at low tide after a storm or strong winter cold front. Otherwise, shells are widely scattered.

Lifeguards: None.

Camping: There are no opportunities for beach camping on Belleair Beach.

Weddings: Belleair is not a hotspot for beach weddings, but if you have accommodations directly on the beach, a smaller, intimate wedding would be easy to arrange.

Belleair Beach and Belleair Shore are two very upscale communities just south of Sand Key Park. Belleair Beach, an upscale community with roughly 2,000 residents, has about 2 miles of shoreline. For many years Belleair Beach did not provide beach access to the general public. Now it provides two public access points. The sand is nearly white, but tends to have quite a bit of minerals in it, giving it a gray tint. This is because it was brought in from offshore to compensate for erosion, as is the case on many beaches.

Belleair Shore consists only of 55 or so private homes on the beach and as of this writing it provides no access points open to the public.

15: Belleair Beach Marina

(GPS: 27.93578, -82.83977) Parking is available in the marina parking lot at 3700 Gulf Blvd., Belleair Beach. There is a fee to park and pay stations are provided. There are no restroom or concession facilities and no lifeguard. The access trail is about 450 feet south of the parking lot, on the north side of the Nautical Watch Beach Resort. It is then another 250 feet to the beach.

16: Morgan Park

(GPS: 27.93003, -82.84196) This public access is located in the 2600 block of Gulf Blvd at Morgan Drive. It has a covered picnic pavilion with two tables and two benches and restroom facilities along with an outdoor rinse-off shower. There is a fee for parking. Park hours are 6 am to 9 pm. This is a small access, and including the word "park" in the name is perhaps a bit ambitious. Pets are not allowed on the beach. No lifeguard. There is no shade other than the picnic pavilion.

Photo: Indian Rocks Beach looking north toward the County Park access.

Indian Rocks Beach

Interstate 275 Exit: 30 (Roosevelt Blvd/S.R. 686), or use exit 31 (S.R. 688) if you are traveling south.

Nearest mainland city: Largo

Major access roads: Interstate 275, Roosevelt Blvd. (S.R. 686), Ulmerton Road (S.R. 688)

Directions: Follow Ulmerton Road west through Largo. Ulmerton merges into Walsingham Road, and then takes you over Indian Rocks Bridge to the beach.

Entrance fee: No entrance fees. Most parking is free. There is a parking fee at the county beach park.

Hours: Varies according to location; generally 6 am to 11 pm.

Pets: Pets are not allowed on Indian Rocks Beach beaches.

Disabled Access: The county beach park is ADA compliant.

Restrooms: Provided only at the county beach park.

Food and Drink: None on the beach, but there are plenty of restaurants within walking distance of most beach accesses.

Alcohol: Not allowed out on the beach.

Shelling: Shelling is average.

Lifeguards: None.

Camping: There are no opportunities for beach camping on Indian Rocks Beach.

Weddings: Indian Rocks Beach is a prime location for beach weddings.

In stark and welcome contrast to Belleair, Indian Rocks Beach provides some of the best public beach access on Sand Key, and much of it offers free parking. The community of Indian Rocks Beach is located south of Belleair Shores and north of the town of Indian Shores, and is across the Intracoastal Waterway from the City of Largo. County Road 688, also known as Ulmerton Road runs east/west through Largo, and then merges into Walsingham Road before connecting the mainland to Indian Rocks Beach.

The town of Indian Rocks Beach (IRB) runs for about 28 blocks (about 3 miles) along the Gulf of Mexico and nearly every street end provides public beach access from 6am to 11pm. Most have free parking, and all are clearly marked as public access points. IRB is a low-altitude community, which is to say it is not dominated by high-rise condominiums. Most homes and beach cottages here are one or two level buildings. Most have been here a long time. Small businesses are many along Gulf Blvd. and fine local restaurants and shops cater not only to the many visitors, but to the locals as well. You won't find fast food restaurants or corporate chain restaurants here. Though it maintains a small-beach-town feel, it is quite busy during the high season. But, you can't get much more laid-back than this while still having many of the big-town amenities.

When you visit IRB you will see that they truly care about preserving their shoreline environment and about making it available to residents and visitors. From the engineered "turtle-friendly" beachfront lighting to the maintenance of sea oats on the dunes, IRB demonstrates its stewardship toward the island. Make no mistake, IRB is still overbuilt. But they are doing the best they can to preserve and enhance what is left. I have indicated throughout this book that free parking is quickly going the way of the dinosaur. But at IRB they are continuing the tradition of providing ample free parking for residents and visitors. Thank you Indian Rocks Beach! The beach accesses have dune walkovers to protect the beach vegetation from being trampled underfoot, and native vegetation is used whenever possible. A bench to sit on, a water fountain, and often a shower to rinse off sandy feet are provided at most accesses. There are no restrooms or lifeguards except at the County maintained beach.

Photo: A typical street-end access boardwalk and beach trail through the dunes.

17: Indian Rocks Beach Street-End Accesses

Indian Rocks Beach runs for about 28 blocks along the Gulf of Mexico. Nearly every street-end has free beach parking and free access to the beach. Most only have a few parking spaces; some have no parking for cars, but provide access on foot. These accesses do not have restrooms or lifeguards, but most have an outdoor shower to rinse sand and salt water from your body. Generally, parking is allowed from 6am to 11pm for the public. For parking after 11pm and before 6am, a permit is required. The shoreline here has mostly rental and residential beach cottages and homes, with a few condominiums here and there. This is a built-out beach community, but there is still plenty of greenery to compliment the real estate, which is small enough in scale to be livable. The beaches are beautiful and the water is just fine.

The following avenues provide beach access with free parking spaces: Central, 1st, 2nd, 3rd, 4th, 8th, 12th, 15th, 16th, 19th, 20th, 21st, 22nd, 23rd, 24th, 25th, 26th, and 27th.

The following avenues provide beach access with no parking spaces for cars: 5th, 6th, 7th, 9th, 10th, 17th, 18th, and 28th.

All of the above have open-air showers and foot washes except 17th, 18th, and 24th.

12th Avenue provides a bike rack. All have one or two benches to sit on near the access.

18: Indian Rocks Nature Preserve

(GPS: 27.89269, -82.84794). 903 Gulf Blvd., Indian Rocks Beach, FL. While it may seem that no part of Indian Rocks Beach was left undeveloped, this wonderful free park on the east side of Gulf Blvd between 9th and 10th Avenue North offers nearly 2,000 feet of nature trail boardwalks through the mangroves and a short fishing pier on the bay. There is plenty of parking, restroom facilities, and a fenced dog park. You could park here and walk to either the 9th or 10th Avenue beach accesses, since neither of those accesses provides parking. From the restroom building in the park, it's roughly a 1,200 foot walk to the beach at 9th Avenue, and about the same distance to the beach at 10th Avenue. Since there is so much parking provided within steps of the beach in this city, the nature preserve does not seem to be heavily used by beachgoers as a parking spot. Nevertheless it is a good place to consider if you want to combine a picnic or birding with some time at the beach, or if parking is difficult to find elsewhere. The park is open from 7 am to 10 pm.

19: Indian Rocks Beach Access (A Pinellas County Park)

(GPS: 27.899904, -82.848378) Located at 17th Avenue, across the street from Guppy's On the Beach Grille and Bar. 1700 Gulf Blvd., Indian Rocks Beach, FL. This is a clean, gated Pinellas County Park with restrooms and outdoor showers. Parking here is not free. The parking spaces are numbered and there are pay-stations located near the restrooms. The parking lot has a narrow entrance and the parking spaces will not accommodate vehicles longer than 20 feet. The lot opens at 7am and closes at dark, which is typically one-half hour after sunset. Wooden boardwalks lead over a low, sea oats-covered dune field to the wide sandy beach. Low-rise condominiums are above the beach on either side of the access, but there is a small, vegetation covered dune field, a few trees, and some low vegetation as a buffer between the buildings and the beach. Of course there are no buildings at the park except for the small restroom building. The park officially has 300 feet of beachfront, but as on all beaches you can walk as far north or south on the beach as you like. The beach sand is white, but is not the fine powdery sugar sand found on some barrier islands. There is no lifeguard and no snack bar, but restaurants are nearby. This access is the closest thing you'll find to a "full-service" public beach in Indian Rocks Beach.

Photo: Indian Rocks Beach County Park access.

Photo: Tiki Gardens beach access.

Indian Shores

Interstate 275 Exit: 28 (Gandy Blvd/Park Blvd/ S.R. 694)

Nearest mainland city: Pinellas Park, Seminole, St. Petersburg

Major access roads: Park Blvd (S.R. 694)

Directions: Follow Park Blvd west through the town of Seminole all the way to the beach at Indian Shores.

Entrance fee: Parking fees apply at Tiki Gardens access. Handicap parking is free.

Hours: Varies according to location.

Pets: Pets are not allowed on Indian Shores beaches.

Disabled Access: Tiki Gardens access is ADA compliant. The 190th access has two handicap spaces. No beach wheelchairs are available.

Restrooms: Tiki Gardens access has restroom facilities.

Food and Drink: Tiki Gardens access has drink vending machines and water fountains.

Alcohol: Not allowed out on the beach.

Shelling: Shelling is average.

Lifeguards: None.

Camping: There are no opportunities for beach camping on Indian Shores.

Weddings: Indian Shores is a small town, so facilities may be limited, but check with area wedding vendors. A wedding can be arranged on most any beach.

Located immediately south of Indian Rocks Beach, and north of Redington Shores, Indian Shores stretches for two and a half miles along the Gulf, from 184th Avenue to a little past 200th Avenue. It is similar to Indian Rocks Beach in character, but lacks the street-end beach accesses. There are no buildings higher than five stories. The public beach access here is at the Pinellas County Park known as Tiki Gardens.

20: Tiki Gardens Access (A Pinellas County Park)

(GPS: 27.854157, -82.845481). 19601 Gulf Blvd., Indian Shores, FL. This is a great public access located at about 195th Avenue, across the street from the Sea Crest condominium. There is a convenience store just south of the parking lot in case you get the munchies. The 200 space parking area, restrooms and a drink vending machine are on the east side of Gulf Boulevard, which means you have to cross Gulf Boulevard to get to the beach, roughly 600 feet away. The county provides a marked pedestrian crosswalk with a signal to stop traffic so you don't have to stand there all day. I've never had a problem crossing the two-lane boulevard here. Just keep your eye on your children. The large, paved parking area provides metered parking (free for the disabled). This ten acre facility is open from 7am until dark. Thick mangroves, ferns, and some exotic vegetation surround the parking area. The walk way to the beach is nicely landscaped and offers two outdoor rinse-off showers and a drinking fountain. A wooden boardwalk crosses the small dune area onto the beach. The beach is white / light gray, wide, and very nice. Above the beach are medium-height condominiums and beach homes, but no major resorts, restaurants or bars.

Photo: The shoreline at Tiki Gardens beach access.

21: 190ᵗʰ Avenue Beach Access

This beach access is located at 190ᵗʰ Avenue, near the intersection of Park Blvd and Gulf Blvd. It has no public parking other than two spaces for handicap parking. They are "van accessible." There is a ramp with a short boardwalk to the beach.

22: 186ᵗʰ Avenue Beach Access

This access, located just south of Park Blvd, has four parallel parking spaces at the beach access. Across the street is plenty of additional parking at the 186ᵗʰ Avenue park, but be warned, crossing the very busy four-lane Gulf Blvd at this location is difficult and dangerous.

Suncoast Seabird Sanctuary

The Suncoast Seabird Sanctuary is located in Indian Shores, at the boundary with Redington Shores. The address is 18328 Gulf Blvd, Indian Shores. Don't drive by without stopping in to visit the birds. This will give you a great opportunity to see our beautiful shorebirds up close and personal. It really will give you a much greater appreciation for the beautiful wildlife we have here. The sanctuary has had serious financial and management problems in recent years and its continued existence is uncertain.

Redington Shores

Interstate 275 Exit: 28 (Gandy Blvd/Park Blvd/ S.R. 694)

Nearest mainland city: Pinellas Park, Seminole, St. Petersburg

Major access roads: Park Blvd (S.R. 694)

Directions: Follow Park Blvd west through the town of Seminole all the way to the beach at Indian Shores. Turn left and drive south one-half mile to Redington Shores.

Entrance fee: Beach access is free but the better parking lots are metered.

Hours: Varies according to location. Main beach parking closed from 1 am to 6 or 7 am every day, as posted.

Pets: Pets are not allowed the beach.

Disabled Access: The main access at 182nd Avenue is ADA compliant.

Restrooms: Clean, modern restrooms are located at the 182nd Street access. Other street accesses do not provide restrooms.

Food and Drink: There are no beach facility snack bars on Redington Shores, but there are restaurants and cafes conveniently located.

Alcohol: Not allowed out on the beach.

Shelling: Shelling is average.

Lifeguards: None.

Camping: There are no opportunities for beach camping on Redington Shores.

Weddings: Redington Shores is a fine place for a beach wedding.

23: Redington Shores Public Access

Mile Marker 12 ½

(GPS: 27.83304, -82.83410). 18200 Gulf Blvd., Redington Shores, FL. This small community has about one mile of beachfront, from 174th Avenue to 184th Avenue. The main public access is at 182nd Avenue at Redington Shores Beach Access. Here Pinellas County provides a very large paved and landscaped parking lot with pay stations. Parking is metered and the lot is open from 7am until dark. This means the gate closes at dark. This beach has restroom facilities and outdoor showers. There is no food concession at the park, but next door and across the street are Bad Ass Coffee of Hawaii which advertises Cuban sandwiches and the Friendly Tavern, with an outdoor deck that seems to be very popular. One feature that is unique to this beach access is the existence of a breakwater (pile of rocks) in the shallow water directly off the beach. It was constructed in 1986 by the Army Corp of Engineers and Pinellas County. The breakwater is roped off, so there are usually people to the north and south of the breakwater, and an assortment of herons, pelicans, gulls, and terns perched on the breakwater rocks. It seems an odd place for a breakwater and its effectiveness is doubtful. Otherwise it is a nice wide beach. As is par for the course in this area, there are low to medium sized condominiums to the north and south of the park.

Photo: Breakwater at Redington Shores

24: 178th Avenue Lot

(GPS: 27.827899, -82.830241) This is a free unpaved parking lot right on Gulf Blvd at 178th Avenue. The beach access trail is one block north at the western end of Atoll Avenue, about 500 feet from the parking lot. There are no public restrooms or any other facilities.

Additionally, there is limited on-street parallel parking along Gulf Blvd. Some parking is limited to two hours or to certain times of the day. Take note of any posted signs.

The only other public access I know of on Redington Shores is adjacent to the Long Pier at 175th Avenue. It is a very narrow fenced access on the north side of the pier parking lot. Parking at the Redington Long Pier is for pier patrons who have paid the pier entrance fee, but there is 2 hour street parking along parts of Gulf Boulevard from 6am to 10pm. The pier extends 1,200 feet into the Gulf. For around five bucks you can park in the pier parking lot and spend an hour on the pier.

25: The Long Pier

Also formerly known as the Redington Long Pier, and the Dubai Pier.

Located at 17490 Gulf Blvd., Redington Shores, FL. (GPS: 27.823983, -82.828358).

I really like this pier because it is old and funky. That's how piers should be---wooden, creaky, fishy smelling, with lots of bird crap and fish blood and scales stuck to the wood. A good pier needs old men with big bellies and beer breath, hairy arms and necks, loud voices, but with a gentle manner and lots of patience. The fish are in no hurry.

And birds. Every pier needs lots of hungry raucous birds flapping and squawking and hopping all over, ready to grab any fish cast aside by a fisherman. The Long Pier has lots of birds—long-necked herons, goofy pelicans, pesky seagulls, flighty terns, and confused pigeons. Being close to the Suncoast Seabird Sanctuary adds to the bird population quite a bit.

The pier isn't crowded because it costs $5 just to walk out onto the pier, and it costs $15 to fish—$20 if you want access to the VIP area at the end of the pier. But if you ask me, it's worth five bucks just to get out over the Gulf and away from all the condos and resorts and traffic. Out on the pier you can catch the breeze, smell the salt water and really breathe. Had a tough day? A tough week? A tough life? Just walk out onto the pier on a warm sunny day. Take something to drink. Sit in the shade on a hard wooden bench and just sink into the wood. Pretend you are a whacky pelican with no place to go. Just sit there and get into the zone. Don't move for at least an hour. No one will bother you. Real fishermen respect your quiet space. That's why they are there too, most of them.

The Long Pier is owned by Tony Antonious, a former New York tax accountant that turned his increasingly frequent Florida vacations into a lifestyle when he purchased the pier in 2000. Pier ownership has not always been smooth sailing though. Storm damage and arguments with city officials over the safety of the pier resulted in Antonious renaming the pier "The Dubai Pier" for a time. But those contentious days have passed; the pier has been refurbished, wounds healed, and the name is now simply "The Long Pier." Neither the birds nor the fish care one way or the other. (Goff, 2012)

Visit their website, TampaBayFishingPier.com, for all the details, prices, hours, and pictures of some awesome fish that have been landed on the pier.

Photo: North Redington Beach looking north toward the Redington Long Pier in Redington Shores.

North Redington Beach

Interstate 275 Exit: 28 (Gandy Blvd/Park Blvd/ S.R. 694)

Nearest mainland city: Pinellas Park, Seminole, St. Petersburg

Major access roads: Park Blvd (S.R. 694)

Directions: Follow Park Blvd west through the town of Seminole all the way to the beach at Indian Shores. Turn left and drive south about two miles to North Redington Beach. Or, follow the directions to Madeira Beach and turn north on Gulf Blvd for about two miles to North Redington.

Entrance fee: Beach access and limited parking are limited, but free.

Hours: None posted, except as noted below.

Pets: Pets are not allowed the beach.

Disabled Access: Not provided.

Restrooms: Not provided.

Food and Drink: There are no beach facility snack bars on North Redington Beach, but there are a few restaurants and cafes conveniently located.

Alcohol: Not allowed out on the beach.

Shelling: Shelling is average.

Lifeguards: None.

Camping: There are no opportunities for beach camping on North Redington Beach.

Weddings: North Redington Beach is a fine place for a small beach wedding, but access and parking are limited.

26: Public Walkways to Beach

This beach community has about one mile of beachfront between 164th Avenue and 173rd Avenue. There are no public beach facilities in North Redington Beach. However, six public walkways to the beach are provided. Each is inconspicuously marked with a small sign, visible at the entrance to each access path located on the west side of Gulf Boulevard. The only parking available is parallel street parking on Gulf Boulevard. Street parking is free. The only limitations I can see are signs posted against parking trailers or motor homes between the hours of 11 pm and 6 am. In other words "no boon docking." Pay attention to posted signs and you'll be fine.

There is a public parking lot on the east side of Gulf Boulevard at Bath Club Concourse (1 block north of 164th), but from 7 am to 6 pm on weekdays parking is limited to three hours. The beach is lined with large condominiums and resorts. The beach access is adequate if you happen to be passing through and want to spend an hour or two at the beach, but it's not really a destination beach for a day trip.

If you want to grab a bite to eat before you hit the beach, I recommend the Frog Pond for a great breakfast, or the Sweet Sage Coffee Café for either breakfast or lunch.

Redington Beach

Interstate 275 Exit: 25 (38th Avenue North)

Nearest mainland city: Seminole, Kenneth City, St. Petersburg

Major access roads: 38th Avenue North, Tyrone Blvd, Bay Pines Blvd.

Directions: From I-275, take the 38th Avenue North exit and drive west to Tyrone Blvd. Turn right onto Tyrone and follow it over the Tom Stuart Causeway (S.R. 666) to Madeira Beach. Turn right onto Gulf Blvd and drive north one-half mile to Redington Beach.

This upscale community has about one mile of private beachfront between 155th Avenue and 164th Avenue. There is no public beach access provided by Redington Beach. Keep on driving, or rent a condo.

Photo: Madeira Beach, looking north from John's Pass.

Madeira Beach

Interstate 275 Exit: 25 (38th Avenue North)

Nearest mainland city: Seminole, Kenneth City, St. Petersburg

Major access roads: 38th Avenue North, Tyrone Blvd, Bay Pines Blvd.

Directions: From I-275, take exit 25, 38th Avenue North, and drive west to Tyrone Blvd. Turn right onto Tyrone and follow it over the Tom Stuart Causeway (S.R. 666) to Madeira Beach.

Pets: Pets are not allowed on the beach.

Disabled Access: Archibald Park and John's Pass beach are ADA compliant.

Restrooms: Public restroom can be found at Archibald Park and John's Pass.

Food and Drink: Archibald Park has an excellent snack bar which also serves beer, wine and frozen drinks. No matter where you are on Madeira Beach you are not far from food and drink.

Alcohol: Alcoholic beverages are allowed on the beach but glass containers are not.

Shelling: Shelling is average.

Lifeguards: Madeira Beach does not offer lifeguards at any of its beach accesses.

Camping: Forget about it.

Mad Beach. That's what they call it. Draw your own conclusions. It occupies the last 2 miles of Sand Key on the south end bordering John's Pass, starting at about 155th Avenue and ending at John's Pass. Madeira Beach is the most commercialized part of Sand Key. It is a beach party town with plenty of local flavor. With very little greenery, this overbuilt hodge-podge of condos, restaurants, bars, and souvenir shops is the antithesis of what I have in mind when I think of an island. But here it is.

The south end of Madeira Beach basks in the capitalist aura of John's Pass, which just happens to have the most trumped-up commercial center on the island and is a fantastic example of what happens when you run out of space for building, but you keep on building anyway. John's Pass is a tourist shopping mecca capitalizing on its reputation for having more grouper brought in by fishing boats than anywhere else in the state, a claim that must surely be increasingly difficult to hang onto in light of the very restrictive grouper "harvest" regulations being imposed on the commercial fishing interests in Florida. In addition to providing many opportunities for spending your money, Madeira Beach is also fairly generous with providing beach access, if you're willing to feed the parking meters.

27: Archibald Memorial Beach Park

Between Mile Marker 9 ½ and 10

(GPS: 27.801967, -82.802925) Located a short distance north of the Tom Stuart Causeway (State Highway 666, formerly Welch Causeway) at about 153rd Avenue. It is not located in the most attractive of settings. Across Gulf Blvd are commercial buildings and shopping centers. On the north and south side of the park are tall condominiums. The beach itself has beautiful soft white sand and about 500 feet of beachfront. Four wooden dune walkovers lead from the paved and metered parking area to the beach. Concrete and rock erosion control groins extend out into the Gulf every few hundred feet, but they are low and relatively unobtrusive. On the north side of the park a covered picnic pavilion sits next to the parking lot but really doesn't even have a good view of the beach since it is located just behind the low dunes. Restroom facilities are located in a small concrete building next to a log cabin-like structure that functions nicely as a top-notch snack bar called "The Old Snak Shak, which serves the usual burgers, hot dogs and ice cream as well as beer, wine and frozen drinks. Tables are outside on the deck overlooking the beach. It's sort of a Tiki-bar, but not quite. The beach, restrooms, outdoor shower, snack bar and deck are wheelchair accessible. Parking meters are in effect from 6am to midnight, 7 days a week. The lot is closed from midnight to 6am. The parking lot would not accommodate trailers or motorhomes.

Photo: Snack bar at Archibald Memorial Beach Park.

28: Madeira Beach Parking and Access (Pinellas County Park)

Mile Marker 9 ½

(GPS: 27.797813, -82.797534) This Pinellas County beach access park is maintained by the City of Madeira Beach and is located at 145th Avenue. On its 1.5 acres there is paved, metered, and nicely landscaped parking for about 100 cars. Restrooms and outdoor showers are the only amenities here. This access has 450 feet of beachfront, but once you are on the beach you can walk as far north or south as you wish. This is a nice access and is my choice for beach access on Madeira Beach unless you need a snack bar, in which case you should go to Archibald Beach Park. Because of the landscaping and narrow entrance you could easily drive right by this access without seeing it.

29: Tom and Kitty Stuart Park

(GPS: 27.794962, -82.793947) Located between 140th and 141st Avenues just south of the County Park, this tiny access has only 5 parking spaces and 1 handicap space. Parking is allowed from 6am to 10pm, 7 days a week. The spaces are metered. This little access is squeezed between small motels but still manages to have a nice wooden dune walkover and small covered deck with 2 wooden picnic tables. On each side of the access are low-rise motels while further down the beach in both directions are motels and condominiums of all sizes. There is little or no vegetation on the beach and generally no dune field at all. This park has no restroom facilities.

30: Madeira Beach Street-End Accesses

In addition to main City and County accesses, additional parking and beach access is provided at many of the avenues ending at the beach. Some have parking and some are only a walking trail to the beach. Try the following avenues for metered spaces: 130th, 131st, 132nd, 133rd, 134th, 135th, and 136th (has outdoor shower). The most parking spaces are to be found at 130th Avenue (about 75 spaces) and 132nd Avenue (about 30 spaces). These are all metered spaces, none is free. None has restroom facilities and all require a walk between condominiums to reach the beach.

31: John's Pass Beach

(GPS: 27.78407, -82.78361) This public access, operated by the City of Madeira Beach, is located at 129th Avenue, on the north side of John's Pass. John's Pass is the outlet for water to flow from the Intracoastal Waterway to the Gulf, and separates Sand Key from Treasure Island to the south. This beach has a large paved lot with metered parking. This facility also has nice restroom facilities and a covered picnic pavilion with wooden tables and boardwalks to the beach. The pavilion is in the parking lot, so does not have a view of the beach, but has a view of John's Pass. A rock jetty with a sidewalk provides fishermen and sightseers with easy access to the pass. It is common to see dolphins playing in the pass near the bridge.

Photo: Standing on John's Pass Bridge, looking north. Beach, left. Shopping and food, right.

The renourished beach here is wide and is manicured by the huge beach rakes, as are many of the Pinellas beaches. I don't care much for the look of a freshly raked beach. I much prefer the look and feel of a natural beach. But beach raking is often used on renourished beaches to keep the sand from becoming a hard packed crust (cementation). A sign cautions against swimming here because of swift currents near the Pass—good advice, but you could walk north for a few minutes and swim safely. Of course, this being Madeira Beach, you are constantly in the presence of large condominiums and there is little or nothing that resembles trees or vegetation on the beach except for a small dune field at John's Pass, a few other spots here and there, and a bit more at Archibald Beach. But that's just the way it is on Mad Beach.

You could come to this beach and relax for a while, get some sun, go for a walk, have a swim, then rinse off with the outdoor showers, put on some dry clothes and walk over to the John's Pass shops and have lunch, do some souvenir shopping, buy a t-shirt for the relatives back home, or perhaps acquire some artwork or craft to remind you of your great day at the beach. You can do all this without driving anywhere. You can climb up stairs onto the bridge and get a bird's-eye view of the pass, or you can walk right under the bridge and go shopping or have lunch at John's Pass restaurants and shops.

Treasure Island

Interstate 275 Exit: Preferred exit would be 24 (22nd Avenue North) See below directions.

Nearest mainland city: St. Petersburg

Major access roads: Central Avenue (S.R. 150), Treasure Island Causeway.

Directions: Central Avenue in St. Petersburg will take you all the way over the Treasure Island Causeway to the beach. If you are already in St. Petersburg, just about any north/south through street will take you to Central. Drive all the way west on Central Avenue.

Pets: Pets are not allowed on the beach.

Disabled Access: Treasure Island beaches are so wide that it could be quite difficult for a mobility challenged person to get from the parking lot to the water, even with a special beach wheelchair. Beach wheelchairs are not currently provided on Treasure Island beaches.

Restrooms: Public restrooms can be found at the municipal beach at 112th Avenue, the county park at 104th Avenue, and at the Treasure Island Beach Center in Sunset Beach.

Food and Drink: The municipal beach facility at 112th Avenue has a snack bar.

Alcohol: Alcoholic beverages are allowed on the beach but glass containers are not. There is an alcohol-free zone in the Sunset Beach area.

Shelling: Shelling is average.

Lifeguards: Treasure Island does not offer lifeguards at any of its beach accesses.

Camping: Not available.

Weddings: Treasure Island beaches are excellent for beach weddings. Be sure to get the necessary permits. There are excellent facilities available and there are wedding vendors to suit most any budget.

From I-275, there is no exit onto central. There are several exits fairly close to Central. Some are not in the best neighborhoods. The "safest" exit in my opinion would be exit 24 (22nd Avenue North). Yes, it is 22 blocks north of central, but as I mentioned, it will take you through the safest neighborhood areas. Go west on 22nd Avenue North to 34th Street (US 19). Turn left on 34th Street and drive south toward Central. Turn right (west) on Central Avenue and continue all the way to the beach.

To the south of Madeira Beach, and separated from it by John's Pass, Treasure Island has roughly 3 miles of beaches stretching to the south and overlapping the northern tip of St. Pete Beach at Blind Pass. Treasure Island is another overbuilt, over-commercialized beach town, where you can't even get a glimpse of the water until you've parked your car and walked past the beachfront resorts and condos. Forget about palm trees in paradise. Whatever trees may have been here have long been bull-dozed and paved over.

The beaches on Treasure Island have been renourished with sand from offshore, and the island boasts of having the largest white sand beach on the Gulf coast of Florida. These artificially wide beaches sometimes result in a situation where the beach near the dunes is at a lower elevation than the beach closer to the water. So, after a heavy rain, or after a storm tide, water can often get trapped in the low spots for several days or more. This means you may have to wade through 6 or 8 inches of water to get to the Gulf. Not a big deal, but it can be awkward if you are dragging gear and kids.

At some point a beach can be too wide. Who wants to drag their beach gear a quarter mile to get to the water on a 90 degree summer day? For me the most positive effect of having a super-wide beach, other than affording extra storm surge protection, is that it puts a lot more space between me and all the cars and condominiums, resulting in a quieter, more relaxing day at the beach.

Treasure Island has one of the widest white sand beaches on the Gulf Coast. Width in this case refers to the distance between the parking lot or hotel and the water's edge. The widest part of the beach, between 104th Avenue and 112th Avenue is 800 – 1,000 feet from the parking lot to the water's edge. By comparison, the widest portion of Fort Myers Beach, near the south end of Estero

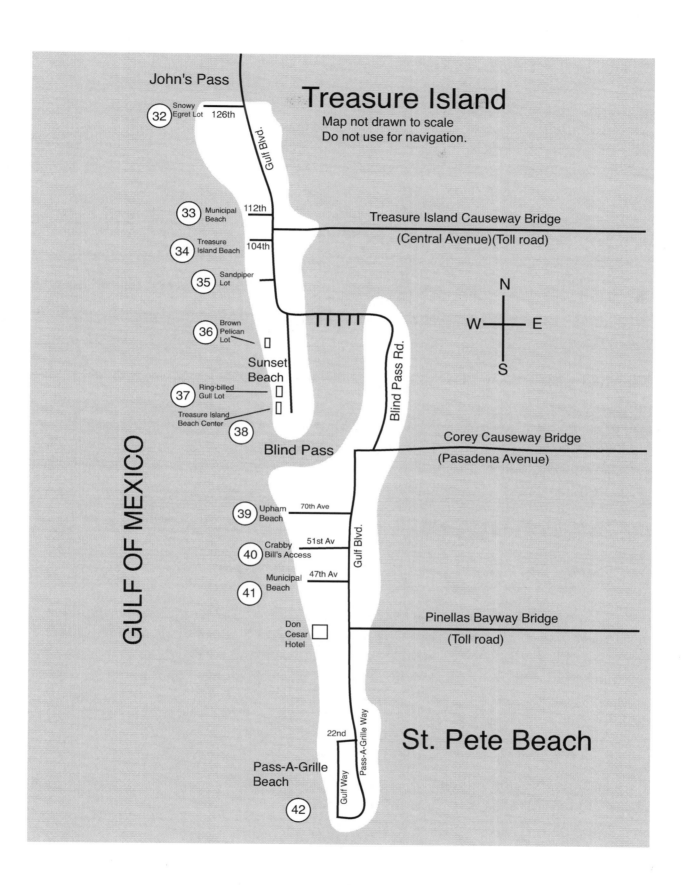

Island, is about 700 feet of white sand. On Marco Island, just south of Tigertail Beach Park, there is a section of beach that is just short of 1,000 feet from the resorts to the water's edge, so both of those beaches are in the same ultra-wide category as Treasure Island beaches. But, currently, Treasure Island has the largest area of wide beach, and they take advantage of it by holding a Saturday evening drum circle, as well as annual events like sand a sculpting competition and a kite festival. They even hold carnivals here, complete with Ferris wheels.

The southern portion of Treasure Island is a community known as Sunset Beach. One of the most popular hangouts for the party crowd is Caddy's Restaurant, which sits right on the beach. This area is known for its hard partying atmosphere, especially on weekends and holidays, and the presence of law enforcement is usually needed to keep behaviors under control during those times. The southern end of Sunset Beach is also a popular surfing spot when the waves are up, particularly at the Tern Parking Lot and with the right swell, down at the jetty (which requires a walk on the beach or boardwalk).

Alcohol Ban

Alcohol on the beach is one of the main catalysts for rowdy and sometimes inappropriate behavior. Treasure Island has instituted a ban on the consumption of alcoholic beverages on the beach between 99th Avenue and 85th Avenue in the Sunset Beach neighborhood, though an exception is carved out for Caddy's Restaurant. This ban is generally in effect from February through September, but is subject to adjustment. Pay attention to the posted signs. Spring Break and holiday weekends would be the times with the most rowdy behavior.

32: Snowy Egret Parking Lot at Sunshine Beach

(GPS: 27.779665, -82.781853) Located just south of John's Pass at 126th Avenue, this access has metered parallel parking spaces. There are a dozen or so spaces here and a wooden dune walk-over to reach the beach, which is referred to as Sunshine Beach. You can walk north for 5 minutes on the beach and arrive at the south jetty at John's Pass. Low-rise condominiums line the shore here, but there are trees and vegetation creating a small buffer zone between the buildings and the beach. I don't recommend swimming too close to the pass. No restroom facilities here. And this is not the super-wide beach you'll find mid-island.

You'll find a few free parking spaces on 127th Avenue and a trail to the beach. This is as close as you can park to John's Pass on the Gulf side of Treasure Island.

At 124th Avenue there is free parking. 124th Avenue has a very nicely landscaped boardwalk to the beach. This is a good access, but there are no restroom facilities.

33: City of St. Pete Municipal Beach at Treasure Island

Mile Marker 7

(GPS: 27.77218, -82.77248) Located at 112th Avenue, just north of the Treasure Island Causeway (where St. Petersburg's Central Avenue crosses the bridge to Treasure Island). A huge paved parking lot with pay stations enforced 24 hours per day, including weekends and holidays. The beach, however, is closed from 1 am to 5 am. This is a wide beach; perhaps even too wide. It is a long walk to the water's edge—almost 1,000 feet. If you have kids and gear in tow, or if you are unable to walk really well on sand, this may not be the best beach for you. On the positive side, once you arrive at the Gulf's edge you are a comfortable distance away from all the Gulf Boulevard noise and congestion. The sand here is pumped in from offshore and is not the powdery sugar sand that I love so, but it is white and clean and is raked regularly. The water is excellent for swimming and wading.

There are major resorts on either side of this huge public beach and there is a profusion of restaurants, including a Waffle House, and small motel apartments everywhere you look. On weekdays it is not unusual to find only a few cars in the paved parking lot that I'd estimate would hold over 100 cars. Most of the people on the beach tend to be resort guests or local people who live within walking distance. Considering the very high population density of Pinellas County, I really would expect to find a full parking lot, particularly considering that the total number of parking spaces on the Pinellas Beaches is rather small.

There is a snack bar and restrooms here (10 am to 5 pm) and rentals of beach equipment, cabanas, and chairs, and there is playground equipment for children and volleyball nets located strategically near the snack bar. The restroom facility has indoor showers (10 am to 4 pm). The snack bar and playground equipment is near the parking lot, not near the water, which is a considerable walk away. There is no shade at this beach other than that provided by the pavilion adjoining the snack bar. There are picnic tables under the pavilion.

Overall, this is a very good beach. The overall appearance of the facility is clean but dated. The landscaping around the parking area and beach entrance is Spartan and there are no trees, other than a few lonely-looking palms.

34: Treasure Island Beach Access (Pinellas County Park)

Mile Marker 6.5

(GPS: 27.76641, -82.76851) This County Park is located at about 104th Avenue on Treasure Island, just south of the Bilmar resort hotel. This is a fully equipped beach facility (restrooms/open-air showers/cabanas and chairs for rent), but does not have a snack bar. But it is directly across the street from a supermarket, so food isn't far away if you get the munchies. Actually there are so many restaurants in the area you will never be far from something to eat. This access used to provide free parking, but no longer. It is now metered. A large paved lot is provided and is open from 7am until dark every day. If you'd like to try for some free parking, there is an unpaved lot one block south on 103rd Avenue that has space for about 20 cars and is still free as of this writing.

This beach access is more attractive than the Municipal Beach at 112th Avenue. It has a landscaped parking area and a nice sea oats-covered dune area between the parking lot and the beach. The facilities are compact, modern, and well maintained. The native Florida palms used for landscaping don't provide any real shade and there is no picnic pavilion here or picnic tables. The beach here is huge, like the Municipal beach, with a few patches of sea oats scattered here and there. The water is great for wading and swimming.

At this beach access you'll find the southern terminus of the Treasure Island Beach Trail, a 4,500 foot long sidewalk roughly 10 feet wide that runs between the dunes and the hotels. It was originally constructed in 1966 and stretches from 104th Street to 119th Street. Treasure Island has tried to extend this paved trail north and south for nearly the full length of the island, but there has been too much opposition from the beachfront landowners. The trail underwent welcome design changes and renovations in 2012.

Photo: This is a portion of the 4,500 foot long Treasure Island Beach Trail.

On Saturday evenings a "drum circle" is held at this beach. It is very popular and attracts people from all over, so parking can be very tight on Saturday afternoons and evenings. Usually the drumming begins an hour or so before sunset and ends sometime between sunset and 10 pm. It's not highly organized so times may vary according to the season and changing local ordinances. www.TreasureIslandDrumCircle.com .

Photo: It's a long way to the water's edge on parts of Treasure Island.

35: Sandpiper Parking Lot

Mile Marker 6

(GPS: 27.759369, -82.765778) Located in the 10,000 block of Gulf Blvd, on the north side of the Island Inn Beach Resort Condominium, this small paved lot squeezed between two condominiums is metered and has no facilities of any kind. A wooden dune walk-over provides access to a wide beach entirely dominated by condominiums. It's fine if you just want to stop and spend an hour or two at the beach.

One block north is free beach parking for 8-10 cars at 101st Avenue and Gulf Blvd.

Sunset Beach Area

There is parking available on many of the side streets south of around 90th Avenue. Pay close attention to posted signs.

36: Brown Pelican Parking Lot (Sunset Beach)

(GPS: 27.753088, -82.763858) This very small parking lot is located on West Gulf Boulevard south of the intersection of Blind Pass Road and West Gulf Boulevard, just south of Caddy's On the Beach restaurant and across the street from Ka'Tiki Tiki bar and grill. There are only a few spaces, and they are metered. This access is in the area of Treasure Island known as Sunset Beach, a largely well-to-do but totally unpretentious residential beach community. No beach facilities or restrooms.

37: Ring-Billed Gull Parking Lot (Sunset Beach)

(GPS: 27.745245, -82.760054) This unpaved lot is located at about 81st Avenue on West Gulf Boulevard in Sunset Beach. It is across the street from the Blue Water Motel and Cottages (a single story structure) and provides about 65 metered spaces. Two dune walk-overs with stairs provide access to a residential beach. Tall Australian Pines line the shore just north of this access, partially obscuring the mostly two-story residences. This access is just a few hundred feet north of the Treasure Island Beach Center, described next.

38: Tern Parking Lot Treasure Island Beach Center (Sunset Beach)

Photo: Treasure Island Beach Center.

(GPS: 27.743905, -82.759132) This is the main beach access for Sunset Beach, at the south end of Treasure Island. It is also marked as the "Tern" parking lot, in keeping with the other lots named after birds. Actually, it isn't quite the end of the island. The southern tip of Treasure Island is owned by a large private condominium development, so the Beach Center is just the end-of-the-line for public parking access. An unpaved lot provides metered parking. Meters are enforced 24 hours a day. However, the beach is closed from 1am to 5am.

This beach is well cared for and is heavily used by the locals. The beach pavilion provides covered picnic tables, restrooms, and boardwalks to the beach. Wheelchair access is provided. At the south end of the Tern parking lot is the entrance to a public boardwalk that will take you along the beach past the condominium development for about a half-a-mile to the south tip of Treasure Island at Blind Pass. There is plenty of beach vegetation here and the view across Blind Pass is of the northern end of St. Pete Beach. There is a rock jetty on both sides of Blind Pass. The jetty on the other side is the northern limit of Upham Beach. I like this beach mainly because it is in a residential area. It is also a popular surfing spot when the waves are up. Blind pass is a good fishing spot and can be accessed from either side. The Upham beach side (south side) jetty is better for fishing, but severe beach erosion sometimes limits physical access to the jetty on the south side of the pass.

The beach pavilion is available for wedding receptions, but may not have electricity available. This is a popular beach for weddings. It is noteworthy that Sunset Beach is well-known as regularly attracting a significant number of gay visitors.

St. Pete Beach

Interstate 275 Exit: Preferred exit would be exit 24 (22nd Avenue North), or 54th Avenue South (Pinellas Bayway).

Nearest mainland city: St. Petersburg, Pasadena

Major access roads: Central Avenue, Pasadena Avenue, Corey Causeway, Pinellas Bayway

Note: Refer to this book's map of Treasure Island, which also shows St. Pete Beach beaches.

Directions: You can take Central Avenue to Pasadena Avenue. Turn left on Pasadena and drive west to St. Pete Beach over the Corey Causeway Bridge. There is no toll on Pasadena.

Pets: Pets are not allowed on the beach.

Disabled Access: Pass-A-Grille Beach offers the best access for the mobility challenged. The Paradise Grille has a special beach wheelchair available at both the Upham Beach and Pass-a-Grille locations.

Restrooms: Public restrooms can be found at Upham Beach, at the Municipal Beach at 47th Avenue, and at the Paradise Grille on Pass-A-Grille beach.

Food and Drink: Upham Beach and Pass-A-Grille both have snack bars.

Alcohol: Alcoholic beverages are NOT allowed out on the beach.

Shelling: Shelling is average.

Lifeguards: St. Pete Beach does not offer lifeguards at any of its beach accesses.

Camping: Some of the best camping in Florida is available at Fort Desoto County Park nearby.

From I-275, refer to the directions for Treasure Island. Again, I would recommend exit 24 (22nd Avenue North) so you will be driving through safer neighborhoods. Take Central Avenue to Pasadena. Turn left on Pasadena and follow it over the Corey Causeway to Gulf Blvd.

Alternatively, you could take exit #17 off I-275 and follow the Pinellas Bayway (54th Ave South) to St. Pete Beach. The Pinellas Bayway is a toll road.

The island of St. Pete Beach, also known as "Long Key," is located south of Treasure Island and has about 4 miles of Gulf front beaches. Long Key is separated from Treasure Island to the north by the narrow Blind Pass. Access to Long Key from St. Petersburg is by Pasadena Avenue (693) over the Corey Causeway, or further south via the Pinellas Bayway (682) toll road. St. Pete Beach is another overbuilt Pinellas County barrier island and on much of the island it's hard to tell you're even near the beach except for the names of the hotels and businesses which use beachy-sounding names. But there are some fine beach accesses here.

39: Upham Beach

(GPS: 27.736322, -82.751304). 6850 Beach Plaza, St. Pete Beach, FL. Upham Beach is a great local beach with a slightly Art Deco façade in the form of a wavy pastel concrete barrier separating the parking lot from the vegetation-covered upper beach. You'll find this beach if you turn off Gulf Blvd at 68th Avenue and drive west to Beach Plaza Road. Upham Beach stretches for several blocks from about 71st Avenue to 67th Avenue; just enough to get the condominiums off your back and give you some space to breathe.

Upham Beach has 4 boardwalks leading from the long narrow pay and park lot to the beach. Parking is metered. Parking fees are enforced from 8 am to 8 pm every day, but as far as I can tell the beach is open all night. Fishermen park here and walk to the jetty and fish all night and there always seems to be someone on the beach. The parking spaces will not accommodate large motor homes or trailers. There are restrooms here and outdoor showers. All the facilities and the boardwalks to the beach are ADA compliant. A special beach wheelchair is available at no charge.

The snack bar, called the Paradise Grille serves breakfast and lunch with somewhat more interesting choices than the typical snack bar. The Paradise Grille is generally open 8am to around sunset and they do serve a good breakfast. Dining is open-air. Beer and wine are served.

There are no gates on the parking lot, so you won't get locked in if you stay past sunset. This is a very popular beach with locals and used to be a surfing hot-spot when the waves were up, but a series of erosion control structures on the beach has largely ruined the surfing opportunities at Upham.

Photo: Geotubes installed on Upham Beach are an attempt to slow erosion of the beach.

Upham Beach has one of the worst erosion problems of any beach in Florida. The problem is caused by the rock jetty constructed at Blind Pass to stabilize the shape and size of the pass, and by the construction of several tall condominiums too close to the high tide line. While the rock jetty at the inlet does stabilize the pass, it also blocks the southward longshore movement of sand from Treasure Island. As sand flows away from Upham Beach, it is no longer naturally replenished by the natural movement from beaches to the north. To make matters worse, the interaction of wave action with the sea wall in front of the condominium exacerbates the erosion problem. The residents in the condominiums naturally suffer from considerable anxiety when they see the beach wash away and observe the waves lapping at their back door. This has resulted in some experimental "t-groin" structures being placed on the beach to try to slow the erosion. These structures are called "Geotubes" and are canary yellow. They are an eyesore, to say the least. The county wants to replace the yellow Geotubes with permanent rock structures but is being challenged by some of the locals and by the Surfrider Foundation. It remains to be seen what the final solution will be.

Fishing is good at Blind Pass at the north tip of the island. It's a short walk from Upham Beach, but when the beach is severely eroded (which is most of the time) it is a treacherous climb along the high sea wall, which I don't recommend.

40: 51st Avenue Access

There are a few metered parallel parking spaces next to Crabby Bill's Restaurant where 51st Avenue meets the beach. There is a dune walkover to the beach, and that's about it. I would not recommend trying to use the restaurant parking lot for beach access parking.

41: St. Pete Municipal Beach

(GPS: 27.722008, -82.740524) This beach access is located on Gulf Blvd at 47th Avenue. There is a traffic light at the entrance. It's across the street from the Dolphin Village shopping center, which has several restaurants and a grocery store. The lot offers metered parking. The park is open 7am until dark; just enough time to watch the sunset, pack up your stuff and leave before the gates close. There are 4 dune walkovers to the beach, which is of course squeezed between a hotel and a condominium. There is no shade here, nor is there a snack bar. There are restrooms and outdoor showers to wash off the sand and salt. The beach has beautiful white sand and the water is great for swimming. Vendors on the beach rent umbrellas, cabanas, chairs, and parasail rides.

42: Pass-A-Grille Beach

(GPS: 27.689067, -82.738196) The beaches of Pass-A-Grille are located at the southern end of St. Pete Beach. Take Gulf Blvd south to 22nd Avenue, then turn right on 22nd avenue and drive one block to one of the best beaches in Pinellas County. There is metered street parking along the beach from 22nd Avenue all the way south to 1st Avenue. There are a lot of parking spaces, but they fill up quickly. Meters are generally in effect from 8 am to 8 pm. The island is quite narrow in the Pass-A-Grille area, so one can easily walk the short block to the bay side of the island. There is metered parking along the bay from 12th Avenue to 1st Avenue. On other streets you may see parking, but it is for residents with parking permits only. On the beach, at 10th Avenue, is the Paradise Grille (900 Gulf Way), where you can eat and drink right on the beach at umbrella-covered tables. The public restrooms are located at the Paradise Grille. They do serve beer and wine. Across the street is the heavily advertised Hurricane restaurant complex, a huge 3 story mansion with a restaurant, bar, and rooftop deck. The rooftop is a popular place for having a drink and watching the sun sink into the Gulf. A block away is the 8th Avenue historic business district with several very good restaurants and a few galleries that display and sell the work of local artists and crafters. Pass-A-Grille's 8th Avenue was once called "America's shortest and most beautiful main street," by Robert Ripley of "Ripley's Believe It or Not." (Hurley, 1989, p. vii)

Photo: Pass-a-Grille Beach looking north from the jetty toward the Don Cesar Resort.

Pass-A-Grille has a tradition of ringing a ceremonial bell at sunset. Most every evening, shortly before sunset, a small crowd gathers by the beach at the Paradise Grille next to a large bell fixed atop a post. The official volunteer bell ringer--recognized by his or her possession of the lanyard needed to ring the bell properly--explains the origins of the ceremony to anyone interested before reciting a dedication and benediction in preparation for the ringing. Often the actual ringing of the bell is delegated to a willing volunteer from the crowd. As the sun sets, the bell is rung and dozens of cameras record the moment. It's a beautiful thing.

A sidewalk parallels Gulf Way for the entire 22 blocks on Pass-A-Grille. This beach town's saving grace is that there are no homes or resorts directly on the beach. All the buildings are across the street, allowing unblocked access to the beach at all points. Also, once you are on the beach, you are behind the dunes and are relatively removed from the business of the town. The neighborhood puts some effort into having an attractive and cared-for island landscape, without being overdone or highly manicured. Overall it is more residential than commercial. There is just one high-rise condo. Pass-A-Grille is my choice for an easily accessible, attractive, and relaxing beach in Pinellas County with all the comforts you need.

The Boca Ciega bay side of Pass-A-Grille is home to the Merry Pier, a great fishing spot and home to several fishing charter boats as well as the Shell Key Shuttle, a passenger ferry that will take you to the neighboring island nature preserve of Shell Key. This small but busy bayside pier is named after Captain Joseph E. Merry, who built a dock at the end of 8th Avenue in 1902 and operated a general store at the end of the dock. It was the center of activity in Pass-a-Grille in the early 1900's. Today the pier offers bait sales, tackle, rod rentals, bike rentals and a fresh seafood market. There is no charge to fish from the pier but you will need a Florida saltwater fishing license. More info at merrypier.com. Some big grouper have been landed right from the Merry Pier (Merry Pier web site).

The southernmost tip of Pass-A-Grille has a rock jetty that extends a short distance into the Gulf at Pass-A-Grille Channel. This jetty is in almost constant use by a few fishermen and sightseers. Do not swim in the pass. Tidal flow currents can be very powerful. Across the channel is Shell Key, accessible only by boat. Camping is allowed on parts of Shell Key, a narrow u-shaped island preserve with no buildings or development. Shell Key has a beautiful Gulf Beach and a sheltered shallow bay. Portions of the island are off-limits to people and dogs because they are protected bird nesting areas.

Island Ferry (www.islandferry.biz) is starting a round-trip ferry service from the Pass-a-Grille Marina to downtown St. Petersburg. Ferry services are scheduled to begin in June 2013. The price is expected to be $25 per person, for a round-trip ticket.

Photo: Bell ringing ceremony at sunset on Pass-a-Grille.

Shell Key Preserve

Nearest mainland city: St. Petersburg

Major access roads: Accessible only by boat.

Note: Refer to the map of Ft. Desoto County Park (following this chapter on Shell Key).

GPS: (27.65494, -82.74644)

Entrance fee: Free.

Hours: Does not close.

Pets: No pets. This is a wildlife preserve.

Disabled Access: No special access provisions.

Restrooms: None provided.

Food and Drink: There is no food, drink, or fresh water on the island. Bring your own.

Alcohol: Alcoholic beverages are not allowed on the island.

Shelling: Shelling is average to very good. Sand dollars are common.

Lifeguards: No lifeguards or beach patrol.

Camping: Primitive camping is allowed on the south end of the island near Bunces Pass but you must get a permit.

Weddings: To have a wedding on Shell Key, a boat would have to be involved since no roads or bridges lead to the island.

43: Shell Key Preserve

Shell Key is a barrier island located between Pass-A-Grille and Fort Desoto County Park. It is accessible only by boat. The Preserve covers 1,755 acres, almost all of which are underwater sea grass beds and mudflats (great kayaking country). Shell Key itself is a 180 acre barrier island managed by Pinellas County under the Shell Key Management Plan. The middle portion of the island is off limits to humans because it is an environmentally sensitive bird nesting area. Overnight camping and campfires are permitted on the southern end of the island but you must have a permit to camp. It is completely primitive camping. No facilities of any kind are provided and there is no drinking water. Whatever you need, bring it with you and take it back out again. There are no access fees or camping fees. Alcohol is not permitted anywhere on the island. Pets are not allowed anywhere on the island.

Shell Key has beautiful, quiet Gulf beaches and a very shallow protected bay, with a large area off-limits to boats with gasoline or diesel engines (to protect wildlife and sea grass beds). The island is quite narrow, but has more than a mile of Gulf beaches. For everything you could possibly want to know about Shell Key, visit ShellKey.org.

To get to Shell Key, you either need to have your own boat, or you can take the Shell Key Shuttle from Pass-A-Grille. The shuttle is a large covered pontoon boat and departs for and returns from Shell Key numerous times during the day. It only takes 15 minutes or so to get to Shell Key via the Shuttle. Pets are not allowed on the shuttle and it is a smoke-free vessel. To get to the shuttle, follow the directions to Pass-A-Grille. Follow Pass-A-Grille Way to 8th Avenue. The Merry Pier where the shuttle docks is right on the bay. Go inside and get your parking pass and boarding tickets. If you are vacationing on the islands, the Suncoast Beach Trolley will also take you to the shuttle.

You can easily paddle a kayak to Shell Key. You could launch from Pass-A-Grille Beach and paddle right across the pass to the northern tip of Shell Key, or you could launch from North Beach at Fort Desoto Park and paddle across Bunces Pass to the south end of Shell Key. Kayaks can also be launched from the Pinellas Bayway that leads to Fort Desoto Park. You can pull off the road on the west side of the Bayway where you see the breaks in the mangroves, right before the toll plaza. Many people launch kayaks from the Bayway. It is a longer paddle from here though; roughly half-an-hour in the best of weather and water conditions, but the trip is mostly sheltered, shallow water. If you choose to paddle to Shell Key from Pass-a-Grille, be very careful as you cross the pass. Boat traffic and kayaks don't mix very well. I wouldn't try it on a weekend or holiday. The water in the pass can get rough when it's windy, especially when the wind direction and tidal flow are in opposition.

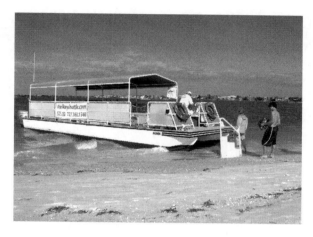

Photo: Shell Key shuttle arriving on Shell Key.

Shell Key is extremely popular on weekends and holidays with boaters who anchor off the beach by the hundreds. Many of them set up camp for the weekend. For a quieter experience, visit Shell Key during the week. The bay side of the island is off-limits to boats with motors in order to protect the sea grasses growing in the very shallow waters, so you can paddle your kayak in that area without being concerned about speeding boats.

Shell Key is divided into three regulated areas: Public Use Areas, Restricted Public Use, and Bird Preservation Area. Refer to the map on the ShellKey.org web site for a visual. Once you arrive on the island, pay attention to the signage. Essentially, there are three public use areas. The northeast tip of the island is open to the public, and the southern third of the island is open to the public, including for camping. There is also a small nub of land about mid-island on the bay side that is designated for public use. It is mainly a place to beach kayaks and cross the island to get to the beach. The Restricted Public Use area allows people to use the beach on the northern third of the island, but not to go above the dunes, due to bird nesting and preservation efforts.

Fort Desoto County Park

Interstate 275 Exit: 17 (US 19 North / 54th Avenue South / S.R. 682 Pinellas Bayway)

Nearest mainland city: St. Petersburg

Major access roads: Pinellas Bayway (682) and S.R. 679

Directions: From Interstate 275, take the 54th Avenue South exit, just north of the Skyway Bridge. Follow 54th Avenue South (Pinellas Bayway S.R. 682) west to S.R. 679. Turn left on 679 and drive south about 5 miles to Fort Desoto County Park.

GPS Coordinates: 27.62312, -82.71387

Entrance fee: Formerly a free park, entrance fees are now in place. Check the Pinellas County web site for current fee schedule. Generally, the entrance fee is $5 per car as of this writing.

Hours: 8 am to sunset.

Pets: Pets are allowed in the park, but not on the beach. Pets must be on a six foot hand held leash.

Disabled Access: ADA restroom facilities are available, and a special beach wheelchair is available from the lifeguard at North Beach. A 2,200 foot (nearly half-a-mile) barrier-free nature trail is located just west of park headquarters. Part of the trail passes along the water's edge. It's a great trail for birding, identifying plants, or just enjoying nature. Trail construction complies with ADA standards.

Restrooms: Yes. Clean, modern restrooms are located at each major beach access in the park. Restrooms have indoor showers and areas for changing clothes.

Food and Drink: Hot food, drinks and limited beach supplies and souvenirs are sold at the Gulf Pier, the fort, and at North Beach. The Bay Pier also has limited refreshments and tackle.

Alcohol: Alcoholic beverages are not allowed in the park.

Shelling: Most productive on the beaches north of the Gulf pier. The best season for shelling is during the winter months after the wind has been blowing onshore for several days, though shells can be found any time of year.

Lifeguards: There is a lifeguard seasonally, as posted on East Beach and at North Beach.

Camping: Fort Desoto Park has one of the best campgrounds in Florida. The camp sites are not on the Gulf beach, but many are on the water facing the bay. Both tents and RV's are accommodated.

Weddings: Fort Desoto is a popular place for weddings. Pavilions with picnic tables may be reserved in advance for a reasonable fee.

The largest park in the Pinellas County Park system, Fort Desoto Park is made up of 5 interconnected islands comprising 1,136 acres. The main island is Mullet Key. The park is named after the fort built on the islands during the period 1898 through 1907 to protect the entrance to Tampa Bay. For anyone wanting an undeveloped Florida island where they can roam and explore freely, Fort Desoto Park is a great place. No, you won't find coconut palms, hibiscus, frangipani, bougainvillea, or any of the other non-native, tropical flowering plants associated with human horticultural pursuits. The park tries to preserve as much native vegetation as possible so the park appears much as it would have in the days of Hernando Desoto and Ponce de Leon. Parking is free throughout the park once you've paid the entrance fee. Now let's talk about the beaches.

44: East Beach

(GPS: 27.624667, -82.710818) As you enter the park you will first pass the entrance to the boat ramp, then you will pass the campground. You will come to a crossroads with Park Headquarters and its large, high-flying American Flag directly in front of you. To get to East Beach, turn left and the huge parking lot will be ahead on your right. East Beach has a huge picnic ground with shaded tables and several picnic pavilions. There is playground equipment for children and very nice clean restrooms. Lifeguards may be on duty seasonally during posted hours. This is a Tampa Bay beach, not a Gulf beach. The water is usually not very clear and the bottom is a bit muddy and there is no

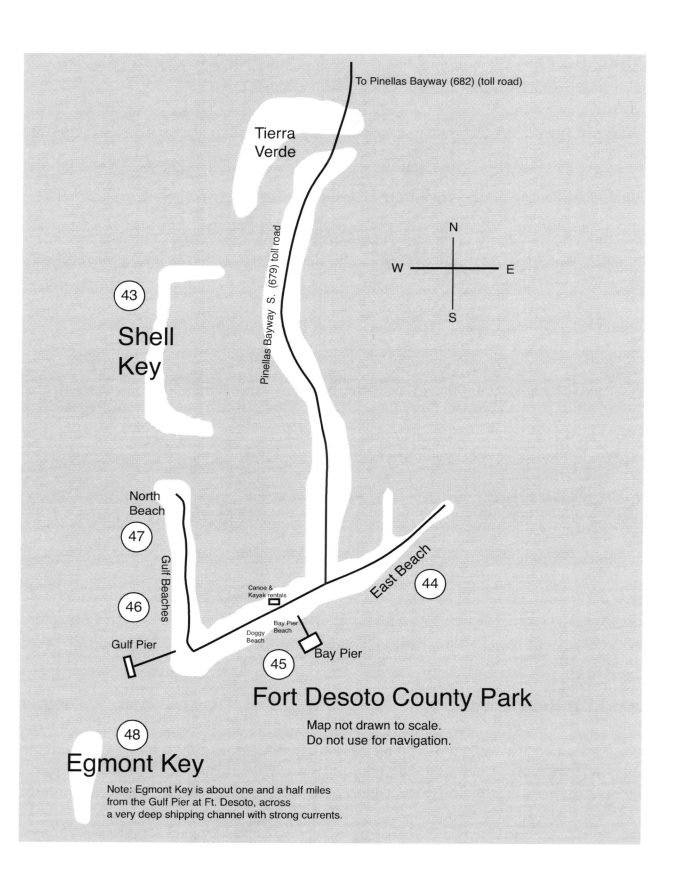

To Pinellas Bayway (682) (toll road)

Tierra
Verde

Pinellas Bayway S. (679) toll road

N
W——————E
S

(43)

Shell
Key

North
Beach

(47)

Gulf Beaches

(46)

East Beach

(44)

Canoe &
Kayak rentals

Gulf Pier

Doggy
Beach

Bay Pier
Beach

Bay Pier

(45)

Fort Desoto County Park

Map not drawn to scale.
Do not use for navigation.

(48)

Egmont Key

Note: Egmont Key is about one and a half miles
from the Gulf Pier at Ft. Desoto, across
a very deep shipping channel with strong currents.

surf here. The heavily used white sand beach is nicely maintained. This would not be my choice for going to the beach, but for a family gathering that needs shaded picnic space and wants to be on a beach, this is an excellent place. If you were to continue east, past East Beach, in a minute or so of driving you would arrive at the eastern tip of the island. This quiet point offers a nice view of the Skyway Bridge, a good place to fish from, or perhaps a place to launch a kayak or go windsurfing. There is also a hiking trail just west of Park Headquarters and long wide sidewalks throughout the park for jogging, skating, and biking. The East Beach picnic area is a popular spot for birding.

45: Bay Pier Beach and Dog Beach

(GPS: 27.617067, -82.726499) To the west of Park Headquarters is the entrance to the 500 foot Bay Fishing Pier. There is also a wide sandy beach on both sides of the pier. There are signs warning against swimming because of strong currents. Since East Beach and Bay Pier Beach are both south-facing beaches, they would be relatively warmer and calmer beaches during the winter months when a stiff north wind is chilling an otherwise warm sunny day. Walk out on the pier and you may be treated to the sight of dolphins playing or catching dinner around the pier. Also, just west of the Bay Pier Beach is Dog Beach, where you can bring Snoopy to frolic on the beach and take a swim. Doggies really love the beach. There is also a doggy park with a large fenced grassy area for Snoopy to play in and a doggy rinse-off shower. Dog beach is pictured below.

The bay pier (above) has a small bait-and-tackle shop and lights for night fishing and offers restrooms and a covered picnic pavilion. The pier closes at 11 pm. No fishing license is needed to fish from the pier because the pier license will cover pier fishermen. The ferry to Egmont Key leaves from this pier.

Birders will be interested in the large spreading mulberry tree at the east end of the parking lot, near the ranger's house. It attracts lots of spring and fall migrants and you can spend hours there identifying the various warblers that stop for a meal of insects or mulberries. Tempting though it may be, the fruit is reserved strictly for the birds.

46: Gulf Pier to North Beach

(GPS: 27.613265, -82.736501) Mullet Key is somewhat in the shape of an arrowhead pointing to the southwest. The Gulf Pier is at the tip of the arrowhead, extending 1,000 feet out into the mouth of Tampa Bay. The beaches begin on the north side of the pier and extend for about 2 miles, in a gentle curve, all the way to Bunces Pass at the northern tip of the island (North Beach). You will see people swimming along this Gulf beach but there are no lifeguards and there are signs warning against swimming because of strong currents. As I mention throughout this book, swimming in or near passes is never a good idea, and the mouth of Tampa Bay is a very large pass. There are restrooms and food and drink at the Gulf Pier. Try their homemade lemonade—it's excellent.

The Fort is located just to the north of the Gulf Pier, within walking distance. The Fort access was completely redesigned in 2012, removing the steep stairs and replacing them with a sidewalk that tacks its way up the steep hill to the top of the Fort. The top of the Fort is definitely the place to be to get a great view of the pier, the beach, and much of the island. As far as the Fort goes, it's rather modest. There are a few cannons on display, and you can go into some of the small, dark rooms that held the gunpowder and shot back in the day. All of the old wooden buildings used by the military on the island are long gone, but the foundations remain, along with informative historical signs and overgrown weeds. You might enjoy stepping into the air-conditioned museum to have a glimpse of what life was like back in the 1800's at the Fort. Oppressive heat, clouds of mosquitoes and no-see-ums, and relentless boredom were the major challenges faced by the soldiers and support staff. The fact that the soldiers had to wear uniforms made of flannel or wool imposed considerable misery on them during the summer.

Photo: Gulf Pier. No fishing license needed. Pier closes at 11pm.

Just north of the Fort is a concession and gift shop which serves the beach and Fort visitors. Various types of bicycles can be rented between the beach and the concession. Riding bicycles is the best way to see the island, and the bike trail makes it easy to get around.

North of the fort are 2 miles of beaches with no lifeguards or facilities. There is plenty of free off-road parking and there are access trails to an extremely wide white sandy beach. This is a very nice beach and is heavily used. There are no buildings along this stretch of beach between the pier and North Beach. It is a very natural area.

47: North Beach

(GPS: 27.63928, -82.73845) Like East Beach, North Beach has a huge paved parking area, a large number of shaded picnic tables, picnic pavilions, and restroom and shower facilities. There are wooded areas on the beach here and some of the nicest shaded picnic tables locations are right on the water, just north of the last parking lot. There is a full-service beach concession, restrooms and lifeguards during the summer season to guard the designated swim area. Directly in front of the concession there is a shallow tidal pool that you have to walk around to get to the Gulf Beach. A special beach wheelchair is available from the lifeguards.

You can walk on the beach all the way to Bunces Pass, overlooking Shell Key. From the main concession it is nearly a mile to the pass. You can shorten the walk by parking in the furthest north section of the parking area. Swimming is good anywhere on the beach as long as you don't get too close to the pass. The lifeguarded area is limited to the beach near the concession.

This brings us to the end of the beaches north of Tampa Bay. Across the bay to the south is Anna Maria Island, just off the coast of the city of Bradenton. The character of the islands and beaches changes dramatically when you cross Tampa Bay. With only a few exceptions, the southern islands are less commercial; they have a lot more trees and vegetation and the water is usually clearer. The barrier islands south of Tampa Bay feel more like communities and a lot less like urban sprawl (again, with a few exceptions). Tampa Bay is bridged by the Sunshine Skyway Bridge, which including the causeway is about 7 miles long.

Egmont Key can only be reached by boat. The next chapter takes you to Egmont Key which is located at the mouth of Tampa Bay between Fort Desoto Park and Anna Maria Island.

Photo: Egmont Key Gulf beach.

Egmont Key State Park

Nearest mainland city: Saint Petersburg, Florida.

Major access roads: Access by boat only, see details below.

GPS Coordinates: 27.59594, -82.76335

Entrance fee: None.

Hours: 8 am to sunset.

Pets: Pets are allowed in the park, but not on the beach. Pets must be on a six foot hand held leash.

Disabled Access: None.

Restrooms: None. The tour boats may have on-board toilets. Inquire before sailing.

Food and Drink: None. The tour boats that take people to Egmont usually either offer or sell some type of food and drink on board the boat. You can bring your own food and drink but must carry all your trash back off the island.

Alcohol: Alcoholic beverages are not allowed

Shelling: Shelling on Egmont is average to very good.

Lifeguards: No lifeguards.

Camping: No camping is allowed. Boats may moor off the beach overnight.

Weddings: Due to the difficulty of getting to the island, the logistics of a large wedding would be discouraging. However, there are local tour boats that will help you arrange a wedding at sea or on Egmont Key. So if that's what you want, go for it!

48: Egmont Key Beaches

Located at the mouth of Tampa Bay, about 2.5 miles north of Anna Maria Island and 1.5 miles southwest of Fort Desoto County Park, this barrier island is accessible only by boat. Since Egmont Key is so close to two major population centers with thousands of boat owners, Bradenton and Saint Petersburg, it has plenty of visitors, especially on weekends and holidays. Both the water and the beaches here are absolutely fantastic. The water is clean and clear and the beaches picturesque and photogenic in that Gulf-Coast sort of way. The sand is white, the water is a clear green, and the island is heavily wooded. The northern beaches are wider and have remnants of the old Fort Dade on the upper beach. The central and southern beaches suffer severely from erosion, with little or no beach available at high tide. The Gulf is lapping at the trunks of the native cabbage palms growing thickly along the shore. At low tide there is a nice clean beach with shady palms to shield you from the scorching sun. Much of the southern and eastern portions of the island are off limits to humans. Those areas are set aside for bird nesting and as a wildlife refuge. No matter, there is still plenty of island left to explore.

Be sure to bring plenty of cold drinks and something to eat. There is no food or water available on the island. During the warm months (April through October) I highly recommend that you bring a beach umbrella or shade of some kind, even though unlike many barrier islands, Egmont Key does have some shady areas in the park and even along parts of the beach there are palms that do provide some shade. But out on the beach there is no shade or shelter.

Egmont Key is a relatively small island (although on foot it seems quite large) and it continues to shrink as the Gulf gradually reclaims the western edge. Originally a 500 acre island, erosion has cut it down to a mere 200 acres and shrinking fast. This actually adds to the allure of the island, particularly for snorkelers. Parts of Fort Dade are now underwater attractions, providing interesting, but not fantastic shallow-water snorkeling. Numerous private excursion boats provide access to the island for beachgoers and snorkelers. There is no camping allowed on the island, and there are no public restrooms or other amenities. Whatever trash you generate you must also remove, as there are no trash cans on the islands. Since this is a state park the collecting of live shells is prohibited. Also prohibited are intoxicants, firearms, fireworks, and spear fishing. Fires are allowed if they are contained in a grill. The park is open daily from 8am until sunset. Pets are not allowed on the bathing beaches (except for guide dogs for the deaf or blind), but are allowed in other areas of the park if kept on a six-foot leash. Artifacts cannot be removed from the park.

Unless you own a boat, getting to Egmont Key involves contacting one of the private excursion boats that make daily trips to the island. You can take a boat for as little as $15, or you can pay more. Several of the excursion boats rent snorkeling gear and sell drinks, snacks, and have toilet facilities on board. Be sure to ask. When the weather is too rainy, windy, or cold, the ferries don't run.

The simplest and shortest trip to Egmont Key is via the Egmont Key Ferry. It leaves from the bay pier at Fort Desoto Park. It's best to call the m for reservations. Visit their web site for more information: www.hubbardsmarina.com/egmont/

Other options to get to Egmont Key include:

www.tropical-island-getaway.com

www.adventurecruise.net

www.dolphinlandings.com

www.islandboatadventures.com

If you're staying on Anna Maria Island or Longboat Key, try Seaduced Watercraft Adventures at www.seaducedagain.com or try www.amishuttleservice.com

For more information about Egmont Key, phone the park directly at 727-893-2627.

Egmont Key has an odd and interesting history mainly because of its strategic location in the mouth of a deep-water port and protected bay. I'm sure you'll want to explore the old Fort Dade and walk the old red brick roadways that seem to lead to nowhere and are now mainly used by hikers and gopher tortoises.

Today, the Tampa Bay Pilots have living quarters on the bay side of Egmont, as does the park ranger. Otherwise the island is pretty much left alone. There is a citizen support organization called the Egmont Key Alliance that works to encourage and coordinate volunteer activities in the Park. Much of the preservation and maintenance work in the park seems to be done by volunteers. I say thank-you to them for their efforts. You can visit this organization's website at www.egmontkey.info. It's a good source of information.

Skyway Bridge

Originally constructed in 1954, the bridge greatly shortened the time and distance involved in traveling between St. Petersburg and Bradenton. My father worked on a survey team on the original bridge before I was born. Because of constantly increasing traffic, a second, parallel span was completed in 1971. Then in May of 1980 a phosphate freighter called the Summit Venture collided with the bridge in a blinding rainstorm, knocking down over 1200 feet of the western (southbound) span, killing 35 people. The northbound span was then used as a two-way bridge until 1987 when the present structure, a "cable-stay" bridge costing $245,000,000, was completed. In 1990, the old main span was demolished and the northern and southern approaches were turned into fishing piers and are now the Skyway Fishing Piers State Park. Skywaypiers.com.

The bridge is located on Interstate 275 across Tampa Bay and connects to Interstate 75. It is also U.S. Highway 19.

49: Skyway Causeway Beaches

There are beaches on the causeway of the Sunshine Skyway Bridge, mainly on the St. Petersburg side. Skyway beaches are not shown on this book's maps. The best of the causeway beaches faces east and is popular with fishermen and families that enjoy the shallow, tranquil bay waters. The causeway beaches on the Saint Petersburg side of the bridge are the most popular beaches in the area for kite surfing and windsurfing. A few Australian Pines provide shade for the picnic areas. There are no lifeguards, but there are restroom facilities and vending machines on the west side of the causeway on the St. Petersburg side, and on the east side of the causeway on the Palmetto side (south side of Tampa Bay).

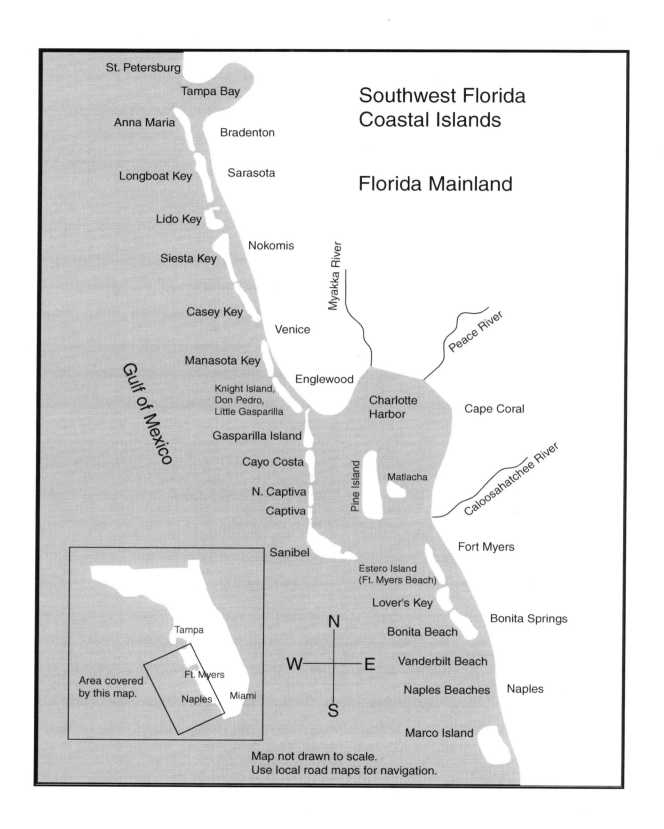

Southwest Florida
Coastal Islands

Florida Mainland

St. Petersburg

Tampa Bay

Anna Maria

Bradenton

Longboat Key

Sarasota

Lido Key

Nokomis

Siesta Key

Myakka River

Peace River

Casey Key

Venice

Manasota Key

Englewood

Knight Island,
Don Pedro,
Little Gasparilla

Charlotte
Harbor

Cape Coral

Gulf of Mexico

Gasparilla Island

Cayo Costa

Matlacha

Caloosahatchee River

N. Captiva

Pine Island

Captiva

Sanibel

Fort Myers

Estero Island
(Ft. Myers Beach)

Lover's Key

Bonita Springs

Bonita Beach

Vanderbilt Beach

N

Tampa

W   E

Area covered
by this map.

Ft. Myers

Naples   Miami

Naples Beaches   Naples

S

Marco Island

Map not drawn to scale.
Use local road maps for navigation.

114

Beaches South of Tampa Bay

South of Tampa Bay the islands have less commercial development overall. Each island has its own personality, but compared to the Pinellas County beaches, there is a lot more greenery, the water is clearer, and between Anna Maria and Manasota Key, beach parking is free. From Englewood Beach/Chadwick Park and most points south, you will generally have to pay to park your car or to enter public beach parks.

Anna Maria is the northernmost in this southwest Florida chain of islands, and is a mostly residential island with some low-rise condominiums. Driving south over scenic Longboat Pass takes you to Longboat Key, an exclusive island of expensive beachfront resorts, high-rise condominiums and few public beach accesses. Just south of Longboat Key is Lido Key and St. Armand's, with easy access to downtown Sarasota. St. Armand's has boutique shopping, fine restaurants, and art galleries. Lido Beach is within a five-minute walk.

South of Lido Key is Siesta Key, another mostly residential island, with a section of high-rise condominiums and the most beautiful beaches with the most beautiful people on the lower west coast. South of Sarasota, toward Nokomis, Venice, and Englewood, the islands are much less developed, except for the City of Venice. Casey Key, the Venice Beaches, and Manasota Key are all very laid-back, almost sleepy islands and beaches compared to those beaches nearer downtown Sarasota.

South of Englewood, Palm Island, along with Don Pedro and Little Gasparilla can only be reached by boat. Gasparilla Island, with the city of Boca Grande, is famous for its fishing heritage and old money. Cayo Costa State Park on La Costa Island is just south of Gasparilla and also can only be reached by boat. It is truly a treasure.

Next are North Captiva, Captiva, and Sanibel Islands which are a world and a life unto themselves. Expensive and exclusive though they may be, nature is protected and development limited. South of Sanibel is Fort Myers Beach, with its Key West party-town atmosphere. Still further south is Bonita Beach, a quiet but upscale beach town that has preserved much of its natural shore with Barefoot Beach Preserve.

South of Bonita Beach the Naples beaches begin, many lined with towering condominiums and sprawling luxurious beachfront estates. Money, money, and more money. At least they don't skimp on the landscaping. With plenty of coconut palms, sea grapes and other beach vegetation, the condos don't seem so overbearing.

Finally, Marco Island luxuriates in the warm calm waters of the southeastern Gulf of Mexico at the doorstep of the Ten Thousand Islands. The world is just discovering this part of Florida. Enjoy it while it is still relatively uncrowded. Change is constant.

Photo: Finding a quiet beach is not difficult on Florida's southwest coast. Casey Key.

Photo: Looking south from Manatee Public Beach, toward Bradenton Beach.

Anna Maria Island

City of Anna Maria, Holmes Beach, Bradenton Beach

Interstate 75 Exit: #220B

Nearest mainland city: Bradenton

Major access roads: Manatee Avenue (Highway 64); Cortez Road (684); Gulf Drive (789)

Directions: Three roads will take you to the island: Manatee Avenue (Highway 64), Cortez Road (684), or Gulf Drive (789) via Longboat Key. Highway 64 is accessible from Interstate 75 at exit 220B. Both Manatee Avenue and Cortez Road lead over two-lane draw bridges which become dreadfully snarled with traffic on sunny winter and spring weekends. The traffic is normally much lighter during summer and fall months. A larger, fixed-span bridge to replace the Cortez Road Bridge has been under discussion for years. It may be years more before anything gets underway.

In 2013, Island Ferry is scheduled to offer round-trip passenger ferry trips from Pass-a-Grille Beach in St. Petersburg to Anna Maria Island. Check their web site for more details. www.islandferry.biz

Entrance fee: All beaches are free and all parking is free.

Hours: The beach is open 24 hours, but public beach parks generally have posted hours.

Pets: Pets are not allowed on Anna Maria Island's beaches.

Disabled Access: Coquina Beach and Manatee Public Beach facilities are ADA accessible.

Restrooms: Public restrooms are provided at Coquina Beach and Manatee Public Beach and on all of the fishing piers.

Food and Drink: Both Coquina Beach and Manatee Public Beach have food concessions. The fishing piers have restaurants. There are plenty of restaurants on the island.

Alcohol: Alcoholic beverages are not allowed on the beaches or in the beach parks.

Shelling: Shelling on Anna Maria ranges from average to good.

Lifeguards: Coquina Beach and Manatee Public Beach have excellent lifeguard coverage during posted hours.

Camping: There are no camping opportunities on the island.

Weddings: Anna Maria Island has excellent wedding facilities and many professional planners, photographers, etc. Each year the island hosts a huge wedding show. Check it out at www.amiweddingfestival.com .

Anna Maria Island is world famous for its white sandy beaches, clear waters and relaxed family-friendly atmosphere. Visitors come here from all over the world to relax and enjoy the beauty and friendliness of the island. It's easy to find the beaches, and although parking is free, it can be hard to find a place to park at the public accesses from January through April.

The island is home to three cities: Anna Maria in the north; Bradenton Beach in the south; and Holmes Beach sandwiched in between. Each city has its own distinct flavor. Anna Maria occupies the northern third or so of the island and is largely residential. The northern tip of the island, known as Bean Point--after early settler George Emerson Bean who built the island's first house--is very quiet with no commercial activity other than the 2 piers on the bay side of the island. Bean Point overlooks the confluence of 4 bodies of water: the Manatee River, Anna Maria Sound, Tampa Bay, and the Gulf of Mexico. It is one of the most beautifully scenic places anywhere in Florida.

Anna Maria doesn't have a beach lined with coconut palms like you'll find in the Miami area, but it is fairly lush with tropical foliage, particularly on the northern third of the island. The sand is pure white quartz, and the water is usually quite clear. If you visit during late spring and early summer, the Gulf water can be nearly swimming pool clear.

Photo: Looking north on Holmes Beach. Anna Maria beaches in the distance.

While many islands on Florida's Gulf coast have succumbed to the lure of tall condominiums and large resorts, Anna Maria has avoided that type of development. In fact, the shoreline looks the same today as it did back in the early 1970's. Many of the older homes on the island have received a facelift over the years, but a person who had not visited the island since the 70's, driving around today, would still find the island much the same now as it was then.

50: Passage Key

In the mouth of Tampa Bay were two islands, Egmont Key, home of Fort Dade, and the now non-existent Passage Key, which is currently just a large sand bar exposed during low tide. Passage Key, located roughly one-half mile off the north tip of Anna Maria Island, was once a 60 acre island with a freshwater lake and was established in 1905 as a National Wildlife Refuge for breeding birds, by executive order of President Theodore Roosevelt. The island was severely decimated by the 1921 hurricane. The roughly 36 acres remaining were designated by Congress as a Wilderness Area in 1970, making it off-limits to humans. However, relentless erosion and the passage of hurricanes, especially the hurricanes of 2004 and 2005, reduced the island to not much more than a large shifting sandbar, covered with water during high tides and inhospitable to nesting birds. The prohibition against humans has been lifted, and this island remnant has now become a popular retreat for nudists, who arrive via boats and spend the day frolicking in the sun on this isolated sand bar. Hundreds of visitors anchor near the sandbar on nice weekends.

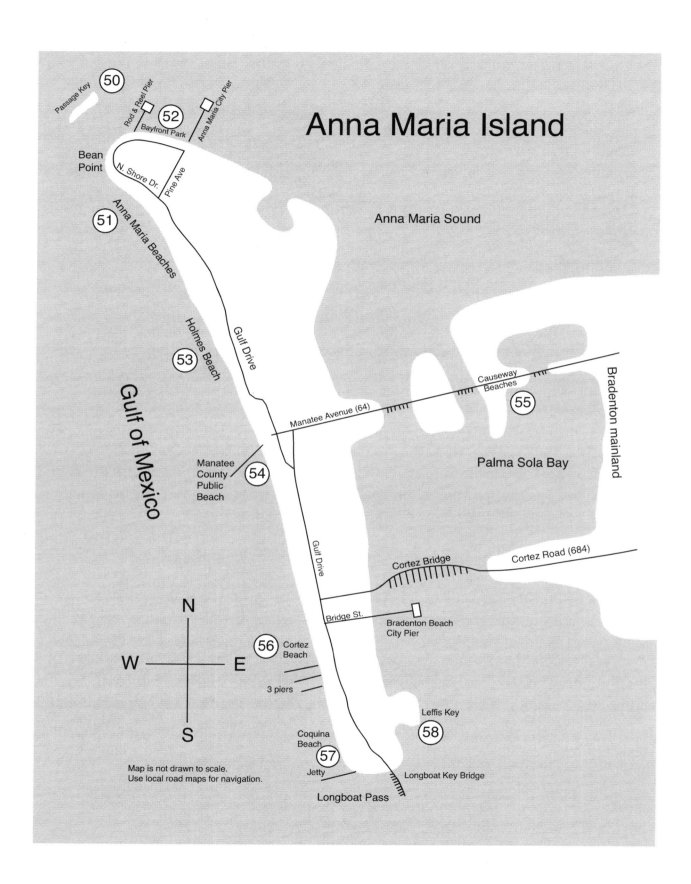

Anna Maria Island

Passage Key

50

Rod & Reel Pier

52

Bayfront Park

Anna Maria City Pier

Bean Point

N. Shore Dr.

Pine Ave

51

Anna Maria Beaches

Holmes Beach

Gulf Drive

Anna Maria Sound

53

Gulf of Mexico

Manatee Avenue (64)

Causeway Beaches

55

Bradenton mainland

Palma Sola Bay

Manatee County Public Beach

54

Gulf Drive

Cortez Bridge

Cortez Road (684)

N

W   E

S

Bridge St.

Bradenton Beach City Pier

56 Cortez Beach

3 piers

Leffis Key

58

Map is not drawn to scale.
Use local road maps for navigation.

Coquina Beach

57

Jetty

Longboat Key Bridge

Longboat Pass

51: Anna Maria Beach

The City of Anna Maria extends from about Beach Avenue to the northern tip of the island, known as Bean Point and offers roughly a mile and a half of Gulf beaches. The beach at Bean Point, the northernmost part of the island, is rarely crowded; and for good reason. The current around the tip of the island is very strong, the water is deep, and there is limited parking. This beach is mostly used by people living or vacationing within a few blocks.

Fishing is good at Bean Point but most fishermen prefer to fish from the Rod & Reel Pier or the Anna Maria City Pier, rather than from the beach. At the tip of the island the view is fantastic: Egmont Key and the sand bar formerly known as Passage Key beckon to adventurers with boats and the colors and hues of the waters change by the hour. It is one of the most scenic spots in Florida. From Bean Point one may walk east for a few minutes and arrive on the bay side of the island, or west and south along the Gulf shore. North Shore Drive is the main road following the curve of the island at the north end. It takes you through a very quiet and very well preserved older neighborhood with beautiful tropical trees and flowers. There are some very nice beach homes, but nothing really extravagant. If you are lucky enough to be here in the month of May you will enjoy the gorgeous red Royal Poinciana trees in full bloom and the fragrant frangipani trees which bloom all summer. There are beach accesses where North Shore drive intersects with Gladiolus, North Bay Blvd., Jacaranda, Cypress, and Fern. There is parallel street parking on Gladiolus, Alamanda, North Bay Blvd., Jacaranda, Fern, Poinsettia, North Shore Drive, Coconut, Sycamore, and Elm. Obey the parking signs. The north end of North Bay Blvd has a beach access with a wooden dune walkover that leads to the tip of the island. There is a bench here under the shade of the Australian pines at what is probably the quietest and most scenic spot on the island. There are several inconspicuous sand trails to the beach all along the northern tip of the island. They are marked with signs.

I don't recommend swimming at the tip of the island because of the strong current, but the Gulf shore is great for swimming. You won't run into throngs of weekend revelers here, only the occasional resident out for a stroll and families vacationing in the beach houses along the shore. The beach here is very wide and powdery, and the homes are set back a considerable distance from the shore. The dunes here are some of the largest anywhere on the lower west coast and are covered with a nice growth of sea oats. The sand is pure white quartz powder.

A mile or so south of the Bean Point is the Sandbar Restaurant on Spring Avenue, a popular hangout for those seeking the total island experience through food, drink, live music, and a view of the Gulf. The Sandbar sits right on the beach and has a large wooden deck where patrons can eat, drink and be entertained while watching the sun go down and the sailboats go by. The Sandbar has tables on the beach, so you can eat and drink with your toes in the sand. If you go for dinner, you will have a wait even with a reservation, and parking is tight. The restaurant is set up to handle weddings and receptions.

The beach along this part of Anna Maria is quiet and residential, but parking and access is limited. In recent years, parallel parking has opened up on certain streets that end at the beach. Generally parking is permitted on one side of those streets. Most streets between Oak Avenue and Magnolia Avenue offer a few parking spaces on the street. Where Magnolia Avenue meets the Gulf, the road loops around to Palm Avenue, then back to Gulf Drive. Parking by the beach is available for people with a handicap permit between Magnolia and Palm where marked. When parking on the street in residential neighborhoods, pay attention to the signs and be careful not to block a driveway.

Parking is always a problem on weekends unless you arrive before 10 am. Understandably, residents don't want their street turned into a parking lot for strangers, nor do they want "their" beach mobbed. Still, for a determined beach bum who doesn't mind arriving early or walking a distance, parking can be found.

The nice thing about Anna Maria Beach is the noticeable lack of high-rise condominiums along the shore. Several miles south, in Holmes Beach, the condominiums have a significant presence, though not to the overwhelming extent that they do on Longboat Key.

52: Bayfront Park

(GPS: 27.53482, -82.735699) As the name indicates, this beach park in the City of Anna Maria is on the bay side of the island. It is located between the Anna Maria City Pier and the Rod & Reel Pier. From Gulf Drive, take Pine Avenue and drive east for about half a mile. When you arrive at the bay, the city pier will be in front of you. Take a left on Bay Blvd., go over the humpback bridge and Bayfront Park will be to your right.

The park is open 6 am to midnight and has no lifeguards. As on most public beaches, dogs and alcoholic beverages are not allowed. This park has bathroom facilities, picnic tables (some covered), shade trees, and playground equipment for the kids. The beach is 20 to 50 feet wide, depending on the tide, and the water is shallow. If the water in the Gulf is too rough for your enjoyment I highly recommend Bayfront Park. If there is no haze on the horizon, the Sunshine Skyway Bridge can easily be seen to the northeast. Bayfront Park is in a very quiet residential neighborhood. If you get hungry and didn't bring food, there are small restaurants on both fishing piers and across the street from the city pier.

53: Holmes Beach

The City of Holmes Beach runs from about Beach Street in the north, to just south of 28th Street, near the Cedar Cove Resort and encompasses nearly 3 miles of Gulf beach. In the City of Holmes Beach, the beach can be accessed at any street end. Parking, however, is another story. Some street ends have a few spots designated for parallel parking. Try 69th street (south of the Bali Hai Resort), 68th, 65th street, 52nd street (south of Martinique condominium), 50th, 48th, 46th, and 45th street ends. There is parallel parking along 2nd Avenue just north of 43rd Street, which is just north of Manatee Public Beach. There is a large church parking lot across the street, but I wouldn't try parking there unless you want to be towed. Of course, there are no restroom facilities or lifeguards at any of the street-end access points.

Photo: Going for a morning walk on Holmes Beach, Anna Maria Island.

South of Manatee Avenue (Hwy 64) and the main public beach, there are several accesses with parking: on the curve at 37th Street is the access closest to the public beach; and another at about 33rd Street. Most street-ends in Holmes Beach between 31st Street and 28th Street offer a few parking spaces either on the street or at the dead-end. Avoid the specific "no-parking" signs and you should be fine.

54: Manatee County Public Beach

Without a doubt, this is the easiest beach access in the city of Holmes Beach. Just drive as far west as you can on Manatee Avenue and you're there (GPS: 27.49846, -82.71214). Usually there is enough parking, but I would strongly advise getting here by 10 am on weekends and holidays.

Photo: Manatee County Public Beach and lifeguard tower.

The public beach is a regular beach scene every day of the week. Everyone mixes and mingles here: northern retirees, families, and teenagers. A concession/restaurant/gift shop serves food and drink, lifeguards are on duty, and the volleyball crowd is in action. The restaurant is called "Cafe on the Beach" and opens daily at 6am. It's a very popular spot for breakfast. On weekend nights there is often live music. Seating is outdoors and is a great way to watch the sun set while you eat and listen to music. If you want to bring your own food there are a few shaded picnic tables overlooking the beach.

This is a very popular beach for taking long morning or evening strolls, or for jogging. You may walk for nearly 4 miles north or south without running out of beach. This beach used to have a concrete pier that extended 300 feet or so into the Gulf. After many decades of use and many poundings by storm surf, the pier was deemed unsafe and was removed. Discussions are underway about whether the pier will be replaced and what type of structure will be built as a replacement. I don't predict that anything will be decided soon. We could end up with another erosion control groin or a 700 foot long full-service fishing pier. It's all about where the money is coming from.

55: Palma Sola Causeway

Palma Sola causeway is on Manatee Avenue (Highway 64) where it crosses Palma Sola Bay. It has a long, narrow beach on each side of the road. The causeway on the east side of the Palma Sola Bridge has quite a bit of shade available. The causeway on the west side of the bridge has only a few palm trees, but there are covered picnic tables and bathroom facilities on the north side of the road. The

124

causeway provides people with a place to work on their tan without driving all the way out to the island.

Since the beach is very narrow, beachgoers drive their cars right down to the water's edge. This is a very popular place for catamarans and jet-skis. Weekends bring a convergence of pickup trucks, vans, hot-rods, motorcycles, and jet-skis. On the northeast section of causeway beach you may see people riding horses along the shore. This has been allowed for many years, but is beginning to become controversial due to the horse droppings sometimes not cleaned up by some horse owners. Camping or overnight parking is not allowed on the causeway, though it would seem like the perfect place for some boon docking. The "no overnight parking" rule is enforced. Alcoholic beverages are not permitted on the causeway beaches.

City of Bradenton Beach

As Gulf Drive snakes south, the island becomes increasingly narrow as you enter the city of Bradenton Beach, which offers about 3 miles of Gulf Beaches, though most of the accesses are found along the southern mile and a half of the island at Cortez Beach and Coquina Beach. There are plenty of beach vacation rentals in Bradenton Beach, and this tiny beach town has a small commercial district centered around Bridge Street, which used to connect the island to the mainland. The historic old wooden bridge was replaced by a fishing pier. Bridge Street is easy to find: A roundabout in the middle of Gulf Drive marks the intersection. There is a big multi-trunk palm tree right in the middle of the road.

The nice thing about staying in Bradenton Beach is that you can get by without a car quite easily. Yes, you do have to cross the fairly busy two-lane road to get to the beach, but everything you need is within walking distance: restaurants, limited shopping, beach supplies, convenience store, fishing pier, and beaches. Need to travel around the island? Take the trolley.

If snorkeling or SCUBA is your thing, an old molasses barge wreck, The Regina, lies in about 20 feet of water about 150 feet off the beach. The wreck is about 200 feet long and is located at about 7th Street, just north of the intersection of Gulf Drive and Cortez Road (traffic light). Parking to dive the wreck is an issue. There is a dive shop nearby called the Sea Kat (www.seakatdivers.com) that may be able to help you with parking. Or you can lug your equipment from Cortez Beach.

56: Cortez Beach

Cortez Beach (GPS: 27.46127, -82.69776) begins a half-mile or so south of Cortez Road, in the city of Bradenton Beach, and just a stone's throw south of Bridge Street. Past all the restaurants, souvenir shops, and convenience stores, the beach comes into full view to the west (to your right if you are heading south). Here, three storm battered concrete erosion control piers stand resolute against the wind, the waves, and the constantly shifting sands. Surfers like it here. Occasional tropical storms and hurricanes cause surf in the summer, and cold fronts bring waves in the winter and early spring. Some surfers even drive down from St. Petersburg and Tampa to catch waves here. Good snorkeling can be found on a hard bottom reef just off the tip of the south pier.

Walking on the piers is prohibited now because the piers are in such a dilapidated state, so that rules out fishing as well. There are no lifeguards, bathrooms, or food concessions here, but there is a substantial parking area and a convenience store up the street in case you forgot your beach supplies. The bathrooms and shaded picnic tables at the north end of Coquina Beach are within walking distance of the southern parts Cortez Beach.

On the east side of Gulf Drive rental beach cottages are built close together. All of them get you close to the beach, which isn't difficult because the island is very narrow here. At the east end of Bridge Street is the city pier which is a very popular place to fish or just take a stroll out over the bay. The pier has a small bait-and-tackle shop and restaurant.

In the early 1900's the southern end of the island was known as Cortez Beach. In its heyday, it had the only bath house and dance hall in west central Florida. In the late 1920's, a reporter for the Bradenton Herald started referring to it as "Bradenton Beach" in his articles. It upset some folks, but the new name stuck (Norwood, 2004, p. 29). Today, it's officially Bradenton Beach, but the beach near the piers is often referred to as Cortez Beach to distinguish it from the adjacent Coquina Beach to the south. Surfers refer to it as "Twin Piers," although there are actually three piers.

Bradenton beach is a frequent beneficiary of beach renourishment because it suffers from constant erosion. Huge quantities of white sand are pumped onto the shore to replace what is washed away by wave action. When I was a teenager in the late seventies, we parked in front of a jagged pile of limestone rock put in place to protect the road from the Gulf waves. Usually at high tide the rocks were awash. To get to the water you had to climb over the rocks. Today after several renourishment projects and the planting of sea oats to create a dune field, there is a lot more beach here. True progress.

The rental cottages end at 13th street south and the road takes a sharp curve. From here to the southern tip of the island nature has the upper hand, at least for now. On the bay side of the island mangroves form a dense protective forest that grows right out into the water. Leffis Key, as it is called, has been restored to a more natural state through the efforts of various organizations, and provides shelter for animals and a quiet respite for humans.

57: Coquina Beach

Coquina Beach (GPS: 27.45108, -82.69287) is named for the small, colorful, clam-like shellfish found at the Gulf's edge. As each surge of water from the breaking waves runs back into the Gulf, millions of live coquina shells are uncovered as the sand is swept away. Then they frantically dig themselves back underground until uncovered by the next surge.

Photo: Coquina Beach features a large shady picnic area and rock groins on the beach.

The sand at coquina beach is brilliant white and squeaky clean, the water is clean and is calm more often than not, and there are plenty of shaded picnic areas and parking spaces. If that's not enough, there are three buildings with bathrooms and outdoor showers, and one with a food concession which was rebuilt from the ground up in 2011.

Coquina Beach is about a mile long and stretches from about 13th street south to Longboat Pass. The beach is separated from the parking areas by a row of sand dunes covered with sea oats, and behind the dunes is a dense stand of Australian Pines. The pines create a shady picnic area that is filled to capacity during spring and summer weekends. Arrive early to get a good picnic table.

The best snorkeling is found in the form of a hard bottom reef just north of the Coquina Beach snack bar. Walk straight west from the snack bar and you'll be in line with the southern end of the reef.

In 2007 there was a big uproar when the county decided to add a paved walking path through the

the picnic area along the entire length of Coquina Beach, from Longboat Pass to 5th Street South. Many of the beloved Australian pines were destroyed to make room for the path. Despite the loss of many pines, the only place where it really had any significant impact on the amount of shade was along Cortez Beach in front of the piers. Overall, it wasn't as bad as people feared, and now there's a paved path that many people enjoy.

As you might imagine, the greatest concentration of beachgoers spread their towels near the food concession. Further south--toward Longboat Pass--the crowd thins out except on those weekends when everybody seems to be at the beach. The water currents near the pass are strong and swimming there is prohibited.

Longboat Pass is a very beautiful place. A rock jetty extends out into the Gulf and used to be popular with fisherman and sightseers, but walking on the jetty is no longer allowed. Most of the fishing in the pass is now done from the small beach under the bridge, or from the bridge itself.

Longboat Pass is a fabulous place to watch the sunset. The beach facing the pass is popular on sunny winter days because it has a southern exposure and is sheltered from the cool north wind. Walking east on this beach will take you right under the Longboat Key drawbridge to the bay side of the island. The pass is a very popular spot and boat traffic can be heavy on weekends. The bay side has a boat launching facility and picnic tables and is a popular launching site for jet skis (aka personal watercraft). Manatees and dolphins also frequent the pass, so be on the lookout for them.

On the other side of the pass is the northern end of Longboat Key--covered with Australian pines, mangroves, and Brazilian pepper trees. If you have any explorer in you at all you'll want to check it out.

58: Leffis Key at Coquina Baywalk

Leffis Key is a nature park created on a manmade island. The center of the island was built up with shell and is elevated far above the surrounding mangroves giving an excellent view in all directions. This is the highest land elevation on the island, possibly in the entirety of western Manatee County. The view of Jewfish Key, to the southeast, is particularly serene. The mound is surrounded by a moat of saltwater fed by the bay waters. Innumerable bay creatures inhabit the waters--mullet, snook, crabs, needlefish, wading birds, kingfishers, pelicans, raccoons, conchs, and whatever else swims, flies, walks, or crawls around these parts. The red mangrove and black mangrove trees surrounding the key reach out into the shallow bay waters, and provide shelter for wildlife. Boardwalks take you across the moat into the mangroves. Several spots on the boardwalk offer fishing opportunities at high tide. It's very shady and quiet among the trees on the boardwalk; the sound of the wind in the trees and the sound of the water lapping at the mangrove roots lulls me into a trance every time I walk there, especially early in the morning. There is no beach on Leffis

Key, but just to the south, between Leffis Key and the Longboat Key bridge there is a bayside beach that is very popular with jet-skiers, kayakers, and families having picnics under the trees.

In summary, Anna Maria Island is a mostly developed island. However, you won't find any large, undeveloped areas, yet neither will you find any huge sprawling luxury resorts. The island is mostly residential, with small commercial areas in each of the three cities. If you are vacationing on the island, everything you need can be found on the island, including a major grocery store. There is no nightlife and no large shopping district. Anna Maria and Holmes Beach are good places to use a bike for transportation. Bradenton Beach is a little too congested and the main streets too narrow for a bike, in my opinion.

Above photo: Anna Maria City Pier.

I feel the need to emphasize that beach parking is becoming quite a contentious issue on the island, particularly in the City of Anna Maria, which has no public beach facility. All of the beach parking in the City of Anna Maria is on-street parking, which fills up very quickly. Some people, when unable to find a parking spot, will resort to parking on private lawns and in private driveways. This angers residents (understandably), and the City will be strongly enforcing parking regulations, perhaps by towing violators in addition to issuing a ticket. This problem is created by day visitors, rather than vacationers who park at their beach house or condo.

The Manatee County Public Beach parking lot in Holmes Beach also tends to fill up early. Often, cars will resort to parking on the shoulder of the road on Manatee Avenue (Highway 64). This is not permitted. The authorities have come to understand that some people just accept the cost of a parking ticket as a cost of going to the beach. So, there are plans to start towing violators. Beware.

It's best to arrive well before 10 am to find a proper parking space, particularly on weekends and holidays during good beach weather.

Photo: Greer Island Park on northern Longboat Key.

Longboat Key

Interstate 75 Exit: 220B (S.R. 64 West), 210 (Fruitville Road)

Nearest mainland city: Bradenton, Sarasota

Major access roads: S.R. 64 (Manatee Avenue) through Bradenton, or John Ringling Causeway via Fruitville Road and US 41.

Directions: You can reach Longboat Key from Bradenton via Cortez Road (684), or from downtown Sarasota via the John Ringling Causeway. If you go through Bradenton, you will first arrive at Bradenton Beach, then turn left on Gulf Drive (789) and head south. You will cross the bridge over Longboat pass to leave Anna Maria Island and arrive on Longboat Key. If you go through Sarasota, when you get to the roundabout at St. Armand's Circle on Lido Key via the John Ringling Causeway, turn north (right) at the first side street in the circle (John Ringling Parkway) and it's a few minutes to cross the bridge over New Pass to Longboat Key. If you want to enjoy the beaches on Longboat Key, I recommend driving onto the Key through Bradenton, since the most accessible beaches on Longboat are at the north end.

Entrance fee: All beaches are free and all parking is free.

Hours: Longboat Key municipal code section 92.10 says beaches are closed from 11 pm to 5 am. Posted signs are in agreement.

Pets: Pets are not allowed on Longboat Key beaches; however some hotels, such as the Longboat Key Hilton, may allow pets in the hotel.

Disabled Access: Accesses at Broadway and several other accesses (see details in this chapter).

Restrooms: Longboat Key does not provide any beach restroom facilities. However, Bayfront Park (4052 Gulf Drive) and Joan M. Durante Park (5550 Gulf Drive) provide restrooms.

Food and Drink: Longboat Key beaches do not have any food or drink sales—not even a water fountain.

Alcohol: Alcoholic beverages are not allowed on the beaches or in the beach parks.

Shelling: Shelling on Longboat Key ranges from average to good.

Lifeguards: Longboat Key has no lifeguards.

Camping: There are no camping opportunities on the island.

The island of Longboat Key is immediately to the south of Anna Maria Island, but is worlds apart. Unlike Anna Maria, Longboat is characterized by high-rise condominiums, exclusive resorts with manicured golf courses, luxurious beachfront estates with jungle landscapes, and long, gleaming white sandy beaches. Longboat Key has an unmistakable air of exclusivity. The miles of white sandy beaches are all but inaccessible to non-residents. The few areas where access is provided by tiny parking areas have no facilities, no picnic tables, no food or drink, and no lifeguards. In short, there are no public beaches with facilities on Longboat Key. Parking is extremely limited and scattered along inconspicuously designated side roads. Streets that allow beach access are marked by small blue signs with white lettering which read "public beach access." Many are only foot paths and do not provide parking.

Residents of Longboat Key shell out big bucks to live here and want to keep the beach private for themselves and for the benefit of the many guests of the island resorts. However, by making their beaches so inaccessible, they have created a very attractive and peaceful beach for those willing to arrive early and stake out a parking spot.

While much of the shoreline (especially the southern shore) is dominated by towering condominiums, there are a few beaches that are somewhat more private and pleasing to behold. These beaches are flanked by homes set back a comfortable distance from the beach and heavily landscaped. None of the beaches on Longboat Key can be described as secluded however, except for Beer Can Island.

59: Whitney Beach and Beer Can Island (Greer Island)

Both North Shore Drive and Broadway Avenue are the public access points for Whitney Beach, which is just south of Beer Can Island. Beer Can Island is on the very north end of Longboat Key. You must walk north from the Whitney Beach access to arrive on Beer Can Island. Don't look for a sign that says "Whitney Beach," you won't find any. Just look for the small blue signs that say "Public Beach Access."

Photo: Pure white quartz sand on Whitney Beach, Longboat Key.

You get to these excellent beaches by taking Gulf Drive to North Shore Road, turning toward the Gulf and driving a few blocks till North Shore Road (GPS: 27.436596, -82.689328) dead-ends at the beach. North Shore Drive is located about 450 feet south of the Longboat Key Bridge (the bridge that joins Anna Maria Island with Longboat Key). Parking on North Shore Road is limited to 20 cars or so, and is only allowed from 5 am until dark. There is a short boardwalk down to the beach. If parking is full here then take Firehouse Road over to Broadway. There is a small parking lot there (GPS: 27.434696, -82.686400) and a nice boardwalk to Whitney Beach, but it's a longer walk to Beer Can Island. The crowd in this area is limited by the lack of parking and the fact that there are no large resorts. Unlike the gray sand on many Longboat Key Beaches, the sand at Whitney Beach is pure white quartz "sugar sand." It is so pure it often squeaks when you walk on it.

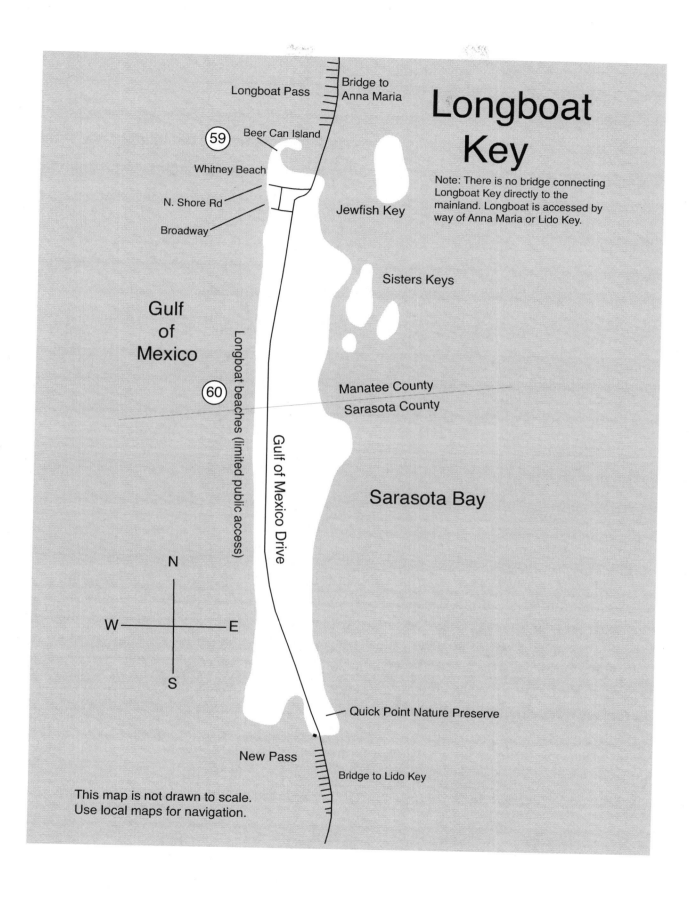

Longboat Key

Longboat Pass

Bridge to Anna Maria

(59)

Beer Can Island

Whitney Beach

N. Shore Rd

Broadway

Jewfish Key

Note: There is no bridge connecting Longboat Key directly to the mainland. Longboat is accessed by way of Anna Maria or Lido Key.

Sisters Keys

Gulf
of
Mexico

Longboat beaches (limited public access)

(60)

Gulf of Mexico Drive

Manatee County

Sarasota County

Sarasota Bay

N

W —— E

S

Quick Point Nature Preserve

New Pass

Bridge to Lido Key

This map is not drawn to scale.
Use local maps for navigation.

133

Once you are on the beach you can walk south unhindered for several hours without running out of beach, or you can walk north to the secluded area known affectionately as Beer Can Island. It is also referred to, especially by local boaters, as the North Longboat Sandbar.

The Beer Can Island area remains in a rather wild state, which adds immeasurably to its beauty. Australian Pines once towered along the shore by Longboat Pass, but now most of them are lying in the sand, roots reaching 10 feet into the air--victims of high tides and heavy surf. In some places their presence creates a maze that makes the beach impassable, so intrepid beachcombers have formed trails around them through the trees.

Photo: Beer Can Island Beach.

Truthfully, and thankfully, Beer Can Island doesn't live up to its name. I've always found it very clean. There are no picnic tables or facilities here, but there are lots of fallen trees to sit on, and there is plenty of shade. Besides, the kind of people willing to go to the trouble to visit this jewel of a spot aren't the kind needing picnic tables anyway. There are trails leading here and there through the Australian pines, mangroves, and Brazilian pepper trees. Ibises and herons stalk along the shore among the fallen trees and driftwood. This is a favorite spot for boaters to bring their families for a quiet day of fishing, picnicking and just lying on the beach watching the crowds of people at Coquina Beach on the other side of Longboat Pass.

On the east side of Beer Can Island there is a shallow, sheltered lagoon suitable for wading, fishing, and learning about the marine life of the area. This is also a great place to observe birds. The yellow-crowned and black-crowned night herons are often seen here.

Erosion is a problem on Beer Can Island. The stand of Australian Pines has been almost completely decimated by the encroaching Gulf. Soon it appears that the Gulf will connect to the backwater lagoon and turn Beer Can Island back into a true island, rather than the peninsula it now is.

Actually it is what's referred to as a "hooked spit." The tip of the island curves back into the bay and continues to form a sort of fish hook shape, creating a very sheltered and very shallow lagoon.

There are currently talks underway regarding what to do about the severe erosion on Beer Can Island and Whitney Beach. The erosion is causing the northernmost condominiums to have greater exposure to storm surges. It appears that at some point in the near future some type of concrete or rock groins will adorn the currently unspoiled white sands and clear green waters of the north tip of the island.

If you are looking for a quiet, secluded beach on Longboat Key, this is the place. Pack your cooler and get here early.

A word of caution: Avoid swimming in Longboat Pass; the current in the pass is very strong.

60: Other Longboat Key Beaches

Though the beaches of Longboat extend the length of the island, most are too difficult to reach unless you are staying in a beach house or condo. There are a few beach accesses here and there along Gulf Drive marked by small blue signs. These accesses have no restroom facilities unless noted otherwise. Block address numbers get smaller as you drive south.

Here is a list, from north to south, of other beach access points and a brief description. I've highlighted the ones I recommend:

- 6399 Gulf of Mexico Drive. This trail access is at Gulfside Road and Gulf of Mexico Drive. GPS: 27.424948, -82.674819. The nearest parking is parallel street parking on General Harris Street about 800 feet away.
- **Recommended:** Atlas Street (unpaved) and Gulf of Mexico Drive. This access has room for about 30 cars and is within steps of the beach. (GPS: 27.400855, -82.650332).
- 4711 Gulf of Mexico Drive at the Hilton. There is public parking and beach access on the south side of the hotel property.
- 4001 Gulf of Mexico Drive. Parking is available at Bayfront Park about 600 feet north of the accesses. This is one of the most scenic stretches of Gulf of Mexico Drive. The highway runs right along the beach for about half a mile. (GPS: 27.386804, -82.640320).
- **Recommended:** 3945 Gulf of Mexico Drive. Unpaved parking right by the beach. Boardwalk to beach. Also has overflow parking in an unpaved lot across the street. (GPS: 27.378286, -82.634786). There is about 1,000 feet of fairly private beach here with some woods above the beach and only a few houses set well back behind the trees. The woods are private property but the beach is public.

- 3355 Gulf of Mexico Drive. This access is at Westfield Street, which is not marked. This unpaved parking lot is right next to the beach and has space for about 20 cars. (GPS: 27.376442, -82.633469).
- 3175 Gulf of Mexico Drive. This access is at Monroe Street, which is not marked. (GPS: 27.373569, -82.631386).
- 2825 Gulf of Mexico Drive. (Parking available up the street at Town Hall, 501 Bay Isles Rd., about 1,000 feet away). This access is practically part of someone's unpaved driveway. It's just a marked sand trail to the beach. (GPS: 27.368249, -82.627337).

A few remarks about the long beaches of Longboat Key (with the exception of Beer Can Island): Longboat Key is a resort island. Sure there are residences here, but mostly they are owned by well-to-do retirees. It is not an island of families and community like Anna Maria. There are lots of exclusive resorts and condominiums with guardhouses and golf courses. The island is heavily patrolled by a very active and visible police force. So, in my opinion, it is one of the safest islands to walk around on, even after dark. But it does not have the same relaxed family "just-folks" atmosphere of Anna Maria Island. The beaches are used by a lot of older retirees and by the tourists and their families, many of them from other countries. None of the beaches could ever be described as crowded, mainly because there just isn't enough parking for off-island day visitors.

Photo: Typical Longboat Key beach access.

If you'd like to do some birding or just go for a nature walk, Joan M. Durante Park at 5550 Gulf Drive is a great place. At the south end of the island at New Pass is Overlook Park, which offers a boardwalk for fishing in the pass. It also provides parking for the Quick Point Nature Preserve (100 Gulf Drive) which you can access by following the boardwalk under the bridge. Quick Point is also good for birding.

At the foot of the bridge over New Pass at the south end of Longboat Key is Ken Thompson Parkway which leads to Mote Marine Laboratory and Aquarium (1600 Ken Thompson Parkway). I highly recommend visiting Mote, which is world famous for its research on sharks. Mote has lots of aquariums and other educational exhibits and is something you will want to see if you are in the area, especially if you have kids with you. Adjacent to Mote Aquarium is the Save Our Seabirds rehabilitation facility located at the former site of the Pelican Man Bird Sanctuary (1708 Ken Thompson Parkway). If you like birds you'll enjoy touring the facility.

Photo: North Lido Beach.

Lido Key

Interstate 75 Exit: 210 (Fruitville Road)

Nearest mainland city: Sarasota

Major access roads: Fruitville Road, US 41, John Ringling Causeway

Directions: You can get to Lido Key from Longboat Key via Gulf Drive (789), or from Sarasota via the John Ringling Causeway. From Interstate 75 you would most likely take the Fruitville Road exit 210. Go west on Fruitville to US 41. Turn left on US 41, then turn right at the next light onto 789 (just follow the signs to the beaches. You must pass through St. Armand's Circle to get to the beaches. After passing through the Circle, the road curves sharply left and becomes Benjamin Franklin Drive. There is parking along the wide avenue here and a small parking lot for North Lido Beach located at the curve where John Ringling becomes Benjamin Franklin. There is no parking on Polk Drive North or any of the street ends of Bryant, Whittier or Emerson. There is public beach parking at both Lido Public Beach and South Lido Beach at the south end of the island.

Entrance fee: All beaches are free and all parking is free.

Hours: Beaches and parks generally close at 10 or 11 pm and open at 5 or 6 am, as marked by signage. People wander the shoreline at all hours, but you can't park in the lots after they close.

Pets: Pets are not allowed on Lido Key beaches. Trained service animals are permitted.

Disabled Access: The main Lido Public Beach facilities are ADA accessible.

Restrooms: Lido Public Beach and Ted Sperling South Lido Park provide public restrooms.

Food and Drink: Lido Public Beach has a food and drink concession. North Lido Beach is within walking distance of the restaurants of St. Armand's Circle.

Alcohol: Alcoholic beverages are allowed on the beach unless otherwise indicated. Glass containers are not allowed on the beach.

Shelling: Shelling on Lido Key ranges from average to good.

Lifeguards: Lido Key offers lifeguards on Lido Public Beach and North Lido Beach. The northern reaches of North Lido do not have lifeguards.

Camping: There are no camping opportunities on the island.

Lido Key seems to have something for everyone, including over 2.5 miles of white sandy beaches. Here you will find natural, mostly undeveloped beaches in the northern and southern parts of the island, and condos, hotels, restaurants, upscale shopping, and a fine public beach in the central part of Lido Key. Also, the world renowned Mote Marine Laboratory on City Island is located nearby on the bay side of New Pass.

61: North Lido Beach

(GPS: 27.31636, -82.58172). This is a beautiful undeveloped beach located right on the curve where John Ringling Blvd curves south into Benjamin Franklin Drive. There are no facilities or food vendors here, just powdery white sand, blue-green water, and a big blue sky. Lifeguards are on duty at the main access point near parking, but the nearest public restrooms are at Lido Beach half-a-mile to the south. The beach is very wide and extends more than a mile north to New Pass. There is a wide expanse of sea oats with a foot/bicycle trail that leads to the northernmost part of the beach bordering New Pass. No houses or condos mar the natural beauty of the beach here. There is no shade here either unless you venture back into the 22 acre wooded North Lido Park with tall Australian pines located a hundred yards or so from the water's edge.

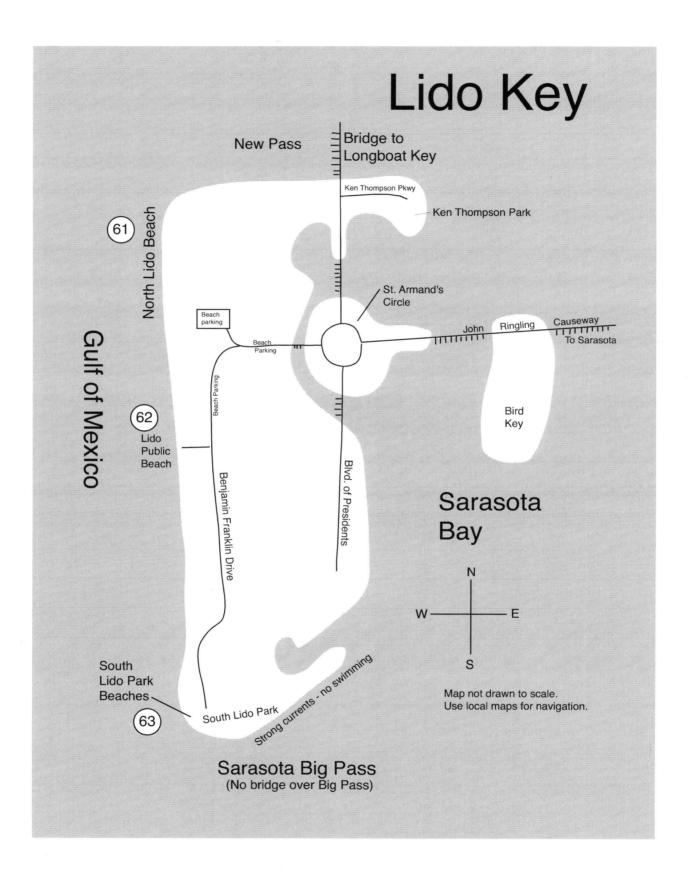

Lido Key

New Pass

Bridge to
Longboat Key

Ken Thompson Pkwy

Ken Thompson Park

(61)

North Lido Beach

St. Armand's
Circle

Beach
parking

John   Ringling   Causeway
To Sarasota

Beach
Parking

Gulf of Mexico

Beach Parking

(62)

Lido
Public
Beach

Bird
Key

Benjamin Franklin Drive

Blvd. of Presidents

Sarasota
Bay

N

W ——— E

S

South
Lido Park
Beaches

Strong currents - no swimming

Map not drawn to scale.
Use local maps for navigation.

(63)

South Lido Park

Sarasota Big Pass
(No bridge over Big Pass)

There is a very small parking area beachside at the end of John Ringling Blvd. Other parking is on-street angle or parallel parking on both John Ringling Blvd and Ben Franklin Drive. If you are dining in the St. Armand's Circle area it's a fairly short walk to North Lido Beach for an evening walk along the Gulf shore.

A walk to New Pass will provide you with a fabulous view of the incredible high-rise condominiums of southern Longboat Key in the distance across the pass, a marked contrast with the left-alone greenery of North Lido. The sand here is soft, white, and powdery and the swimming is great. I do not recommend swimming in the pass, however I often see people go in the water at the pass on an outgoing tide and let the current carry them around the tip of the island to the Gulf beach. There are no lifeguards on that part of the beach, so conduct yourself accordingly.

Photo: Trail and park above North Lido Beach.

Quite a few years ago North Lido was a beach where women frequently went topless, but it is now officially against the law for ladies to be topless on the beach. It is a very liberal beach however, and it is popular with gay couples and singles. If you walk north for five minutes toward New Pass you will start to see quite a few same-sex couples on the beach and in the dunes. Above the beach, North Lido Park for many years was known as a gay hook-up area, although authorities are reported to have cracked down on this behavior. The web site gayinsarasota.com refers to North Lido Beach as "a unique homo-haven on the sand."

62: Lido Public Beach

(GPS: 27.31190, -82.57640) 400 Benjamin Franklin Drive. Located adjacent to and immediately to the south of North Lido Beach, Lido Public Beach is narrower than North Lido along much of its length. It offers beach equipment vendors, restroom facilities, food and drink concessions, covered tables for people ordering food at the concession, lifeguards, and a public swimming pool. There is a small fee for swimming in the pool. The restroom facilities and beach are ADA accessible.

Lido Public Beach has a few shaded picnic tables behind the dune, and a number of covered tables near the snack bar. It has a large paved parking lot and several wooden dune walk-overs. There are no condos or houses along the shore of the public beach; they are set back on the east side of Ben Franklin Drive.

Photo: Lido Public Beach.

Immediately south of Lido Public Beach the condominiums and hotels line the shore. They dominate the shore for quite a distance--all the way to South Lido Park. The beach along here is very nice, and the hotels make a nice weekend getaway as well as a vacation spot. Remember that all the beaches on Lido Key are connected. A beachcomber can walk from the northernmost beach to the southernmost beach in about an hour.

63: Ted Sperling Park at South Lido Beach

(GPS: 27.30009, -82.56696) 2201 Ben Franklin Drive. Ted Sperling Park, also known as South Lido Park, is more than 100 acres of picnic paradise at the very end of Ben Franklin Drive at the southern tip of Lido Key. Acres of Australian pines provide dense shade, a necessity in spring and summer. There are plenty of picnic tables and grills. New ADA compliant restroom facilities are under construction along with additional sidewalks, scheduled for completion in spring 2014. The park has shaded playground equipment for kids in the picnic area.

Here on the south end of Lido Key the beach faces the Gulf of Mexico for several hundred yards, then curves to face Sarasota Big Pass. Siesta Key is on the other side of the pass, to the southeast. The part of Siesta Key visible from Lido is the residential area, which is nearly void of condominiums. So the view is mostly of greenery and very nice beach homes.

The current is very strong in the pass, which makes swimming unwise. Even swimming in the Gulf near the pass can be treacherous. I once spent the weekend at a hotel near South Lido Park, went swimming in the Gulf, and found the current uncomfortably strong even in 3 feet of water. That was nearly a quarter mile north of the pass. My recommendation is that this park is best for fishing, sun bathing, and picnicking, rather than for swimming. Posted signs warn against swimming, but you will see people in the water.

Photo: Ted Sperling South Lido Park, on the bay side of the island near the picnic area.

Although swimming is not recommended here, there is a usually a very large beach here for sunbathing, especially on the Gulf side. The beach along the pass is a popular stopping place for boaters, and attracts quite a few fishermen as well. Nature trails lead through a forested area of Australian Pines and mangroves along the bay and backwaters.

Pets are not allowed on the beach. Alcoholic beverages are allowed, but glass containers are not permitted on the beach. There is no lifeguard. The parking area is unpaved, spacious, and has limited shade. Parking is free. The park is closed to vehicles from 11 pm to 5 am.

South Lido Park is within easy walking distance of several hotels and within easy biking distance of anywhere on Lido Key. A second entrance to the park (190 Taft Drive), on Taft Drive about ¾ of a mile north of the main park entrance, leads to a kayak launch area on the bay. Several local kayak adventure companies launch tours from this location in the park.

Photo: Siesta Key Public Beach.

Siesta Key

Interstate 75 Exit: 210 (Fruitville Road), 207 (Bee Ridge Road), 205 (Clark Rd / SR 72)

Nearest mainland city: Sarasota

Major access roads: Fruitville Road, Bee Ridge Road, Clark Rd / Stickney Point Rd, US 41 (Tamiami Trail).

Directions: Siesta Key is in Sarasota County, just south of Lido Key, but there is no bridge from Lido Key to Siesta Key. In fact, there is no bridge connecting Siesta Key to any other island. You have to access Siesta Key from mainland Sarasota. You can use any of the Sarasota exits off of I-75 to reach US 41. From US 41 you can take either Siesta Drive to the northern part of the key, or Stickney Point Road to the southern part of the Key. If you are coming from I-75, take the Clark Road (S.R. 72) exit, # 205 and go west. When you cross US 41, Clark Road becomes Stickney Point Road and takes you directly to Siesta Key.

Entrance fee: All beaches are free and all parking is free.

Hours: Beaches and parks generally close at 10 or 11 pm and open at 5 or 6 am, as marked by signage. People wander the shoreline at all hours, but you can't park in the lots after they close.

Pets: Pets are not allowed on Siesta Key beaches. Trained service animals are permitted.

Disabled Access: Siesta Key Public Beach facilities are ADA accessible.

Restrooms: Siesta Key Public Beach facilities and Turtle Beach provide public restrooms.

Food and Drink: Siesta Key Public Beach has a food and drink concession.

Alcohol: Alcoholic beverages are allowed on the beach unless otherwise indicated. Glass containers are not allowed on the beach.

Shelling: Siesta Key generally has fewer shells than most beaches. This is one of the reasons it is so nice for walking on with bare feet; there are no shell piles to crunch through.

Lifeguards: Siesta Public Beach offers excellent lifeguard coverage and an active beach patrol. It is a very safe beach though, so lifeguards spend most of their time helping parents locate adventurous children that have wandered away. Turtle Beach does not offer lifeguards.

Weddings: Siesta Key provides the perfect beach for weddings and there is no shortage of wedding service providers.

Camping: Turtle Beach Campground, run by Sarasota County, is located directly on Turtle Beach, behind the dunes and under the shade of tall Australian pines. It's really more suited to RV's, but tent camping is allowed. They pack them in pretty tight, but you are camping within steps of the beach. See the description of Turtle Beach for more details.

Like Lido Key, Siesta Key is partly residential and partly overtaken by resorts and condos. The island offers two small commercial centers, one on Ocean Blvd. in the Siesta Village area, and the other where Stickney Point Road joins the island. The northern part of the Key is largely residential. And some fine residences indeed grace the sand here. Large tropical shade trees, rambling tropical flowers and foliage, and tall palm trees obscure the private and luxurious homes that one can only glimpse through gates, fences, and thick greenery. Private shell driveways disappear into tropical landscapes, leading to homes that I can only imagine.

The middle portion of the island is dominated by beach resorts and condominiums. One could almost mistake this part of the island for Longboat Key, except that on Siesta Key there is less space devoted to lawn and landscape. The largest condos and resorts are mostly confined to the area between Stickney Point Road and Siesta Public Beach.

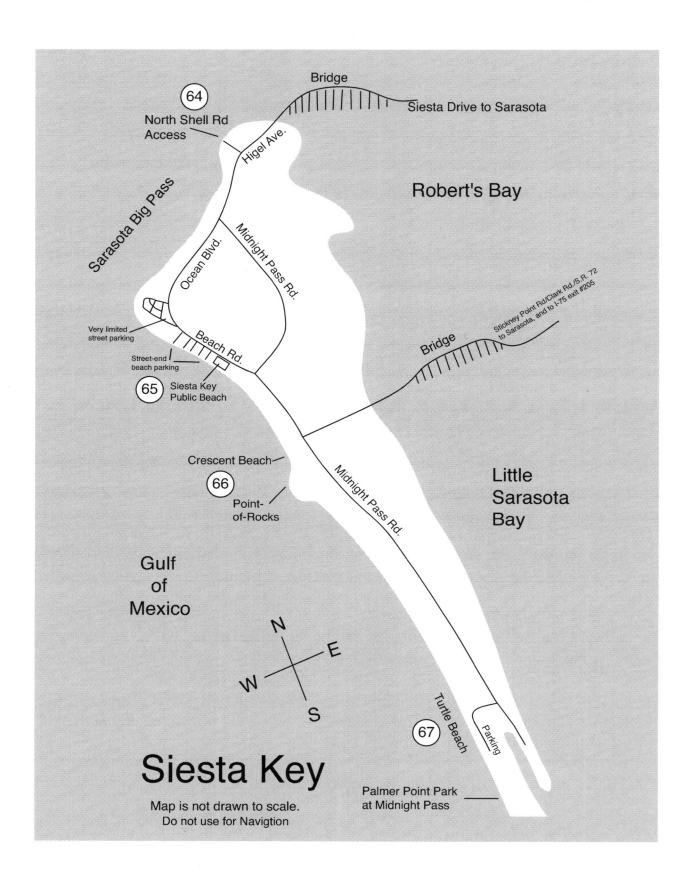

Bridge

64 North Shell Rd Access

Siesta Drive to Sarasota

Higel Ave.

Sarasota Big Pass

Robert's Bay

Ocean Blvd.

Midnight Pass Rd.

Very limited street parking

Beach Rd.

Street-end beach parking

65 Siesta Key Public Beach

Stickney Point Rd/Clark Rd./S.R. 72 to Sarasota, and to I-75 exit #205

Bridge

Little Sarasota Bay

Crescent Beach

66 Point-of-Rocks

Midnight Pass Rd.

Gulf of Mexico

N
W E
S

Siesta Key

Turtle Beach

67 Parking

Map is not drawn to scale.
Do not use for Navigtion

Palmer Point Park at Midnight Pass

The southern half of the island is much narrower than the northern half, and is devoted to residences, some of which are quite palatial. There are a few small beach resorts on southern Siesta. The Key ends at Turtle Beach and Palmer Point Park North. A few low-rise condominiums have been squeezed in at the southern end as well.

Siesta Key is physically connected at its southern end to Casey Key, but there is no road connecting the two islands. An inlet called Midnight Pass used to separate the two islands, but filled in years ago.

All the beach access points on Siesta Key are numbered, except for the two largest: Siesta Public Beach and Turtle Beach.

64: North Shell Road Access (Access #1)

(GPS: 27.29877, -82.559553) On the northern part of Siesta Key there is a small and fairly narrow beach on North Shell Road that borders Big Pass and is used mostly by the locals. There is very limited parking here. Parking is on the very shady street in front of homes. If you arrive on the Key via Siesta Drive, you will curve onto Higel Avenue. Watch to the right for North Shell Road. Turn right and you're there. There are a few choice parking spots right by the beach. Otherwise you'll be parallel parking on the street, which is allowed from 6 am to 9 pm. Be careful not to block anyone's driveway. It's a short walk to the beach. There is a fantastic view of Big Pass, and on the other side, South Lido Beach Park. If you visit the beach here regularly you will see the same faces frequently. Dogs are common on the beach here too. If the tide is low, you can walk about 600 feet to the south, but rock armoring along the beach prevents further passage. This is a nice place to stop, especially for the view, but the homes are very close to the beach, which itself is very narrow. It's a good place to view a winter sunset. During the summer, the sun sets behind Lido Key, so you won't see it sink into the water. Since this beach borders Big Pass, I don't recommend swimming here because of possible strong water currents.

Numbered Siesta Key Beach Accesses

Use these access points if you want to enjoy Siesta Beach but prefer to avoid the big crowds at the main public beach access facility. None of these access points has any restrooms, lifeguards, or other facilities. They all have brilliant white sugar sand, and shallow calm water. All but accesses 1, 2, 3, and 4 have a very wide beach. They are all located between Siesta Village and Siesta Public Beach except for access #12 and #13, which are located south of Stickney Point Road. At the time of this writing, access #6 and access #11 do not exist. I have indicated the accesses that I particularly like and recommend. Note: The access numbers below (1-13) do not correspond to any numbers on this book's maps.

Access #1 - North Shell Road – see separate description above.

Access #2 - At the west end of Avenida Messina, near Siesta Village.

Access #3 - This is just a sand trail to the beach. Located across the street from 131 Beach Road, near Siesta Village. Used by people living nearby to get to the beach. There is no parking.

Access #4 - Beach Road and Avenida Navarra. Has parking for about 4 cars.

Access #5 - **Recommended**. This access is on the curve where Ocean Blvd and Beach Road intersect in the Siesta Village. Narrow parking lot has space for about 30 cars. The beach is wide, so you'll have to walk about 500 feet to get to the water. The advantage to this access is that it is located within a few hundred feet of all the restaurants and shops in Siesta Village. Very convenient for lunch or dinner.

Access #7 – **Recommended**. Located at Beach Road and Calle de la Siesta. Parking for about 20 cars. Nearly 900 feet down the sand trail to a fairly quiet beach.

Accesses - #8 and 9 - Recommended. Located at Beach Road and Plaza de las Palmas. These two lots are within 150 feet of each other. Each has room for about 15 cars. It is roughly a 1,100 foot walk to the water from the parking lots.

Access #10 - Located at Calle Del Invierno. No parking for vehicles. It's more than a 900 foot walk from Beach Road to the water's edge on a sand trail.

Access #12 – **Recommended**. Located about 275 feet south of the intersection of Stickney Point Road (from Sarasota) and Midnight Pass Road on Siesta Key. This is the access to the south end of Crescent Beach and Point-of-Rocks. The parking lot is very narrow. If you plan to go snorkeling or fishing at Point-of-Rocks, this is the access you'll need to use. Get here before 11 am. Earlier on weekends.

Access #13 – This access is in the Point-of-Rocks neighborhood, south of Stickney Point Road. This is the closest access to the snorkeling area at Point-of-Rocks, but there is no parking for vehicles here. It is used by people who live in or are vacationing in the neighborhood. Good access for anyone on foot or bicycle.

65: Siesta Public Beach

(GPS: 27.26674, -82.55202). 948 Beach Road. Just follow the signs to Siesta Public Beach. If you're coming from the north, you will drive through Siesta Key Village, a small shopping and restaurant district on Ocean Blvd. At the public beach there is also parallel parking along the street in addition to a large paved parking lot (which fills up quickly). On this 40-acre public beach there is a food concession, restroom facilities, tennis courts, and a large shaded picnic area with tables and grills just south of the concession. There are lots of volleyball nets and playground equipment for kids. Best of all, it has excellent lifeguard coverage. The beach is huge, the sand is soft and pure white, the water is calm, clear, and shallow, and everything you need to be comfortable for the entire day is available right here at the beach facility.

ADA access note: A special beach wheelchair is available to help people with impaired mobility get across the soft sand. Once you've used the wheelchair to get you to your destination, it is to be returned so someone else can use it. If you prefer to have a beach wheelchair for your unlimited use, Siesta Sports Rentals offers them by the day or by the week (941-346-1797).

In recognition of all it has to offer the public, Siesta Beach was chosen by Dr. Stephen Leatherman (Dr. Beach) as the best beach in the nation in 2011. The sand is mineral quartz and is so pure that it squeaks when you walk on it. Imagine yourself walking on a beach covered with fine sugar and you'll have the picture. If you've ever visited any of the beaches in the Florida panhandle, you know that they are also brilliant white quartz beaches. The main difference is that the sand grains on Siesta Beach are much finer, almost like powder.

Most people do not know that the area of low dunes and vegetation about 300 feet north of the public beach is actually a conservation area. It is roughly one-and-a-quarter acres of undeveloped dune and beach that were donated in 2008 to the Conservation Foundation of the Gulf Coast which oversees the preservation of the tract.

Photo: Siesta Beach has a wide, soft, pure white quartz sand beach.

Siesta Public Beach truly is a magnificent beach. The sand near the water's edge is packed hard enough to make walking or jogging long distances a pleasure. I've even seen baby carriages being pushed along the beach down near the water where the sand is most firm. The beach is very flat and slopes gently into the water, making it very friendly to children or to people who have difficulty walking in soft sand or on steep or uneven surfaces. The shoreline to the north of the public beach has a very wide beach and no condominiums for quite a distance. Although there are vacation homes along the shore, they are set back a considerable distance. The crowd thins out quite a bit as you walk north from the main public beach toward public access numbers 7, 8, and 9.

Siesta Public Beach is where the beautiful people go to the beach, so it is one of the best beaches in the state for people watching. It may attract as many as 30,000 people during a weekend with good beach weather. Alcoholic beverages are allowed on the beach, but glass containers are not. Lifeguard protection is excellent, and law enforcement maintains a presence on all parts of the beach. This is an extremely safe beach. Lifeguards spend a lot more time looking for "lost" children than in performing rescues.

Immediately south of the public beach the condominiums rise out of the sand behind the wide sandy beach. The monoliths stretch for two miles or so before giving way to a more eye-pleasing coastline of greenery and hidden beach houses south of the Point-of-Rocks neighborhood. This is a very popular jogging and strolling beach.

You can easily walk or bike unobstructed on the beach from roughly Columbus Blvd. all the way to Point-of-Rocks, a distance of not quite 3 miles. It is common for people to walk from Siesta Public

Beach to Point-of-Rocks and back. If you don't like to look at condominiums and resorts, you can walk to the north where there is a larger separation between beach and buildings.

If you're on Siesta Key on a Sunday evening, come on over to the public beach and check out the drum circle. It starts a couple of hours before sunset and winds up around 10 pm. There's lots of drumming, dancing, and socializing. It happens near the main pavilion, but can be heard all over the beach. It's a lot of fun and attracts plenty of interesting characters who come to express themselves. You don't have to dance or drum, just show up and watch!

Even though Siesta Public Beach is a top-notch beach facility, plans are in the works for major improvements, including a pedestrian walkway the length of the park, a bigger and better parking lot, improved restrooms, upgraded concession, a new multiuse shelter, a lawn for special events, and general renovation. Construction is generally set to begin in 2013.

66: Crescent Beach and Point-of-Rocks

(GPS: 27.25005, -82.536934). This is a beach you could easily miss. How unfortunate for you that would be. Crescent Beach is located south of Siesta Public Beach. It is dominated by large condominiums and resorts, but the beach and water are beautiful. The problem, unless you are staying at one of the beach resorts, is finding a place to park. Crescent Shopping Center is located nearby, but be warned about using it for beach parking. A designated parking area at beach access #12 is sandwiched in between the Sea Shell resort and the Siesta Breakers where Stickney Point road intersects Midnight Pass road. (GPS: 27.251264, -82.535235). It's just a narrow alley, so don't try to park an RV here. There is probably space for 30 cars or so. Get here early. That means by 9:30 am on weekends.

Once you've secured a parking spot you have it made. It's a short walk to the wide, white powdery beach. You'll be sharing the beach here with the vacationers in all of the resorts along the coast here, but there's plenty of room. The water is beautiful and shallow and the swimming is fantastic. Here at Crescent Beach you are within a five-minute walk (1,500 feet) of the best snorkeling to be found in this area of the state. The south end of Crescent Beach is called Point of Rocks, and has an unusual feature for a coastline characteristically defined by white sand. Flat, smooth beach rock shelves lie under the shallow water here and provide an ideal habitat for the bright Red Boring Sponge (often mistaken for coral), closely cropped sea plants, and a very interesting fish population. The water is very shallow--three to six feet--and there are acres of rocks and crevices to explore. Fish you are likely to see include mangrove snapper, sheepshead, pompano, various species of jacks, grouper, sergeant major, snook, mullet, redfish and much more. Dolphins and manatees are a common sight. The visibility underwater is probably best during May and June, before the summer rains begin. On a really good day, visibility is about ten feet, which is fine when you're in only three to six feet of water. After heavy rains or during turbulent weather visibility may be reduced to two feet because of sediment suspended in the water.

At Point of Rocks there is a sea wall about eight feet high along the shore with a decorative mural painted on it. Past the sea wall and you will find a rather rough and narrow 2,000 foot long sand and broken shell beach above the flat limestone rocks. There is a narrow ledge on the seawall that you can walk on and there are steps to the beach at the end of the wall, but they are usually awash during high tide and are nearly impossible to navigate if the water is rough. There are homes along the beach here, but they are perched on a bluff twelve or more feet above the beach. Wooden steps lead from each home, hidden behind foliage, down to the beach. In the distance to the south, you can see Turtle Beach.

Photo: Point-of-Rocks showing beach rocks exposed at low tide.

67: Turtle Beach

(GPS: 27.21944, -82.51715). Driving south for several miles on Midnight Pass Road will take you to Turtle Beach. This beach facility has a park setting and is next door to a small campground. It is markedly different from the white sand beaches on the northern half of Siesta Key. In the middle of the park is a murky lagoon—part of a former inlet called Blind Pass—surrounded by covered and shaded picnic tables, a volleyball net, a small boat ramp, and restroom facilities. There is a good-sized parking lot near the dunes. The beach is hidden from view by dunes covered with sea oats. Wooden dune walkovers provide access to the beach, which suffers rather badly from erosion, so when you visit it may be very wide or it may be narrow. Regardless of the width, it is a very popular beach. The sand here contains a lot of fine crushed shell and dark minerals and so is quite coarse. Do not expect a soft fluffy white sand beach here.

152

Because of the shell content on the beaches south of Point-of-Rocks, the sand does not pack firmly and makes walking long distances a chore. The sand also has dark specks of minerals and fossilized materials (including shark teeth) mixed with the quartz grains and shell. Depending on the shell-to-fossil ratio at any given time, the sand may appear either light brown or light gray.

Another thing you'll notice that's different about Turtle Beach is that the beach near the water's edge is steeper than on beaches further north on Siesta Key, and when you enter the water there is a quick drop off, then a gradual slope. This is not a dangerous geographical feature, but does make it more difficult for people with balance or mobility issues to get into the water. It also makes this beach less safe for small children, since the water goes from ankle-deep to mid-thigh (adult) deep very quickly. On a positive note, this drop-off is really nice when you just want to get in the water and swim or cool off without having to wade 100 feet out to find water that's deep enough.

Photo: Turtle Beach on southern Siesta Key.

If you choose to trudge north on the beach for a half-mile or so you will find yourself on a very quiet beach with some very luxurious beach houses hidden behind the thickly growing landscape. In some places there are Australian pines trees growing close to the water, providing a nice place to stop and enjoy the serenity. Look north and you can see Point of Rocks. In the summer, when all the homeowners have gone back north, this can be a very quiet place. However, for even more quiet and private remoteness, read on.

If instead of walking north from Turtle Beach, you walk south, you will walk past a number of condominiums before reaching a very quiet beach with no homes or condos. This is Palmer Point Park. Behind the beach is a waterway which is a remnant of a former inlet and is a popular anchoring spot for the pleasure boaters that frequent the beach at Palmer Point. Midnight Pass used to cut through here, separating Siesta Key from Casey Key, but Midnight Pass has been filled in with sand and now the two islands are connected. However, no road connects the two islands, so you can't drive to Casey Key without going back through Sarasota. Sometimes it is not possible to easily walk south past the condominiums. The condos have rough rocks piled on the beach the length of the building to serve as a breakwater. This has caused the erosion of the beach. So except during really low tides you may have to wade through a foot or two of water to get past the condos. This could be dangerous if there are any waves. A better plan would be to visit Palmer Point Park by kayak. Closest launches would be Turtle Beach lagoon, Blackburn Point Rd, or Vamo Drive.

Since it's such a long walk to Palmer Point Park, it's not a crowded beach. Boaters come here for the day, especially on weekends, and a few people find the unspoiled beach to be worth the trek. There are no buildings or facilities at Palmer Point Park, only Australian pines and beach vegetation. South of Palmer Park, the beach on Casey Key is also nearly deserted. The reason: there is no beach access on this part of Casey Key. The only way to get here is to walk from Turtle beach, come by boat, or live on Casey Key. And not many people could even hope to live on Casey Key. Just take a look at the palaces along the beach here and you'll see what I mean. It's worth the walk just to behold the opulent excess of America's upper strata, and wonder what your life would be like if you had created Facebook or Google. Another feature of the beach along Palmer Point and Casey Key is that a wonderful variety of flotsam and jetsam seems to wash up on the beach here, from expired marine life to various nautical paraphernalia. I once found a very interesting clay smoking pipe washed up on the beach here.

Turtle Beach Campground

If you don't mind camping in very close proximity to your neighbors, Turtle Beach has a campground that is operated by Sarasota County. The campsites are arranged on each side of a narrow road that runs from Midnight Pass Road almost to the dunes, a distance of about 500 feet. The entrance to the campground is 180 feet north of the entrance to Turtle Beach. You can easily see the RV's and trailers from the parking lot of Turtle Beach. Although tent camping is allowed, most of the "campers" are living in large trailers or motor homes. I don't know how they do it, but some folks can back a forty-footer into the RV sites. The entire campground isn't even 150 feet wide, including the road.

The campground has 44 campsites with rates ranging from $32 to $60 per night as of this writing. Weekly and monthly rates are available. The closest campsites to the beach are about 200 feet from the sand. Pets are not permitted in the park.

For more information, visit the campground web site at www.scgov.net/turtlebeachcampground or call the office at 941-349-3839.

Photo: Nokomis Beach on Casey Key.

Casey Key

Interstate 75 Exit: 205 (Clark Road / SR 72)

Nearest mainland city: Sarasota, Nokomis

Major access roads: Clark Road / SR 72, US 41, Blackburn Point Rd, Albee Road

Directions: Casey Key is in Sarasota County and is joined to Siesta Key at the point where old Midnight Pass, the former inlet, used to be. The pass was filled in with sand in 1983. However, you still cannot drive directly from Siesta Key to Casey Key. There is no connecting road. To get from Siesta Key to Casey Key you must go back into Sarasota and take US 41 to Blackburn Point Road or Albee Road. If you are coming from I-75, take the Clark Road exit #205 and go west to US 41. Turn left (south) on 41 and drive south for 15 minutes or so to Blackburn Point Road or further to Albee Road. If you want to tour the whole island, which I highly recommend, use Blackburn Point Road. If you just want to go straight to Nokomis Beach or to the North Jetty, use Albee Road.

Entrance fee: All beaches are free and all parking is free.

Hours: Beaches and parks are open from 6 am to midnight every day.

Pets: Pets are not allowed on Casey Key beaches.

Disabled Access: Nokomis Beach facilities are ADA accessible and North Jetty Park facilities are being upgraded to be ADA compliant with a scheduled completion date of January 2014.

Restrooms: Nokomis Beach and North Jetty Park beach each provide restrooms.

Food and Drink: Nokomis Beach has a food and drink concession. North Jetty Park has a small snack shop in the bait shack located on the Venice Inlet. The Casey Key Fish House restaurant is located on Blackburn Point Road near the bridge.

Alcohol: Alcoholic beverages are allowed on the beach unless otherwise indicated. Glass containers are not allowed on the beach.

Shelling: Casey Key has an average selection of shells. Shark teeth and other fossils may be found on the beaches.

Lifeguards: Nokomis Beach and North Jetty Park both have lifeguards year-round during posted hours.

Weddings: Casey Key is an excellent location for beach weddings.

Camping: There are no opportunities for camping on Casey Key.

Casey Key is an unusual island. I can describe 95 percent of the Key by using two words: luxury homes. Unlike many of the barrier islands, Casey Key does not have east-west avenues that dead-end at the beach where a beach access trail is provided. It has but one road: Casey Key Road, which runs the length of the island. The only public access to the beaches on Casey Key is at the southern portion of the island. To really explore the central and northern beaches of Casey Key, I recommend a kayak. Under Florida law, the beach is public up to the high tide line, so you can beach your kayak and enjoy the lower portion of the beach without penalty.

The Key is just across the Intracoastal Waterway from the town of Osprey and just south of Siesta Key. There are two roads leading to the Key. The first, Blackburn Point Road, takes you across a narrow one lane draw bridge and leaves you with a choice: turn left or right. Turn right and you will follow North Casey Key Road north along a winding path through beautiful beachfront residential estates. The narrow road continues north for about two miles to Palmer Point Park, but the public only has access to the first mile of road. Although the road does pass directly along the Gulf beach for quite a scenic distance, there is no parking allowed anywhere. The island residents discourage the public from taking this scenic drive by making the road very narrow, and by posting signage warning that on this dead-end road there is no place to turn around.

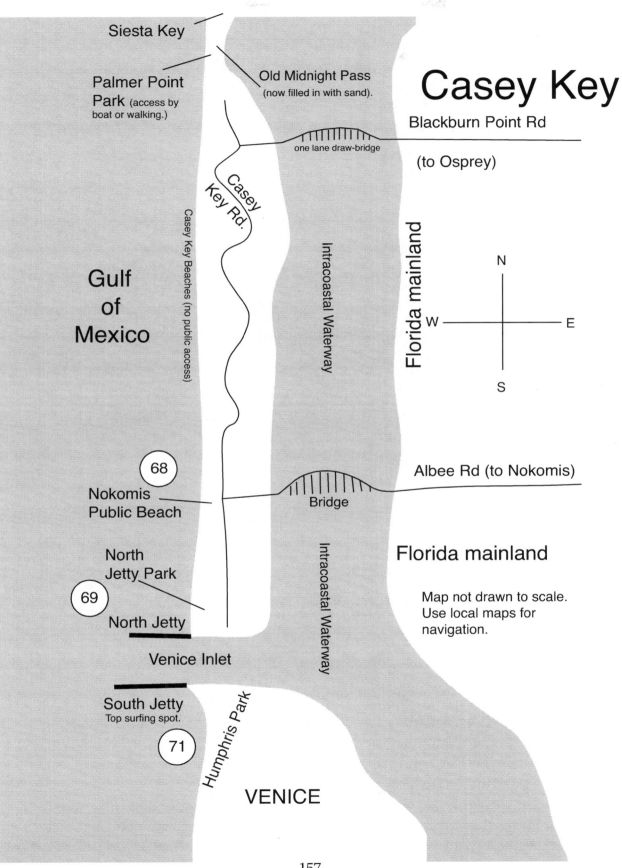

Casey Key

Siesta Key

Palmer Point Park (access by boat or walking.)

Old Midnight Pass (now filled in with sand).

Blackburn Point Rd

one lane draw-bridge

(to Osprey)

Casey Key Rd.

Gulf of Mexico

Casey Key Beaches (no public access)

Intracoastal Waterway

Florida mainland

N
W   E
S

(68)

Nokomis Public Beach

Albee Rd (to Nokomis)

Bridge

Intracoastal Waterway

Florida mainland

Map not drawn to scale. Use local maps for navigation.

North Jetty Park

(69)

North Jetty

Venice Inlet

South Jetty
Top surfing spot.

(71)

Humphris Park

VENICE

157

However, there are plenty of private driveways one could use as a turnaround as some of the houses are set so far back in the foliage you can hardly see them. My recommendation is that you explore this beautiful mile of scenic road on your bike to get the most enjoyment. If you want to do this, there is a small park on the bay side of the island right after you cross the Blackburn Point Road Bridge. You can park your car there and begin your bike ride. Be quiet and respectful of the neighborhood and you should not have any issues. Don't try to access the beach from North Casey Key Road.

Photo: Scenic North Casey Key Road.

If you turn left (south) from Blackburn Point Road and head south you will follow a winding, twisting route south through homes fit for kings, with landscapes that are carefully cultivated, but still have a wild and natural presence. The Key is narrow, and many homes have their back yard on the bay and their front yard on the Gulf. The road seems like an intruder; the cars are the only noise breaking the silence in this cultivated island refuge for the well-to-do. After fifteen minutes or so of twisting and turning, Casey Key Road leads you through a small and unexpected collection of modest beach rental cottages just north of Albee Road before arriving at the public beaches.

If you don't want to take such a circuitous route to the beaches as is provided by Blackburn Point Road, take the other route to the Key, Albee Road, which will take you from US 41 directly to the public beach accesses on Casey Key.

68: Nokomis Beach

(GPS: 27.12429, -82.470549). 100 Casey Key Road. Nokomis Beach is located at the west end of Albee Road. The beach is separated from the parking area by plant covered dunes. Access is provided by wooden dune walkovers and boardwalks along 1,700 feet of Gulf beach. This beach park encompasses 22 acres that also includes access to the intra-coastal waterway and to an excellent boat ramp. This beach has excellent restroom facilities, a covered pavilion and covered picnic tables, a snack bar, and beach volleyball. The beach sand has a high content of tiny shell fragments which makes the sand coarser than on the white powder beaches on Siesta. The sand is a beautiful off-white, slightly golden color. There are lifeguards on duty and it's a short walk south on the beach to North Jetty Park.

The unique beach plaza structure, originally built in 1956, was designed by Jack West, an architect from Illinois who had gained his knowledge of this European-influenced minimalist 1950's architecture by working with the local firm of Twitchell and Rudolph, a firm associated with the design work typical of the Sarasota School of Architecture during that period.

Each Wednesday and Saturday evening, this beach is the site of the Nokomis Beach Drum Circle which attracts many hundreds of people, filling the parking lot with cars and the air with the sound of tribal drums. You'll see all kinds of free-form dancing, belly dancing, and all kinds of hand-held musical instruments accompanying the drum rhythms. This free event starts an hour or so before sunset. Visit www.nokomisbeachdrumcircle.com .

69: North Jetty Park

(GPS: 27.114346, -82.467462). 1000 Casey Key Road. Located at the southernmost end of Casey Key, just south of Nokomis Beach, North Jetty Park is right on Venice Inlet, the narrow pass between Venice and Casey Key connecting the Gulf and the bay. Within the park's 18 acres there are plenty of shaded picnic tables, restroom facilities, and a small fish-camp type store with snacks/bait/tackle, etc., and picnic tables overlooking the inlet. The park generally is a place where retirees hang out during the week, but with an influx of some families on the weekends. The bay side of the park has several kayak launch beaches and some shaded picnic areas.

The beach is the same as Nokomis Beach; it's just three-quarters of a mile further south. The jetty here at the inlet is a long pile of huge granite rocks bordering each side of the inlet. Asphalt was poured over the top of the rocks to hold them together and provide a flat surface for fishermen and sightseers to walk on. There is a jetty on both the north and the south sides of the inlet, although the north jetty seems to be the most popular with fishermen, perhaps because it is a bit easier to get to from Sarasota. It has a bait shop too. Look for dolphins, manatees and large rays in the inlet. The dolphins and rays may jump completely out of the water. Surfing is good on the north side of the north jetty during a south or west swell.

The color of the water near the jetty can change with the tide. On an outgoing (ebb) tide, tannin-stained water from the inland waterway mixes with the clear Gulf waters. The transition zone can be quite striking in appearance at times. On the incoming (flood) tide, the inlet and surrounding waters take on the clear, green color typical of the Gulf of Mexico.

Photo: Venice Inlet and jetties.

The beach is protected by lifeguards, and wooden dune walkovers provide passage across the dunes, which are heavy with vegetation. The park area has some very large sea grape trees that provide shade, along with the Australian pines. The scenic view from the jetty makes it easy to compare the condominium-heavy Venice shoreline to the south with the tranquil, tree-lined shore of Casey Key. An adventurous beachcomber could walk north for miles along Casey Key without running out of beach, but the beach here is not hard-packed enough to ride a bike.

North Jetty Park is, during 2013, undergoing a $1.4 million renovation. The park will get new, larger ADA compliant restrooms and a concession. Parking lots will be improved and there will be paved walkways with crosswalks and paved ADA parking. The park will remain open during construction but there may be some inconveniences. Completion date is set for January 2014.

Driving the length of Casey Key I always try to imagine what it would be like to live here. It is quiet, except for the occasional cars passing by. There is no town center or shopping center. It is a beautiful island with beautiful homes, all valued at more than a million dollars, and all of which have a beach right across the street. However, to me it is noticeably missing one thing in particular: a sidewalk. There is no good way to travel on the island except by car. The road is narrow and lacks a shoulder and there are too many blind curves for me to feel comfortable walking or riding a bike except during times when traffic is very sparse. A wide sidewalk to stroll and bike on would tremendously enhance the experience of living on and visiting this island.

Photo: Venice Municipal Beach looking north.

Venice

Interstate 75 Exit: 193 (Jacaranda Blvd)

Nearest mainland city: Venice beaches are mainland beaches in the city of Venice.

Major access roads: Jacaranda Blvd, Venice Avenue.

Directions: Venice is located 15 minutes south of Sarasota and Nokomis on US 41. From I-75, take the Jacaranda exit #193 and follow Jacaranda Blvd. to Venice Avenue. Venice Avenue will take you right through downtown Venice and straight to Venice Municipal Beach.

Entrance fee: All beaches are free and all parking is free.

Hours: Beaches and parks are open from 6 am to midnight every day, except Paw Park which is open from 7 am until dusk.

Pets: Pets are not allowed on the beaches, except at Paws Park just south of the Venice fishing pier. Service dogs are generally permitted.

Disabled Access: Venice Municipal Beach, Brohard Park (by the pier), and Caspersen Beach have restrooms that are ADA compliant, and provide boardwalks with ramps to the beach. However, at the time of this writing, only Venice Municipal Beach offers beach wheelchairs.

Restrooms: All public beach parks provide restrooms.

Food and Drink: Venice Municipal Beach, Humphris Park (at the jetty), and Sharky's Restaurant at the Venice Fishing Pier all provide food and drink on the beach. There are plenty of restaurants on Venice Avenue off U.S. 41, just a few blocks from the beach.

Alcohol: Alcoholic beverages are allowed on the beach. Glass containers are not allowed on the beach.

Shelling: The Venice beaches have a selection of shells that ranges from average to very good. Shark teeth and other fossils are found on the beaches and in the water.

Lifeguards: Venice Municipal Beach offers lifeguards year-round during posted hours.

Weddings: Venice Beach is an excellent location for beach weddings.

Camping: There are no opportunities for camping on Venice beaches.

70: Venice Municipal Beach

(GPS: 27.10046, -82.459748). 101 The Esplanade, Venice, FL. Take Venice Avenue as far west as you can and you will see Venice Municipal Beach right in front of you. The street that runs north and south along the Gulf is called The Esplanade. Venice Beach has lifeguards on duty during posted hours, and a beach pavilion with a striking winged design houses a food concession and restrooms. Venice Beach is a great spot to find fossilized shark teeth. Look for them down by the water's edge. As Sanibel Island is famous for its shells, Venice is famous for its shark teeth. You will see many people sifting through the sand in search of the dark colored teeth. Because of the heavy fossil deposits located just offshore, Venice has a natural black sand beach. It isn't really all black, but it is very dark because of all the tiny pieces of fossils mixed in with the sand. The offshore fossil deposits attract SCUBA divers who are able to collect the fossils before they are worn down by wave action on the beach. The really big shark teeth are found off the beach in about 15 to 20 feet of water.

In April each year, Venice hosts the Shark Tooth Festival on the airport grounds not far from the beach. It draws quite a crowd. You can see, touch and buy shark teeth and fossils of all kinds. Visit

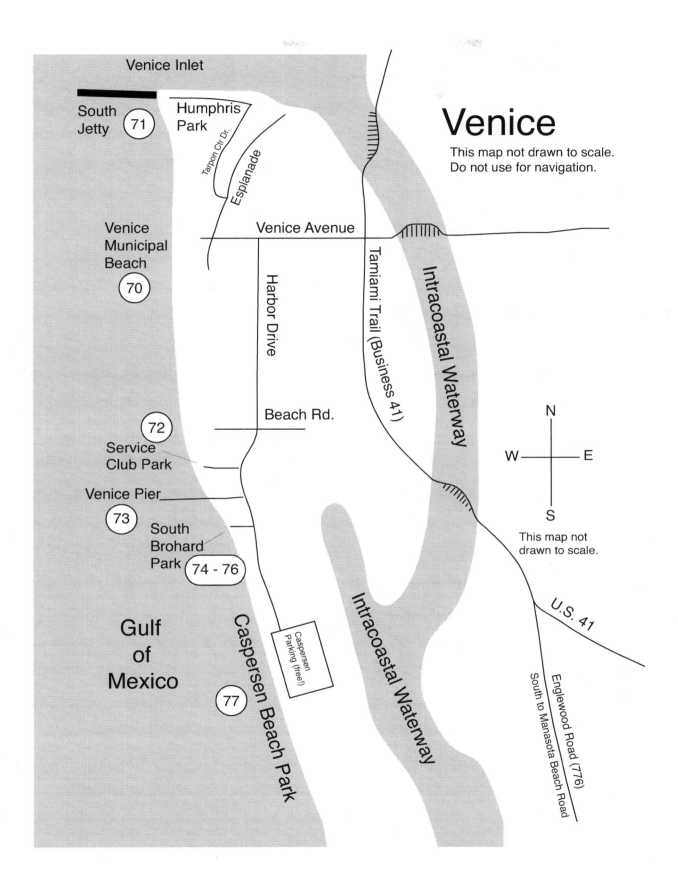

Venice Inlet

Venice

This map not drawn to scale.
Do not use for navigation.

South Jetty (71)

Humphris Park

Tarpon Ctr Dr.

Esplanade

Venice Municipal Beach (70)

Venice Avenue

Harbor Drive

Tamiami Trail (Business 41)

Intracoastal Waterway

N
W — E
S

This map not drawn to scale.

Beach Rd.

(72)
Service Club Park

Venice Pier
(73)

South Brohard Park
(74 - 76)

Gulf of Mexico

Caspersen Beach Park

Caspersen Parking (free!)

(77)

Intracoastal Waterway

U.S. 41

Englewood Road (776)
South to Manasota Beach Road

their web site at sharkstoothfest.com. When sand is added to the beaches during infrequent beach renourishment projects, large sections of the black sand beach may be covered with lighter colored sand, but the fossils still can be found at the water's edge and in the water. Hunting for shark's teeth along the Venice beaches is so popular that local sporting goods stores sell special scoops—sometimes referred to as "Florida snow shovels"—for sifting the sand. In a few hours of collecting, anyone can find hundreds of teeth and other fossils.

Venice beach is flanked by condominiums which house a large retirement population. The city attracts quite a few European visitors, and it is not unusual to hear Italian being spoken on the beach. Many of the street names are Italian. Venice, Florida refers to itself as the "sister city" of Venice, Italy.

71: South Jetty (Humphris Park)

(GPS: 27.11233, -82.46663). 2000 Tarpon Center Drive, Venice, FL. Follow The Esplanade north to Tarpon Center Drive. Turn left on Tarpon Center Drive and follow it to its natural end at the Venice Inlet and the south jetty, officially named Humphris Park. Popular with fishermen all year, this jetty is one of the best surfing spots on the west coast on a north or west swell, which usually happens during winter cold fronts. The park is nearly surrounded by water, with the Gulf on the west and south side, and the inlet on the north side. From south jetty you can access the beach, but this is really more of fishing or surfing spot than a beach. A short trail leads to the beach, passing under some Australian pines with some very healthy prickly pear cactus as ground cover. The beach here is fairly steep and is dominated by condominiums. The beach crowd is mostly retirees, except when the surf is up and surfers come from all over to catch waves. From south jetty you can walk to any beach in Venice if you are a serious beach walker. Walk all the way out to the end of the jetty and you'll have a great view of the coast.

The park's concession sits just feet from Venice Inlet and is a popular place to hang out and grab a bite to eat, or just sit with a cup of coffee and enjoy the view. It also provides public restrooms.

There is no lifeguard on duty at Humphris Park. There is plenty of free parking, except when the surf is up and surfers and their vehicles arrive from all over the state. The unpaved parking lot is closed to vehicles from midnight to 6 am. Camping is not allowed. No animals are allowed in the park or on the beach and no fires are permitted in the park.

Brohard Park Area

Brohard Park encompasses 67 acres of beachfront parks on Harbor Drive, south of Beach Road. It includes Service Club Park, Venice Fishing Pier, Maxine Barritt Park, and South Brohard Beach. Descriptions of each beach access follow.

72: Service Club Park

(GPS: 27.07869, -82.45083). 1190 S. Harbor Drive, Venice, FL. From Venice Avenue, go south on Harbor Drive. After driving a mile or so, you'll see a sign pointing the way to the beaches. Service Club Park is easily overlooked. It's on the right and is marked by a sign. It has restroom facilities, covered picnic tables, and some limited playground equipment for small children. The restrooms and the boardwalk, including the picnic tables, are wheelchair accessible, but to get down to the sandy beach requires descending about a dozen wooden steps.

Photo: Picnic tables on the boardwalk, Service Club Park.

The park has no food concession and no lifeguard. The parking area is paved, but is not very large. The area between the parking lot and the beach is very thickly wooded with saw palmettos and pine trees. A 350-foot long boardwalk leads from the parking area to the beach through an area thickly wooded with saw palmetto and pine trees. Also situated on the boardwalk are several covered picnic tables.

You can walk south on the beach to Brohard Park and the Venice Fishing Pier in just a few minutes. This is a favorite fossil hunting place for some people. I've seen people create some very interesting devices for separating fossils from sand and shells using some type of wood or metal frame and various types of screens. Some people buy and sell shark's teeth in quantity. It is not unusual to see SCUBA divers entering the water here to search for fossils offshore.

Service Club Park is gated, and it closes between midnight and 6 am. RV's over 20 feet in length are not allowed in the park. Alcoholic beverages are allowed in the park, but glass containers are not.

A word of caution: There are a number of ditches, ponds and low-lying areas near the Venice beaches south of the pier. Alligators do live in those wet areas.

73: Venice Fishing Pier / Brohard Park

(GPS: 27.07428, -82.45020). Continuing south on Harbor Drive, past Service Club Park you will see the sign at Sharky's Restaurant. Sharky's is a nice place to eat while listening to tropical music and gazing upon the water and the fishing pier. You can eat on the deck or inside. It's a bit pricey though, even for a hotdog. But it's right on the beach, what do you expect? There is an outdoor deck, including an upper level, which is great for cooling off in the afternoon sea breeze. Get more info at www.SharkysOnThePier.com . Parking and beach access are free. The beach near the pier is great and has the dark sand characteristic of Venice beaches. The water is usually a chalky green near shore, but is clearer further out.

Photo: Venice Fishing Pier.

Some very serious fishing takes place on the 700 foot long Venice fishing pier. Papa's Bait and Snack Shop located out on the pier keeps the fishermen well-supplied from 6 am to 9pm. There is no fee to access the pier which is open 24 hours a day every day of the year, though the beach park is closed from midnight to 6 am. You can rent fishing gear if you need to (or rent a Florida snow shovel to sift the sand for shark teeth). No fishing license is needed to fish from the pier, but if you want to fish from the beach, you'll need a Florida saltwater fishing license. The pier was originally built in 1966 and has been rebuilt twice since then (1984 and 2004). The pier makes a great foreground for sunset photographs. Get more info at www.VeniceFishingPier.com .

Here's a tip for the penny pinchers: A cheeseburger with fries at Sharky's is $10.50; a cheeseburger at Papa's Bait shop on the pier is $3.50.

The Brohard Park public beach facilities are just north of the pier and share the same access driveway. The restrooms are new and modern and are ADA compliant. Outdoor rinse-off showers are provided. There is no picnic area, but there are several covered picnic tables at the pavilion overlooking the dune and beach. RV's are not allowed in Brohard Park's parking lot.

74: Maxine Barritt Park

(GPS: 27.07141, -82.44808). 1800 S. Harbor Drive, Venice, FL. This is a relatively new park situated immediately to the south of the Venice fishing pier. It is a nice park, with its own lake and lots of sidewalks and a few covered picnic tables. Clean, modern restrooms and a large picnic pavilion offer great facilities for gatherings, but it is not a good beach access point. Though the park has 1400 feet of beautiful beachfront, the only two access points are at the north end by the pier, and at the south end via the dog park. There are several beach overlooks on the boardwalk, but they do not provide for beach access. The parking area is separated from the beach by the lake, so the shortest distance from the parking area to the beach at the north end of the park is about 800 feet. At the south end the beach is accessed by entering the dog park. Essentially, the south end of Maxine Barrett Park functions as overflow parking and restroom facilities for Paw Park. There is no food concession and no lifeguard.

If you'd like to stop and do a little birdwatching, the lake attracts quite a few water birds. The sidewalk which circumnavigates the lake offers a meandering walk for a distance of two-thirds of a mile, nearly half of which is just behind the dunes and offers several overlooks to stop and enjoy the view of the beach and Gulf.

75: Paw Park at Brohard Beach

(GPS: 27.06971, -82.44703). 1600 Harbor Drive S., Venice, FL. This is the best dog beach park on the peninsular west coast of Florida. It is rivaled only by the dog park at Fort Desoto County Park in Pinellas County, and I suppose one could argue about which is superior. The fenced park has a place to rinse off your dog, a picnic shelter with tables, and a path to the Gulf beach. Entrances and exits from the fenced area are double-gated. Dogs are allowed in a restricted area on the Gulf beach and are not required to be leashed. The Gulf is about 700 feet from the fence area with drinking water, so consider taking some drinking water out onto the beach for your dog. Swimming in the salt water will make them thirsty. The park is open from 7 am to dusk.

Photo: Paw Park, south of the Venice Fishing Pier is one of the best dog beaches in Florida.

76: South Brohard Park

(GPS: 27.06694, -82.44714). Just around the corner from Paws Park, this park provides a large paved parking area, restrooms, and two boardwalk trails to the beach. There are no food concessions or lifeguards. This access is good for people who don't want to hang out by the pier or drive down to Caspersen beach, but it is just a few hundred feet from the dog beach, for those concerned about dogs running loose. The parking lot is rarely full, and you could most likely find a spot for an RV around the edges of the lot. The restroom has a ramped entry and one of the dune crossover boardwalks is wheelchair accessible. If you just want easy beach access and want to avoid the crowd around the pier, this is an excellent access.

77: Caspersen Beach Park

(GPS: 27.05647, -82.44262). 4100 Harbor Drive South, Englewood, FL. From South Brohard Park, Harbor Drive follows the coast south for half-a-mile, just behind sand dunes that spill onto the roadway. It ends at a large parking area with restroom facilities. This is Caspersen Beach Park. The park has an extensive 1,400 foot boardwalk system providing access to the beach. The beach in front of the boardwalk is rocky, with areas of soft sand. At the south end of the boardwalk the rocks give way to nearly two miles of soft sandy beach in varying shades of gray and near-black.

With major improvements to all of Venice's beach facilities in recent years and with the continued promotion of the area, this is not the remote and quiet park it used to be. Weekdays during the summer months are the least crowded time to visit, but you can usually find a quiet spot by walking south on the beach any time of year.

Photo: Caspersen's "black" sand beach, looking south toward Manasota Key.

Since this beach is located so close to Venice Airport you will discover that there always seems to be an airplane within ear shot. No jets; just the sometimes annoying buzz of small single propeller aircraft. After a while you get used to it. If you're shooting video on the beach, the plane noise always seems to end up in the audio.

In 2011/2012 Caspersen Beach Park facilities were renovated in a big way. The new restroom facilities have larger restrooms and a separate family restroom. The restroom facilities are ADA compliant. Access to the facilities is made easier with paved parking spaces and sidewalks, and sloped entry ramps with grab rails. There is a handicap access dune crossover with ramps near the handicap parking and restrooms, although there is not, as of this writing, a beach wheelchair available to get you across the sand to the water's edge.

The system of boardwalks along the beach has been greatly improved and enhanced. The boardwalk meanders along 1,400 feet of the beach through vegetation, past numerous stair cases or ramps to the beach. This is one of the most scenic beach boardwalks in Florida. The beach is very rocky in front of the boardwalk and is an excellent place to look for shells, shark teeth and other fossils. When the water is clear and calm, it is also an excellent place for snorkeling. There are five rocky reefs just 50 feet or so off the beach extending as far as 150 feet from shore. The northern segment of the boardwalk has handicap parking spaces right next to the boardwalk to minimize the distance to the beach.

The bay side of the park now has restrooms, a large covered picnic pavilion and children's playground, and a kayak launch area.

Caspersen Beach Park is a trailhead on the Venetian Waterway Park paved multi-use trail, which begins at the Venice Train Depot and runs south along each side of the Intracoastal Waterway. The western trail terminates at Caspersen Beach. So you can bring your bike along to do some trail riding. The trail also connects to Venice's Legacy Trail, which runs north from the Venice Train Depot.

Harbor Drive is closed to traffic about 500 feet from where it dead-ends at the beach. The last 500 feet of roadway make a great walking or bike path toward the quieter parts of this beach. At the southern end of Harbor Drive, as far as the eye can see there is nothing but water, sand, and trees. The completely undeveloped portion of the beach continues south for nearly two miles before you start seeing houses on the beach. So if you are planning to take a lengthy stroll along the beach, or to explore the trails in the woods above the beach during the warmer months, I strongly urge you to carry plenty of cold water. Insects are not usually a problem, but on very still, humid summer days the no-see-ums and biting flies can sometimes be bothersome until the afternoon sea breeze kicks in.

Caspersen Beach has a sand bluff above the beach leading to a very large wooded area crossed with walking trails. There are no homes or buildings of any kind along the park's shoreline. Consequently, wildlife is abundant. There are gopher tortoises in the woods and the beach is strewn with raccoon footprints. In the early summer, beginning in May, you can see lots of sea turtle tracks and nests on Caspersen beach. The turtles come out of the Gulf at night and crawl up the beach, leaving bulldozer-like tracks behind them. They dig a large hole, lay their eggs, and cover the hole before heading for the water again. So they leave two tracks--one coming and one going--leaving the impression of a bulldozer coming up out of the water.

Caspersen Beach is a great place to look for shells, and a great variety of sea life washes up on the beach. Various sea grasses, sponges, corals, bones, carcasses, fossils, fishing floats, ropes, you name it. Don't miss it. Bring your fishing pole, a shell rake, a cooler, a beach tent, a kayak, a ball, a

Frisbee, a kite, whatever. Spend the whole day. If you want to get away from the crowd, quiet portions of the beach are just a short walk away.

Photo: Rocky area off Caspersen beach is suitable for snorkeling.

On a final note, I feel I must mention that because of its secluded—bordering on remote—location, Caspersen Beach attracts some folks who want to engage in certain activities in a natural environment. To be blunt, in addition to attracting a contingent of benign and discrete naturists (nudists) who discretely use the southern remote areas of the park, Caspersen Beach has a well-documented problem of certain gay men hanging around trying to hook-up with other men, sometimes exposing themselves inappropriately and engaging in sex acts in the woods above the beach and on the beach in some not-so-secluded areas.

Most beachcombers agree that we should not allow this situation to keep us from enjoying this wonderful beach. If you see inappropriate behavior, report it to the Sherriff's Department. Just to be clear, I do not conflate discrete nudity on a remote beach with inappropriate public sexual activity. They are two completely separate issues.

There are many families that bring their children here and enjoy the beach near the boardwalk and parking area and never have a problem. On weekends and holidays when there are plenty of people around, you are much less likely to encounter inappropriate behaviors. However, if you come to Caspersen Beach during the week, especially earlier in the morning or later in the afternoon and evening, your chances of encountering inappropriate behavior are increased, especially if you walk south for half a mile on the deserted beach or go into the woods above the beach. It goes without saying that children should not play unsupervised in the wooded or remote areas, which is good advice for any location.

Photo: Manasota Key looking north from Manasota Beach Park.

Manasota Key

Interstate 75 Exit: 193 (Jacaranda Blvd.)

Nearest mainland city: Venice, Englewood

Major access roads: Jacaranda Blvd, SR 776 (Englewood Rd), Manasota Beach Rd.

Directions: Manasota Key is located south of Venice near Englewood. Access is gained by following Englewood Road (S.R. 776) to Manasota Beach Road. From I-75, take the Jacaranda exit #193. Follow Jacaranda to Englewood Road (S.R. 776). Turn left (south) on 776 and drive several miles to Manasota Beach Road. Turn right and follow Manasota Beach Road to the beach. From Venice or Nokomis, follow US 41 south to Englewood Road (S.R. 776), which will take you to Manasota Beach Road.

Entrance fee: All beaches are free and all parking is free.

Hours: Beaches and parks generally close at 10 or 11 pm and open at 5 or 6 am, as marked by signage. People wander the shoreline at all hours, but you can't park in the lots after they close.

Pets: Pets are not allowed on Manasota Key public beaches. Trained service animals are permitted. I do see dogs on the northern private beaches of the key, but those beaches are only accessible to residents and guests.

Disabled Access: Manasota Key Public Beach provides the best disabled access. All the public beaches offer some provisions for the disabled.

Restrooms: All public beach parks offer restrooms.

Food and Drink: There are no food and drink concessions on the beach. There are restaurants across the street from Englewood Beach.

Alcohol: Alcoholic beverages are allowed on the beach unless otherwise indicated. Glass containers are not allowed on the beach.

Shelling: Shelling is good. Manasota Key is a very good place to find fossilized shark teeth.

Lifeguards: None.

Camping: There are no camping opportunities on the island.

The northern part of Manasota Key is very narrow. On this quiet stretch of beach there are about seventy beach houses worth several million dollars, most of which have the beach as their front yard and the bay as their back yard with a private dock. There is a private unpaved road that provides gated access to the homeowners. The only way to explore the beach north of Manasota Beach Park is by walking north from Manasota Beach Park, or south from Caspersen Beach Park. The sand is quite soft, so walking long distances does require some effort. Exploring by kayak is an attractive option. Between Caspersen Beach Park and the northernmost homes on Manasota Key there are nearly two miles of completely undeveloped island and beach. Other than Cayo Costa State Park and North Captiva Island, I'd say that stretch of beach is probably the quietest on the peninsular Gulf coast of Florida.

Here's a secret way to get to the super quiet beach on northern Manasota Key: The South Venice Civic Association operates a small ferry from a dock at 4800 Lemon Bay Drive, Venice. (GPS: 27.03987, -82.42756) It will take you on a five minute ride to Manasota Key where the South Venice Beach Endowment Trust maintains 1300 feet of undeveloped Gulf Beach. (GPS: 27.036894, -82.429342). The South Venice Beach Ferry runs every half hour every day but Wednesday and certain holidays. Here's the catch: Although this private nonprofit ferry is open to the public, there are no day passes. You have to buy a monthly or yearly pass. Visit www.southvenicebeach.org for more info.

Between Manasota Beach Park and Blind Pass Park, four miles to the south, is a fairly quiet two-lane road that meanders through the residential neighborhood. Many of the homes are nearly invisible behind thick jungle landscaping. One of the most scenic parts of the drive down Manasota Key is just north of Blind Pass where Manasota Key Road passes just behind the dune for about 2000 feet and offers a sweeping view of the Gulf of Mexico. A sharp dogleg in the road marks the Blind Pass beach access. This Blind Pass filled in with sand a very long time ago, so there is no longer any water flowing through it.

You might wonder about the origin of the name "Blind Pass." It happens that there are a number of inlets in Florida which bear that name. It came from the nature of certain small inlets to orient themselves in an oblique angle relative to the shoreline, making it impossible to see the inlet from the perspective of a ship offshore. A lookout on a ship would see a continuous line of trees on the horizon rather than a break in the trees characteristic of an inlet that runs perpendicular to the shoreline.

The area to the south of Blind Pass Beach is especially wooded, and the only evidence of homes is their narrow winding sand and shell driveways disappearing into the jungle. Several sections of the road are completely covered by large trees, plunging overheated travelers into dense cool shade for several hundred yards.

Further south, once Manasota Key road enters Charlotte County the scenery changes drastically. Small hotels and beach cottages line both sides of the road. Past Englewood Beach/Chadwick Park there is a more typical residential district of modest homes. The road ends at Stump Pass Beach State Park, formerly known as Port Charlotte Beach State Park.

78: Manasota Beach Park

(GPS: 27.01051, -82.412109) Located off SR 776, Manasota Beach Road takes you directly to Manasota Beach Park at 8570 Manasota Beach Road. When you drive over the bridge to Manasota Key, notice how undeveloped the shore is on both sides of the narrow Lemon Bay.

As soon as you cross the bridge, Manasota Beach Park is directly in front of you. In 2013 Manasota Beach held its grand re-opening to show off a newly completed $1.5 million improvement project. A much larger restroom facility is the architectural and functional centerpiece of the improvements, which also included upgraded picnic pavilions, a larger and upgraded system of boardwalks over the dunes, and fantastic handicap access provisions. The new restroom facility includes a "unisex" restroom in addition to the traditional "men's" and "ladies" rooms. There is also a room for the lifeguards to use. This forward-thinking beach facility has gone "green" with a rainwater catchment system.

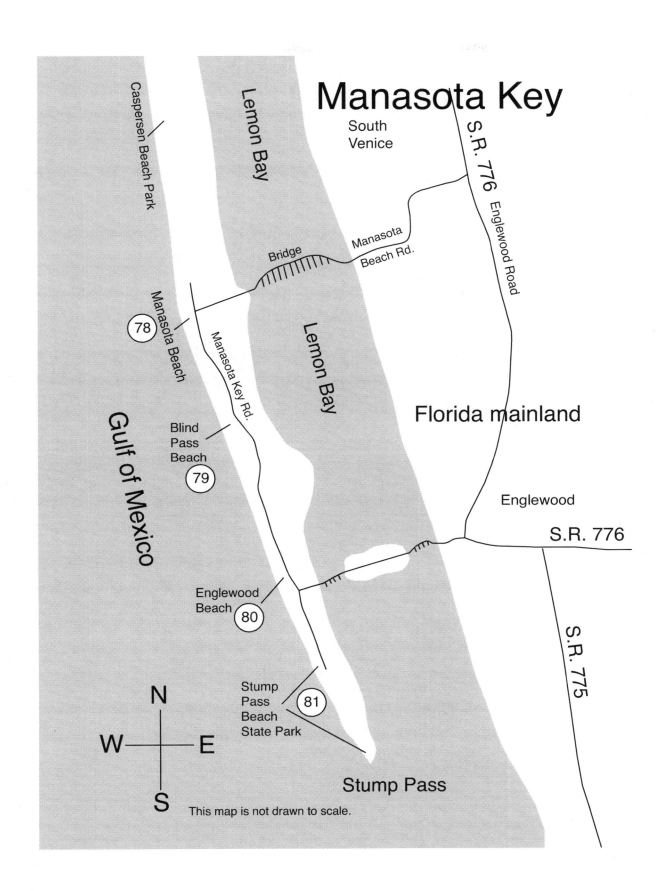

Manasota Key

South
Venice

S.R. 776

Englewood Road

Caspersen Beach Park

Lemon Bay

Manasota
Beach Rd.

Bridge

Lemon Bay

78

Manasota Beach

Manasota Key Rd.

Florida mainland

Blind
Pass
Beach

79

Gulf of Mexico

Englewood

S.R. 776

Englewood
Beach

80

S.R. 775

Stump
Pass
Beach
State Park

81

N

W   E

S

Stump Pass

This map is not drawn to scale.

The unpaved parking lot is across the street from the beach and has been significantly expanded. There is a circular drive on the beach side next to the restrooms and picnic tables that allows for temporary loading and unloading of passengers and gear, and provides ample free parking for ADA access. Barrier-free sidewalks lead to all covered picnic tables and restrooms, and the boardwalks to the beach are ramps, not stairs. Unfortunately, as of this writing there are no big-wheeled beach wheelchairs available on site to the public. So, to get from the boardwalk ramp to the water's edge, you're on your own. I hope this oversight will be corrected soon.

This beach facility does not have a snack bar or vending machines, but does have water fountains, outdoor rinse-off showers, lifeguards, and good picnic facilities, including a large pavilion.

Photo: The beach gets crowded near the public access.

Of course you are not limited to the official public beach boundaries. You can walk north or south along the beach as far as you like. The beaches on Manasota Key are very much like Caspersen Beach to the north, but have homes along the shore. This really does not detract much from the sense of serenity because the homes are hidden behind dense greenery. The beach foliage here is not the carefully cultivated landscape typical of many populated islands, but rather a wild and windblown tangle of sea grape, cabbage palms and Australian pines. Wooden steps lead down the sand bluff from the homes to the beach, and some of the homes have some pretty cool looking beach shacks perched on the small bluff above "their" beach. This is also a beach popular with egg-laying turtles, and if you visit May through July you'll likely see many fresh nests, all carefully marked and dated by authorized volunteers who keep track of the nests.

The beach on Manasota Key has a small drop-off, called the "plunge step" that is the collection point for many of the best shells and fossils, including shark teeth. That's where you'll see most collectors concentrating their efforts.

Manasota Beach Park is one of my favorite beaches, especially when I want to walk for several hours and see few people. Many of the homes along the shore here are very interesting and show something of the owner's personality. Most of them are not typical barrier island monoliths built as testaments to the owners' wealth.

Of course it isn't necessary to walk long distances when you visit this beach. You can simply cross the dune to the beach and park yourself right there with everyone else. But feel free to explore. Once you are a few hundred feet away from the public access in either direction you are likely to have the beach nearly to yourself.

The beach from South Jetty at the Venice Inlet all the way south to Stump Pass at Englewood beach is one continuous beach. That distance represents nearly 17 miles of beach and it would easily take a whole day or more to walk its entire length. Fortunately, you can drive from place to place in a much shorter time.

79: Blind Pass Beach

(GPS: 26.96353, -82.38456) This beach, also known as "Middle Beach" because it is near the midpoint of the island, is located at 6725 Manasota Key, Road, slightly less than 4 miles south of Manasota Beach Park on Manasota Key Road. The free sand/shell parking area is on the east side of the road. You must walk across the road (which is not heavily traveled) and follow the boardwalks to the beach. The Blind Pass beach entrance is located on a blind curve that makes for some difficulty in seeing oncoming cars, so exercise care. This is a natural wooded area and is very quiet. The beach and water are beautiful and the shore above the beach is thickly wooded. You can walk north or south as far as you like. The bathroom/changing facilities here are generally well maintained, but there is no snack bar or vending machines. There are no lifeguards on duty.

Handicap access parking spaces are located next to the road, but still require you to cross the road. A special boardwalk is provided for ADA access to the beach and to the restrooms, but there is no beach wheelchair available as of this writing. The beach is open from 6 am to Midnight every day of the year.

This is one of the better beaches for finding fossilized shark teeth. Venice Beach gets all the publicity, but lots of serious collectors like to come here to search. In addition to the Gulf beach, the park also has a children's playground behind the parking area and several spots to launch a kayak. And, Blind Pass beach has been the location of a 4th of July fireworks display for more than 20 years.

There is public dock on the east side of the park for those who may arrive by boat.

Meandering through the thick mangroves on the north side of the parking area is the Fred Duisberg nature trail, which was designed so nothing manmade would be visible from the trail.

Photo: Blind Pass Beach access.

Blind Pass beach has quite a bit of interesting history, a remnant of which sits immediately to the south of the public beach facilities. The Hermitage Artist Retreat is a collection of historic buildings that today are owned by Sarasota County and leased to the Hermitage, a nonprofit concern which brings accomplished artists to the beach for a creative retreat. While here, the artists contribute their talent to the local community by performing two free programs. One of the most interesting architectural aspects to me of the historic property is the pair of wooden cisterns that adorn the southern edge of the retreat beneath the shade of a large strangler fig. They were built in the early 1940's by one of the property owners. The most memorable use of the Hermitage property was its two year tenure as a nudist colony back in the late 1930's. It was known as "The Florida Sea Island Sanctuary." www.hermitageartistretreat.org

80: Englewood Beach/ Chadwick Park

(GPS: 26.92527, -82.36087) This park is located toward the southern end of Manasota Key where S.R. 776 crosses Lemon Bay. This part of the island is in Charlotte County and is significantly different from the Sarasota County portion of the island. As soon as you cross over into Charlotte County the greenery ends and the hotels and cottages begin. Englewood Beach is located across the street from several small stores. The park has a very large paved parking lot, but you have to pay to park here, though it is not expensive. There are many covered cement picnic tables. Some pavilions large enough for several families.

Photo: Englewood Beach. The boardwalk provides easy access to all parts of the beach.

The beach is a mix of light and dark gray sand. The official public beach area offers roughly 1800 feet of beach front. A wooden boardwalk parallels the beach for 1000 feet between the parking lot and the small grass covered dunes above the beach. Steps lead from the boardwalk to the beach. There are also two ADA accessible ramps providing access from the boardwalk to the beach and to the restrooms. A special beach wheelchair is available. Check with the beach umbrella vendor or call Charlotte County Community Services at 941-625-7529 for assistance.

Once on the beach, you can walk north unhindered as far as you like. You may be able to walk south all the way to Stump Pass, depending on the tides, the surf, and the width of the beach. This is a very popular beach because of its easy access from the city of Englewood. For you beach-bar lovers, Flounders Restaurant and Tiki-Bar is right across the street from the beach. You can't miss it.

81: Stump Pass Beach State Park

(GPS: 26.910401, -82.352277) This wild and scenic beach is located at the south end of Manasota Key. Follow the main road, Manasota Key Road, south past Englewood Beach/Chadwick Park. Take Gulf Blvd south and you will drive right into the Park, which now has a pay station (bring dollar bills), an unpaved lot, and wooden boardwalks to the beach. This park used to be known as Port Charlotte Beach State Recreation Area and originally boasted a grand total of four parking spaces. Fortunately someone came to their senses and now Stump Pass Beach has been made truly accessible by the much improved parking facilities. Parking is a couple of bucks per day per car and the park is open from 8am till sunset. Florida State Park rules are in effect. Don't bring your dog or camp overnight, neither is allowed. Alcohol is not allowed on the beach. Fires are not permitted on the beach.

Photo: Stump Pass Beach State Park, looking south toward Stump Pass.

There are excellent restroom facilities, drinking water, and cold drink vending machines, but there are no lifeguards on duty and there is no snack bar. Stump Pass beach is very secluded and this part of the island is extremely narrow—you could cross the island by walking about 100 paces. A narrow portion of Lemon Bay (great for kayaking) is to the east and the Gulf is to the west. On the bay side shoreline, mangroves create a forested area that extends most of the way to Stump Pass. Boaters love to pull up onto the bayside beach under the overhanging trees and anchor their boats while they visit the Gulf beach.

The state park occupies the entire southern tip of the island. It's a little over a mile of beach and forest. The beach sand here has a very high fossil content and is a light-gray color, as is typical of the Venice area beaches. It also has a high content of crushed shell, which makes for somewhat difficult walking. Behind the low dunes is a thick forest about 50 - 100 feet deep with a nature trail. The forest is now mostly mangrove trees and other small Florida native species.

Australian pines have been eradicated. All that's left of them is a dwindling number of dead tree trunks. The pines did provide nice shade, but they choke out native species very quickly and do not provide good protection against erosion as they are easily blown over or undermined by storm waters. Removing Australian pines is a controversial practice, but it is the state's policy on state-owned land.

Stump Pass State Park Beach is heavily used by nesting shorebirds and by nesting sea turtles. It's a great place for birdwatching and beachcombing. If you visit this area, please observe signs warning you to avoid the areas roped off for the nesting birds. They actually lay their eggs right in the sand. Disturbing the birds exposes the eggs to the blazing sun and to hungry sea gulls.

The southern tip of the island is on Stump Pass, a narrow inlet that is constantly shifting with the currents. If you have a kayak you could easily paddle 300 to 400 feet across the pass to Knight Island.

There are a few multi-level beach houses visible on Knight Island (also known as Palm Island), but it is a peaceful island with a very quiet beach, particularly between May and December. Knight Island is part of a four-island group. Thornton Key, Don Pedro Island and Little Gasparilla are the other three. You can only reach them by boat. Don Pedro Island is the home of Don Pedro Island State Park. The northern island, Knight Island, is private and is occupied by the Palm Island Resort.

Photo: Don Pedro Island State Park beach. Gasparilla Island is visible on the horizon.

Palm Island Archipelago

Interstate 75 Exit: 193 (Jacaranda Blvd)

Nearest mainland city: Cape Haze

Major access roads: SR 776, SR 775

Note: Refer to the map in this book's chapter on Gasparilla Island, following this chapter.

Directions: The Palm Island archipelago (group of islands) is located south of Stump Pass, north of Gasparilla Island, and just west of Cape Haze. To get to this group of islands, take US 41 south to Englewood Road (SR 776). Follow Englewood Road south to Placida Road (County Road 775). Turn right on CR 775 and drive 20 minutes or so to Panama Blvd. Turn onto Panama Blvd and you find parallel parking along the street. You can leave your car there and catch the Palm Island Ferry to the island. A secure (fenced) parking lot is also available from the Island Park Cooperative, which offers daily, weekly, and monthly rates (call 941-697-8809).

The ferry runs every ten minutes or so. It is unlikely that you would want to bring your car onto the island via the ferry as the fee is over fifty dollars per car. The fee for pedestrians (including bicyclists) to ride the ferry is less than ten dollars. Understand that whatever water and food you need, you'll have to bring with you, and the only public restrooms are located at Don Pedro Island

State Park, which is a 2.25 mile walk from the ferry landing, although you could ride your bike the first mile to a beach access point on South Gulf Blvd.

Entrance fee: All beaches are free and all parking is free, but getting your car onto the island is expensive. Don Pedro Island State Park has an entrance fee.

Hours: Don Pedro Island State Park closes at sunset. Other beaches do not have posted hours.

Pets: Pets are permitted in the state park but are not allowed on the state park beaches. Pets are not officially allowed on the beaches per county ordinance, but well-behaved pets are generally tolerated by the islanders, especially on Little Gasparilla and Don Pedro, but not on the Palm Island resort beaches.

Disabled Access: There are no provisions that I'm aware of for disabled access.

Restrooms: The only public restrooms are located at Don Pedro Island State Park.

Food and Drink: There are no food and drink concessions on the beach or on any of the islands in the archipelago. There is a restaurant in Palm Island Resort for guests.

Alcohol: Alcoholic beverages are allowed on the beach unless otherwise indicated. Glass containers are not allowed on the beach. Alcohol is not allowed in the state park.

Shelling: Shelling is average. Shark teeth and other fossils are commonly found.

Lifeguards: None.

Camping: There are no camping opportunities on the island.

The Palm Island archipelago really is designed to be conveniently enjoyed by residents and resort guests, not by the general public. So if you truly want to appreciate the laid-back island lifestyle I recommend that you rent a beach house or spend some time at one of the resorts here. The off season—May through December—brings weekly rentals into the affordable range. The main reason I've included this island's beaches in this book is that I realize there are a few people (just a few) like me who don't mind overcoming a few obstacles to enjoy a beach.

The first obstacle is finding the darn thing. My directions above, along with a good map of the Englewood area, should solve that problem. If you don't have a boat docked conveniently at a nearby marina, you will need to take the ferry to the island. You can park your car along Panama

Blvd. and walk a few hundred feet to the ferry dock, pay your six or seven bucks and ride two hundred feet across the bay and disembark on Knight Island. You can walk anywhere you like that isn't private property, which limits your choices severely. My recommendation is that you bring your bicycle across on the ferry, along with plenty of water and some food and snacks. With a bicycle you can easily see all of Don Pedro Island and the public half of Knight Island without wearing yourself out. Walking takes a lot of time and energy that should be spent relaxing on the beach. If you are a high-roller and don't mind shelling out the ferry fee (currently $55), go ahead and bring your car over on the ferry.

The Palm Island archipelago is made up of four islands, Knight Island, Thornton Key, Don Pedro Island, and Little Gasparilla Island, creating 7 miles of beautiful quiet beaches. Although the islands were at one time separate from each other, they are all now connected in various places through the natural movement of sand and with a helping hand from people. Walking along the beach, it seems like one big island. Island politics and economics are a different story and are beyond the concern of the casual visitor.

About half of Knight Island is owned by the Palm Island Resort, which also owns the Palm Island Transit ferry providing the main access to the islands. Because of the fame of the resort, the entire island group is commonly referred to as Palm Island. This practice is met with some disdain by residents of the other half of Knight Island as well as residents of the other three islands who don't like being overshadowed with the identity of the resort, though as time passes I think most folks are becoming more accepting of all the islands being generally referred to as "Palm Island."

Knight Island (aka Palm Island)

Knight Island, located at the north end of the group, is half occupied by the Palm Island Resort which is private. You will need to be staying at the resort or be a guest of the resort to explore the northern end of Knight Island, though the Gulf beaches are open to the public from end to end. The resort is gated. Guests leave their cars outside the resort and use golf carts for transportation on its unpaved roads that meander for roughly one mile past modern beach houses, tennis courts, and the only restaurant on the island, Rum Bay. The north tip of the island overlooks Stump Pass, a narrow inlet the island shares with Englewood's Stump Pass State Park on the north side of the pass. The pass beach is very dark and quiet at night and is a great spot for those resort guests who might want to be alone. If you like to watch for meteors and stars, Stump Pass beach is a great spot. An important point to keep in mind is that while all Gulf beaches are "public," access to the beach may or may not be provided.

The remainder of Knight Island, outside of the resort, is residential, but does at least offer limited public beach access. Beaches on Knight Island are white quartz with some fossilized material and shell mixed in. The beaches are usually grayish-white and have the darkest sand down by the water's edge. It is not unusual to find fossilized shark teeth in the shallow water. Beaches accesses in the Palm Island Resort are private—for guests only. Outside the resort there are three public access points, one of which offers enough parking for a dozen cars or so.

Photo: Beachfront condos and homes in the Palm Island Resort.

82: Knight Island Beach Access Points

To get to the Knight Island public beach access points from the ferry landing, simply follow Gulf Blvd. You will pass the intersection with S. Gulf Blvd. then you'll pass Palm Drive. About 400 feet past Palm Drive you'll see a Public Beach access sign. (GPS coordinates 26.872145, -82.321331) If you are on foot or bicycle, this will be a good place to access the beach. It has no shade, no bathroom, no water, and no lifeguard. It's just a sand trail to the beach between two houses. This access is about half a mile from the ferry landing. If you are driving a car, or if you prefer to be a bit further from homes, go on to the next access.

Continuing north on Gulf Blvd, the next public access (GPS coordinates 26.875266, -82.323804) is located on a 500 foot wide beachfront lot with low, grass covered dunes. There are two sand trails across the dune to the Gulf beach. Parallel parking is available on the shoulder of the road. The access is marked with a small sign. There is no shade, no restroom, no drinking water, and no lifeguard. This would be my choice for beach access on Knight Island. It is about 3/4ths of a mile from the ferry landing. This access is pictured in the following photo (next page).

Further north, just outside the entrance to the Palm Island Resort is the third public beach access (GPS coordinates 26.879425, -82.326493). There is enough space to park a couple of golf carts, but I don't think it would be a great place to park a car. To get to the water's edge will require a 600 foot hike across the dune and beach. This access is right next to a large home with a tennis court. This is as close as you can get to Stump Pass without entering the resort. The access is located about one mile from the ferry landing. It has no shade, no restrooms, no drinking water, and no lifeguard.

Photo: Knight Island public beach access with parking.

Thornton Key

Thornton Key is east of and is connected to Knight Island but has no Gulf beach at all. The northern end of Thornton Key has some unpaved roads and a few homes, and the southern end has a few homes with docks, but most of the middle section of the island is a 31 acre nature preserve that protects one of the few remaining tropical hardwood hammocks in southwest Florida. Thornton Key Preserve is only accessible by boat. It has a nature trail loop that is slightly less than one mile in length. There are no facilities of any kind in the preserve. It's just a place to get out of your kayak or small boat and stretch your legs a bit while enjoying the nature. It would be a good place for birding, especially during migration. As far as I'm aware, camping is not allowed on Thornton Key, however if you are interested in camping on an island in the general area, there is a seven acre private island in Gasparilla Sound that allows primitive camping. It has four campsites and the price is right. Arrange camping through Grande Tours Kayak Center in Placida at grandetours.com. The owner of Grande Tours, Captain Marian Schneider, is well-known in the area. Nobody knows more about the local nature and waterways than she does.

Don Pedro Island

Don Pedro Island is south of Knight Island and has private homes and beach houses, many for rent, and is also home to Don Pedro Island State Park. Unlike Knight Island, Don Pedro is not owned by a resort company. It is a community of private homeowners, some of whom live there year-round, and is the most developed and populated island of the group. Most of the roads are unpaved and the homes are each as different as their owners. Landscaping is tropical and natural with plenty of coconut palms. You won't find bushes trimmed in the shape of squares here. There are cars on Don

Pedro but there is nowhere to go so most of them remain parked in the owner's driveway until they need to travel off-island. When moving around the island to visit friends, or when going to the resort for dinner, most people use golf carts or bicycles. The island is so quiet and laid-back, especially from May through December, you could easily think you'd gone back in time to 1920.

Photo: Beach houses on the Gulf of Mexico on Don Pedro Island.

83: Don Pedro Island Beach Access

From the ferry landing, follow Gulf Blvd for about 1200 feet and turn left on S. Gulf Blvd. You'll drive over a one-lane bridge onto Don Pedro Island. There are two beach public beach access points on Don Pedro, outside of the state park.

The first access (GPS 26.865770, -82.317625) is right around the curve on S. Gulf Blvd. The access is about 3100 feet from the ferry landing and has enough space to park a car on the shoulder of the road. Mostly you'll see golf carts parked by the access. There is no shade, no restroom, no water, and no lifeguard.

The furthest south public access is located another 1400 feet past the first access. It is across the road from a tennis court and consists of a narrow trail to the beach along the south side of a swimming pool. (GPS: 26.862288, -82.314944). There is no place to park a car, but you could probably lock your bike to the "beach access" sign. It's unlikely you'd need to lock your bike on this island, but I usually do anyway. This is as close as you can get to Don Pedro Island State Park without a boat. From this access it would be a 1.3 mile walk to the restrooms and water fountains at the state park.

84: Don Pedro Island State Park

(GPS: 26.84674, -82.303404) Even though the state park is located on Don Pedro Island, there is no way to drive a car to the state park since the only thing that might pass for a road to the park crosses private gated property. The only way to visit is by walking along the beach from a public access on Don Pedro, or by arriving via private boat, or charter. As of this writing, there is no regular ferry service to this state park. However, you can arrange a boat ride to and from the park by calling Pirate's Water Taxi at 941-697-5777. You should give them a couple of days advance notice if possible, especially if you are visiting on a weekend.

Photo: Don Pedro Island State Park beach, looking south toward Gasparilla Island.

A simple way to visit Don Pedro Island State Park is by kayak. The park has a "land base" on the mainland at 8450 Placida Road, Cape Haze, FL, where you can park your car and launch a kayak across the narrow, shallow backwater and arrive on Don Pedro after paddling less than one mile. There is a boat dock as well as a kayak rack on the island where you can store your kayak and lock it if you feel inclined and if you have a cable and lock. The island is very narrow so it only takes a couple of minutes to walk 600 feet on the sandy trail from the dock on the bay side to the Gulf beach. The only shade in the park is provided by the covered picnic pavilion with about 12 picnic tables overlooking the Gulf. The park has restrooms, drinking fountains and barbeque grills. The vegetation is mostly grasses and small bushes and trees like mangrove and sea grapes, muhly grass and sea oats. The only thing to do in the park is enjoy the beach and nature. You can walk on the beach in either direction as far as you like. Although the park seems quite remote, plenty of folks in the area have boats, so weekends and holidays can see quite a few people visiting the park's beach and using the picnic facilities. It is not a large park. It offers about one mile of beach front and the island is only 1200 feet wide at its widest point. As on the rest of the Palm Island Archipelago, the beaches are light brown or gray sand with some dark fossilized material mixed in. The dry sand is soft and relatively free of shells. The wet sand near the water's edge is hard packed and great for walking.

The park does have an entrance fee which is on the honor system. A small pay station with envelopes and numbered receipts allows you to pay the fee. Exact change is required. Check the parks web site for current fees, but as I write this the fee is two dollars per person for island access. The land base has a separate fee. The park is open from 8 am to sunset, every day of the year. There are no lifeguards on duty and no ADA access accommodations. Pets and alcoholic beverages are prohibited in the park and on the beach. Ground fires are prohibited; you must use a grill.

If you are vacationing on Don Pedro Island, the walking distance to the state park is between one and two miles, depending on where your house is located. From the public access trail on South Gulf Blvd., it would be a one-and-a-half mile walk along the beach to the picnic pavilion and restroom facilities in Don Pedro Island State Park. As far as riding a bike on the beach, some sections of beach are firm enough, but others are not, so you'll find yourself walking the bike at least part of the distance, based on my personal experience. If you have a really low gear and really big balloon tires, maybe you'll do better than I did.

85: Little Gasparilla Island

Little Gasparilla Island occupies the southern two miles of this four island complex and has private homes, rental beach houses, and two small resorts. It is only accessible by boat. Although it is physically connected to Don Pedro Island, private property prevents passage by dirt trail from Don Pedro to Little Gasparilla, though you can certainly travel from one island to another by walking along the beach. There are no cars on Little Gasparilla, other than the occasional service vehicle. Transportation is provided solely by your two feet, a bicycle, or a golf cart.

Little Gasparilla has no real road, but does have wide sand trails that the locals walk and ride golf carts on. The number of full-time residents varies between 60 and 250, depending on who you talk to, and with 350 homes the island is about 50% built-out (which means there is still room for you to build your dream house). The population swells considerably on weekends and holidays. Many owners who come for weekend getaways are from Tampa and Lakeland. Since there is no water supply piped in from the mainland, many homes have rain catchment systems that can store 2500 gallons or more. There are also desalination plants on the island that provide drinking water.

Photo: Little Gasparilla Island Beach, looking north toward Don Pedro Island State Park.

The beaches are beautiful and offer a good view of Gasparilla Island (Boca Grande) to the south. Other than the residents and guests staying on Little Gasparilla, the only people you'll see on the beach are those who've arrived by boat. The southern tip of the island is a very popular spot for weekend boaters to anchor and wade ashore and can get a bit crowded on nice weekends. Pirate's Water Taxi operating out of Eldred's marina on the Boca Grande Causeway provides ferry service to Little Gasparilla for guests.

Since there are no stores or restaurants on the island, you'll need to bring whatever food and drink you plan to eat while you're visiting. There are no public restrooms anywhere on the island; so generally, the best place to come ashore is at Don Pedro Island State Park. You can easily walk down to Little Gasparilla in about 20 minutes to have a look around.

Well behaved dogs are tolerated on the Little Gasparilla beaches, though officially, dogs are prohibited on Charlotte County beaches. There is no prohibition against alcoholic beverages.

If you like to get away from it all, Little Gasparilla may be what you're looking for.

190

Photo: Lighthouse on Boca Grande Pass beach.

Gasparilla Island

(Boca Grande)

Interstate 75 Exit: 191 (River Road)

Nearest mainland city: Placida and Cape Haze. Englewood is the nearest larger city.

Major access roads: SR 776, CR 775, CR 777

Directions from I-75: Take exit #191 (River Road). Go west on N. River Road. Cross US 41 onto S. River Road. Turn left on Pine Street, which becomes Placida Road after you cross S. McCall Road. Follow Placida Road south until you get to the Boca Grande Causeway entrance. It's about 23 miles from I-75 to Boca Grande Causeway. You'll have opportunities for gas and groceries in both Englewood and Placida.

Directions from U.S. 41: Take US 41 south to Englewood Road (SR 776). Follow Englewood Road south to Placida Road (County Road 775). Turn right on CR 775 and drive 20 minutes or so to the sign pointing to Gasparilla Island.

Pets: Leashed dogs are permitted on the beaches, except for the state park beaches. Seventh Street has a small dog park right next to the beach, located at the Gasparilla Inn's soccer field. Lighthouse Park, at the southern tip of the island allows dogs in the park, but not on the beach.

Disabled Access: Lighthouse Park and the #1 Sandspur access have disabled-friendly access. Lighthouse Park has one beach wheelchair available on a first-come, first-served basis.

Hours: The state park accesses open at 8 am and close shortly after sunset. Other beaches do not have posted hours.

Restrooms: Public restrooms can be found at Lighthouse Park and at the #1 Sandspur Beach access. The other state park accesses have portable toilets. South Beach Bar and Grill has restrooms for customers and is located at the #3 Seawall Access.

Food and Drink: None of the beaches offer food concessions, however South Beach Bar and Grill is right next to a state park beach access. Lighthouse Park has a drink vending machine.

Alcohol: Open containers of alcoholic beverages are not allowed on Gasparilla Island beaches.

Shelling: Gasparilla Island beaches are very good for shelling and beachcombing in general.

Camping: There are no beach camping facilities available on Gasparilla Island.

Lifeguards: There are no lifeguards on Gasparilla Island. Conduct yourself accordingly.

Weddings: Gasparilla Island is excellent for weddings. Gasparilla Island State Park's lighthouse park has a chapel available for weddings. Banyan Street is also a popular location.

You will have to pay a toll to the private Gasparilla Island Bridge Authority to drive onto the island. Currently the toll is $6.00 per car but don't be surprised if it's another dollar or two higher when you visit. The bridge to Gasparilla Island is the only operating "swing" bridge in Florida. It was built in the mid 1950's. There are actually three bridges to cross to get across the causeway to the island: the swing bridge, center bridge, and south bridge. As of 2013, center bridge has been replaced and a new south bridge is under construction. Plans are underway to replace the old swing bridge with a taller swing bridge that will meet the state's requirements to withstand a 17 foot storm surge.

Gasparilla Island, referred to interchangeably as "Boca Grande," is quite out of the way. You don't really stop by here on the way to somewhere else. You have to make up your mind to drive here. The island is a very special place for the few fortunate islanders who live here, and for the many guests who vacation here. It is remarkable for its uniqueness, its remoteness, and its worldwide reputation as a Tarpon-fishing bonanza. Suitably narrow tree-lined roads are accompanied by paths for golf carts, pedestrians and bicyclists. Lush, tropical foliage in all shades of green hides professionally maintained residential island homes and lawns glowing with tropical blooms.

Fences and walls surround the most luxurious homes whose scale is dwarfed only by the huge banyan trees that tower above everything. In short supply are banana, papaya and mango trees that one would expect to find on an island so favorable for the sweet fruits that please. One might speculate that for the many residents and visitors who can afford, without a thought, to fly in any exotic fare they desire, the idea of waiting for a mango to slowly ripen on a tree in the corner of the estate might be too much bother.

The public beaches are not the most prominent feature of Gasparilla Island. In fact, the beaches take a back seat to fishing, boating, and golf on the Gasparilla Island Chamber's web site. Compared to the beaches of Bradenton, Sarasota, and Venice, public access is limited though it has improved in the last decade, but the character of the island makes it worth the trip, and the beaches are beautiful, quiet and family oriented. Swimming is O.K. at all the beaches except for those in Lighthouse Park on Boca Pass at the southern tip of the island. Water currents are too strong for swimming near Boca Grande Pass.

Photo: This beach is accessible from street-end accesses along Gasparilla Road.

The water on Gasparilla Island can be an extremely clear luminous green and very inviting, especially during the spring months. It's a great place for snorkeling too, when the water is clear. The bottom does tend to drop off a bit more quickly on Gasparilla Island than on most of southwest Florida's beaches. So you'll go from ankle deep to waist deep fairly quickly.

Although Gasparilla Island does have roughly seven miles of sandy Gulf beaches, many of the beaches are very narrow because a rocky sea wall runs for miles along the coastline. Beginning at about 1st Street there are about 1.75 miles of good, wide walkable beaches served by three public accesses with parking. Added to that is another half-mile of beach on Boca Pass at Lighthouse Park.

The first half of Gasparilla seems rather unfriendly. You are never out of sight of a No Parking/No Trespassing sign, though there are numerous places that would prove interesting to explore. Parking is strictly prohibited on the causeway, which is privately owned by the Gasparilla Island Bridge Authority (GIBA). The first sign of visitor friendliness is the paved bike path that runs the entire length of the island, and some small signs pointing to limited beach access at street ends between 19th street and 5th street. Fifth Street marks the northern edge of Boca Grande Village. The Village has a small shopping district with numerous fine casual eateries and interesting stores to browse in; it's well worth a couple of hours exploring. The Island Bike'n Beach shop is located on Park Avenue. Here you can rent bicycles, roller blades, strollers, golf carts (to drive around on the island), umbrellas, mask & fins, rollaway beds, and cribs. This is a fantastic island to explore on a bicycle and is very visitor-friendly. Traffic is light, especially during the summer and fall and I've already mentioned the bike path.

While Park Avenue takes you through the middle of "town," Gilchrist, just one block to the west, is a more naturally scenic route. Gilchrist has a very wide, grassy median and is lushly landscaped with coconut palms. The homes along the Gulf are extraordinarily beautiful, and as large as they are, they are dwarfed by the huge tropical trees surrounding them.

And don't miss riding or walking down Banyan Street. It is shaded by towering Banyan trees on each side of the road that grow together at their uppermost branches. The gray, twisted, aboveground roots and the gigantic cement-like trunks and branches put you in a different world entirely. It's easy to imagine that you are somewhere in South America. The subdued light, the swaying of the branches and the rustling of the leaves, the birds calling, and the coolness of the shade will make you want to sit down and spend the day right there.

86: Street End Beach Parking

Along Gasparilla Road, before arriving at the Village of Boca Grande, many of the street ends have public parking and access to the beach. Specifically, the street-ends at 19th, 17th, 14th, 13th, 12th, 11th, 10th, 9th, and 7th, have very limited free parking on the street. Signs indicate "Public Parking," and "Beach Access" on streets where access and parking are available. These beach access points offer a few, mostly unmarked parking spaces, a couple of trash cans and a path to the beach through the tropical foliage. The main strategy is to find some shade, get as close to the beach as possible, and avoid blocking anyone's driveway. There are no restroom facilities, no water fountains or rinse-off showers, and no lifeguards. On some streets, parking may also be available on the opposite side of Gasparilla Road.

A larger public parking lot is available at the west end of 5th street, next to the Gasparilla Inn Beach Club. However a tall seawall prevents all but Spiderman from getting down to the beach. From the

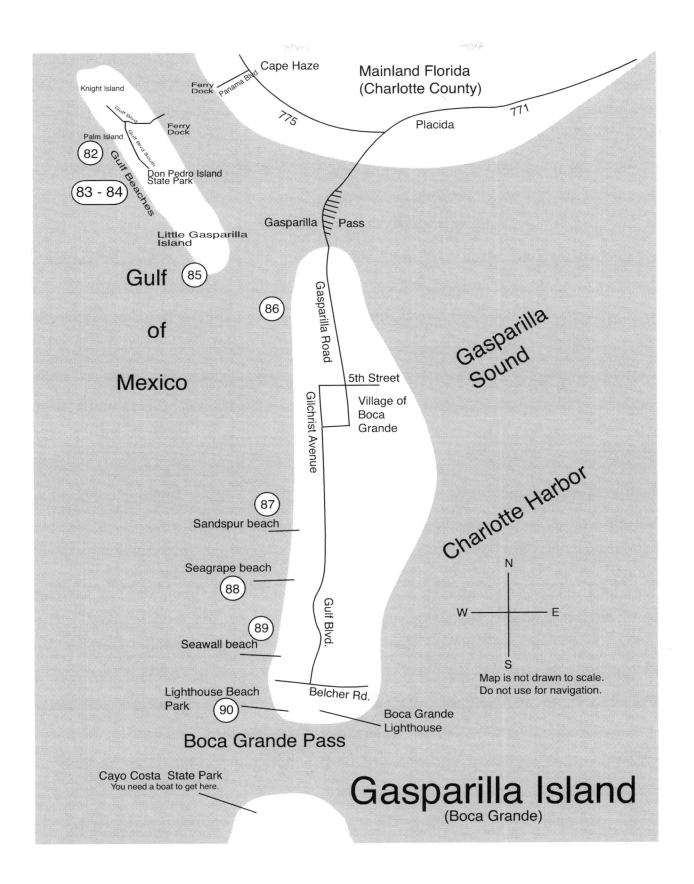

Mainland Florida
(Charlotte County)

Cape Haze

Knight Island

Ferry Dock

Panama Blvd

775

Placida

771

Gulf Blvd

Ferry Dock

Palm Island

82

Gulf Beaches

Gulf Blvd South

83 - 84

Don Pedro Island
State Park

Gasparilla Pass

Little Gasparilla
Island

Gulf

85

of

86

Gasparilla Road

Gasparilla
Sound

Mexico

5th Street

Village of
Boca
Grande

Gilchrist Avenue

87

Charlotte Harbor

Sandspur beach

Seagrape beach

N

88

W   E

89

Gulf Blvd.

Seawall beach

S

Map is not drawn to scale.
Do not use for navigation.

Belcher Rd.

Lighthouse Beach
Park

90

Boca Grande
Lighthouse

Boca Grande Pass

Cayo Costa State Park
You need a boat to get here.

Gasparilla Island
(Boca Grande)

seawall on 5th street, it is possible to walk north along the seawall for about 600 feet toward 7th street to gain access to a navigable beach trail.

Continuing south on Gilchrist, all streets ending at the beach between 5th street and 1st street, including Banyan Street, have free parking. Unfortunately, the high sea wall above the beach tends to thwart easy access to the sand. But if you are agile, you can clamber down to the narrow beach.

Boca Grande Beach Accesses

Gilchrist Avenue becomes Gulf Blvd once you get south of 1st street, which is where you'll find the first of the four main public beach access points on the island. They are all part of the Gasparilla Island State Park system. The first three accesses provide parking, limited facilities, and access to roughly 1.75 miles of sandy beach. The accesses are open from 8am till dusk. The three access points on Gulf Blvd are:

87: #1 Sandspur Beach, Gasparilla Island State Park

(GPS coordinates: 26.743371, -82.263456) This access is just outside Boca Grande Village between 1st street and Wheeler. A small paved parking lot is the only parking for the beach, and it comes with a $3.00 per day parking fee. You place your fee in a special envelope and tear off a numbered tag which is hung on your vehicle's rearview mirror. It is good for any of the Gasparilla Island State Park beach accesses on the same day. There are restrooms and covered picnic tables with BBQ grills. The beach is not far from the lightly traveled road, but is hidden from the road by sea grape trees, sea oats, and other beach vegetation. The beach is strewn with a collection of seaweed, sticks, shells, driftwood, and various sea creatures that have washed ashore. Boca Grande beaches are not manicured with heavy equipment the way some beaches are, so what washes ashore is left for the beachcombers, birds and crabs.

The southern end of the parking area offers several handicap parking spaces with easy access to the restrooms and to one of the picnic shelters. There is also a special mat that provides a wheelchair-friendly ramp to the beach. However there is no beach wheelchair available and no lifeguard or ranger on site.

You'll notice a small lighthouse on the beach here where Wheeler Road intersects Gulf Blvd. This is the Boca Grande Rear Range Light. It's a "pyramid skeleton tower," which was less expensive to build than the big brick or stone lighthouses. It was also portable upon disassembly. This one was moved from service in Delaware and was reassembled on Boca Grande in 1927. It was lit in 1932. It continues to work in conjunction with an offshore light to steer ships into the Boca Grande shipping channel (LighthouseFriends.com).

Photo: Sandspur Beach showing picnic shelters and lighthouse. Gulf is at right.

88: #2 Sea grape Parking Area, Gasparilla Island State Park

(GPS coordinates: 26.72498, -82.26309) About 1.25 miles south of the Sandspur Beach access on Gulf Blvd is a second beach access which is part of the state park system. It offers one picnic table, a dune crossover, and only a portable outhouse for facilities. There are no beach shelters here, and although there are a few handicap parking spaces, there are steps up and down to the beach and no ramp suitable for a wheelchair. The beach is hidden from the road by dunes and vegetation. This is a very quiet beach access. The state park entrance fee applies.

89: #3 Seawall Parking Area, Gasparilla Island State Park

(GPS coordinates: 26.721041, -82.263214) A short distance further down Gulf Boulevard is the third state park access. The state park entry fee applies. This small unpaved lot partially shaded by sea grape trees is located on the south side of the South Beach Bar and Grill. It offers one shaded picnic table, portable toilets, a sand trail to the beach, and easy access to the South Beach Bar and Grill restaurant, which has both indoor and outdoor seating. It's a great place to watch the sunset.

The southern boundary of the beach is a physical barrier provided by rocks and a high sea wall, marking the private property of Boca Bay.

90: Lighthouse Beach Park, Gasparilla Island State Park

(GPS: 26.71912, -82.26159) The Boca Grande lighthouse is located at the southern tip of the island on Boca Grande Pass, in Gasparilla Island State Park. The lighthouse is open to the public, but does have limited summer days and hours. It contains a small but fun museum and gift shop. Even if the museum is not open when you visit, be sure to climb the steps of the lighthouse and sit on one of the gliders on the veranda. The views of Boca Pass and Cayo Costa Island on the other side are magnificent.

Photo: Lighthouse Park beach, looking south toward Boca Pass and Cayo Costa Island.

If you are just passing through and don't have time to go in the park, you can turn right at the park entrance, on Belcher, and drive a block to the Gulf where there is a scenic overlook that's great for a quick look at the beach and the lighthouse; it's a great photo opportunity.

Currently the state park accesses on Gasparilla Island have an envelope and hang-tag pay system upon entering the park. Leave your entrance fee in the envelope and hang the paper tag from your rear view mirror. You'll need dollar bills or exact change for the (currently) $3 fee. There is a parking lot as soon as you enter the park with restrooms and two boardwalks to the Gulf beach. It also serves the small chapel. Follow the dirt road back past the first parking lot and it will take you a short distance to the picnic area, and to another parking area at the Boca Pass beach, and to the restrooms and the lighthouse.

The picnic area has a shaded pavilion with multiple tables and a large grill as well as uncovered tables and grills. Outdoor rinse-off showers are provided and the restroom building has a drink machine. For the disabled, several handicap spaces are located next to the restrooms and outdoor shower and a special mat leads out onto the sand. A beach wheelchair is available on a first-come, first-served basis. It is kept under the park administration building located between the restrooms and the lighthouse. During summer 2013 a new elevated restroom facility was completed to provide additional restrooms closer to the Gulf beach.

During Tarpon fishing season the pass is full of boats trying to catch a trophy-sized Tarpon. And there are always lots of fishing boats in the area because of the relatively productive waters of Charlotte Harbor. In fact, sitting on the Boca Pass beach can be a spectator sport during the spring and summer season with fishing boats jockeying for position. And, if you have a sharp eye and patience you'll see some really big fish (and the occasional shark) breaking the surface of the water. The pass is deep and wide with strong currents. There are some really big fish swimming through.

You may have guessed by the preceding paragraph that swimming at this park is ill-advised. Don't do it. There's plenty of beach to walk and the shelling and beachcombing are great. You might want to bring a pair of binoculars to watch the birds, the boats in the pass, and to check out Cayo Costa Island State Park on the other side of the pass. Cayo Costa is only accessible by boat.

Photo: View of La Costa Island one mile away across Boca Grande Pass. Photo was taken from the Gasparilla lighthouse deck with a telephoto lens.

Photo: A tranquil and scenic crescent shaped beach on northern La Costa Island.

La Costa Island

(Cayo Costa Island State Park)

Interstate 75 Exit: 161 (Jones Loop Road) or exit 143 (Pine Island Road, SR 78)

Nearest mainland cities: Cape Coral, Punta Gorda, and Fort Myers.

Major access roads: Pine Island Road (SR 78), Stringfellow Road.

Directions to Pineland Marina: From I-75, take exit 161, North Jones Loop Road, west. Keep driving west and after about a mile you will US Highway 41 (Tamiami Trail). After you cross US 41, N. Jones Loop Road becomes Burnt Store Road. Follow Burnt Store Road about 18 miles to Pine Island Road (SR 78). Turn right onto Pine Island Road and drive about five-and-a-half miles to Pine Island. At the four-way stop turn right onto Stringfellow Road and drive 3.25 miles to Pineland Road. Turn left on Pineland Road and follow it to Pineland Marina where the Tropic Star is docked. The Tropic Star passenger ferry will take you to Cayo Costa (more information below). From I-75 you could also take exit 143, Pine Island Road (SR 78), but you have to drive through more congestion and traffic lights. Using Burnt Store Road will save you about half-an-hour, until the area becomes more developed (and it is well on its way).

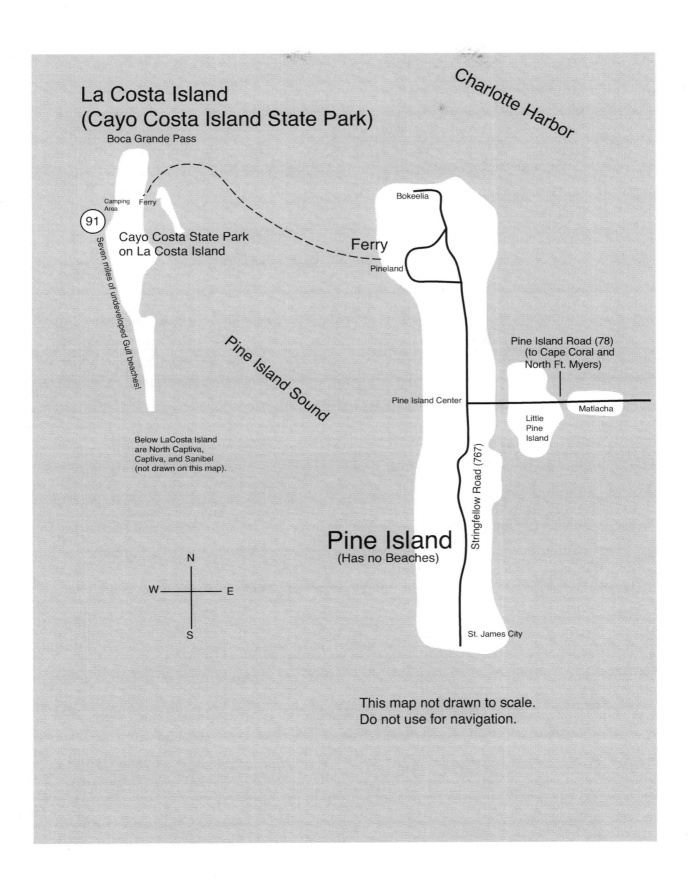

La Costa Island
(Cayo Costa Island State Park)

Charlotte Harbor

Boca Grande Pass

Camping Area

Ferry

91

Seven miles of undeveloped Gulf beaches!

Cayo Costa State Park
on La Costa Island

Bokeelia

Ferry

Pineland

Pine Island Sound

Pine Island Road (78)
(to Cape Coral and
North Ft. Myers)

Pine Island Center

Matlacha

Little
Pine
Island

Below LaCosta Island
are North Captiva,
Captiva, and Sanibel
(not drawn on this map).

Stringfellow Road (767)

N

W———E

S

Pine Island
(Has no Beaches)

St. James City

This map not drawn to scale.
Do not use for navigation.

Cayo Costa Island State Park is on La Costa Island, an undeveloped barrier island about seven miles long and one mile wide at its widest point. La Costa Island is between Gasparilla Island and North Captiva Island, and is five to six miles west of Pine Island. The state park occupies the northern 2.5 miles of this seven mile long island. The northern end of the island happens to have the most land mass as the island is wide at the north end and very narrow toward its southern end. The remainder of the island is mostly owned by the state and local government except for a handful of private lots with homes, mostly near the southern end.

You may visit the park for the day, or you can camp on the island (reservations required). It is a large island and would take the better part of a week to explore it all.

The only way to reach the island is by boat. If you don't have a boat, there are several services that will take you to Cayo Costa. I have always used Tropic Star Cruises (www.tropicstarcruises.com). They are very friendly, always helpful, and their prices are reasonable. Be sure to call first to verify prices, times, and departure locations. The Tropic Star is the official concessionaire for Cayo Costa State Park, making several trips every day to bring day visitors or campers to and from the island. They will haul your camping gear and even your kayak to the island and bring you back when you're ready to come home.

You could also kayak to Cayo Costa from either Pine Island or Gasparilla Island. From Pine Island it would be at least a twelve-mile round trip across the sound in relatively protected and shallow water. From Gasparilla Island you could launch your kayak at Lighthouse Park on Boca Grande Pass and paddle half-a-mile across the pass to the north tip of Cayo Costa (Quarantine Point). The Boca Pass crossing is recommended only for very experienced kayakers using capable sea kayaks with spray skirts and should not be made during tarpon fishing season because the boat traffic in the pass is just too busy. The pass is deep and the current is strong. It can get very rough.

Upon arrival on the island you have to pay a small per-person entry fee per day. If you've arrived at the dock on the bay side of the island, a tram will carry you and your beach gear about one mile across the island to the Gulf beaches. The tram runs from 9 am to 4pm. You will ride through a beautiful oak-palm hammock on your way to the beach. The island today is very much the way it was a hundred years ago. Most of the Australian pines that used to provide copious shade on the island were either blown over or severely damaged by Hurricane Charley in 2004. Since the state was already in the process of removing invasive plant species, it finished Charley's work by removing the remaining pines. Unfortunately, with the Australian pines gone there is not much in the way of shade near the beach, so if you are visiting during warm weather, be sure to bring your own shade, such as a large beach umbrella, tarp, or beach tent. Otherwise it will be one very long and hot day with a guaranteed case of sunburn and risk of dehydration. Do not underestimate the Florida sun.

Pets must remain on a leash and must remain in designated areas. Pets are not allowed on the beach. Alcoholic beverages are allowed in designated areas. Call the park for more specific info. Glass containers are not permitted out on the beach. Bonfires are not allowed out on the beach. There is no lifeguard on duty.

91: Beaches of La Costa Island

There are no specific named beaches on La Costa Island like you would find on most islands. The beach is accessible the entire seven mile length of the island. Unless you have a boat, or are camping and have several days to explore, there is a lot more beach here than you will be able to see in one day. But don't worry; the beach where the tram drops you off is an absolutely gorgeous crescent shaped mile of nearly deserted sand and clean water. As I mentioned, there is no shade on the beach, but if you walk north for three-quarters of a mile, toward Boca Grande Pass, there are several places where the native cabbage palms provide shady spots in the woods above the beach. The water here in the spring months is absolutely gorgeous and clear. You just have to see it to appreciate it. The beach sand is a mix of quartz and crushed shell, has a slightly gray color and is easy to walk on. The island has a reputation for having excellent shelling, particularly after a day or two of strong onshore winds. If you don't see a lot of shells on the beach, put on your mask and snorkel and step into the shallow water. Just a few feet from the sand, right where there is a small drop-off (called the "plunge step") is where you'll find lots of shells and maybe some sand dollars.

Raccoon tracks are everywhere on the beach as could be expected on an undeveloped island. There are feral hogs on the island and alligators in some areas. About mid island, a thousand feet south of the camping area, there is an enclosed shallow salt-water lagoon created by a sand bar or shoal. It's about a mile long and 1,200 feet wide at its widest point. The lagoon is open to the Gulf by a narrow pass at its southern end. There is a sign warning against swimming in the lagoon because of alligators. I have heard that at least one saltwater crocodile is sometimes seen in the Pine Island area. With that in mind I would be inclined to limit my swimming activities to the Gulf and avoid swimming in the inland ponds and backwaters. Check with a ranger if you are concerned, but don't let it prevent you from coming to enjoy Cayo Costa. Remember that nearly every golf course in Florida has a pond with alligators in it and it doesn't stop the golfers.

Camping on Cayo Costa Island State Park

Most people are surprised to find that arranging a beach camping trip in Florida is difficult. Very few beaches allow camping directly on the beach. While Cayo Costa does not allow camping directly on the beach at the water's edge, it does provide plenty of camping opportunity on the upper beach, about 500 feet from the Gulf of Mexico and within sight of the water.

Photo: Tent camping at Cayo Costa State Park.

The island park offers 30 sites for tent campers and 12 small, rustic cabins. Both camping areas lack shade. Unless you have your own boat, the only way to get your camping gear to the island is by using the Tropic Star ferry. This means you'll need to drive your gear to the Pineland Marina on Pine Island where the Tropic Star is docked. You can leave your car at the marina (for a fee) and load your gear onto the Tropic Star which will ferry you to the island. From the dock on Cayo Costa, a tram will help you cart your gear to the camping area. It's slightly less than one mile from the dock to the camping area.

On Cayo Costa there is a ranger station with a very tiny nature museum and gift shop. You can buy firewood and ice, and they have bicycles for rent. There are no paved roads on the island but some of the trails will accommodate a bicycle.

Neither the cabins nor the tent camping area has electricity. Flush toilets are available in the camping area and there is cold running water. The cold-water showers are outdoors and are mainly suitable for rinsing off. The campground area has very little shade and the campsites do not have much privacy.

There is a covered picnic pavilion between the tents and the cabins. It has several wooden picnic tables and is often used by people waiting for the return tram to take them back to the docks.

In summary, La Costa Island is the largest undeveloped island on the peninsular Florida Gulf Coast. It has a colorful history, abundant wildlife, great fishing, nature trails for hiking and biking, gorgeous beaches, clean and often clear water, and has the best rustic beach camping (no campers or motor homes) on the peninsular Florida Gulf Coast.

Photo: Primitive beach cabin in Cayo Costa State Park. Reservations required.

Photo: Turner's Beach on Captiva Island at Blind Pass.

Sanibel and Captiva Islands

Interstate 75 Exit: 131 (Daniel's Parkway)

Nearest mainland city: Fort Myers

Major access roads: Daniel's Parkway, Six-mile Cypress, Summerlin Road

Directions: The easiest way to get to Sanibel Island by car is to take the Daniel's Parkway exit #131 near Ft. Myers off Interstate 75. Drive west and follow the signs pointing the way to Sanibel and Captiva. The way is clearly marked. Follow Daniel's Parkway to Ben C. Pratt/Six-mile Cypress; continue for several miles to Summerlin Road. Turn left on Summerlin Road (869) which will take you all the way to Sanibel.

Pets: Dogs are allowed on Sanibel's beaches (including the causeway beaches) but, by law, must be on a leash no longer than 8 feet. Pets are not allowed on Captiva beaches.

Parking Fees: Entry to all beaches is free, but parking is not. As of June 2013, a $2.00 per hour fee applies to all beach parking on both Sanibel and Captiva. The pay stations located in each parking lot generally accept coins, bills, and credit cards. The pay stations do not make change. Parking is free for those with a valid handicap permit. Beach parking fees are a significant revenue source for the island with more than $1.3 million in revenue collected from the pay stations and more than $50,000 in parking fines collected in 2011.

Disabled Access: Sanibel provides handicap parking spaces at all public accesses, but does not currently provide any beach wheelchairs. The Sanibel Police department (239-463-4588) will make arrangements to have a beach wheelchair at any of the Sanibel beach locations. Billy's Bike Rental at 1470 Periwinkle Way on Sanibel has beach wheelchairs available for rent (239-472-5248).

Restrooms: Public restrooms can be found at all public beach accesses.

Food and Drink: Sanibel and Captiva beach parks do not have snack bars. They do have water fountains. Bowman's Beach has a soda machine. Picnic tables are found at Gulfside City Park and Bowman's Beach.

Alcohol: Alcoholic beverages are NOT allowed out on the beach after dark between December 15th and May 15th, unless otherwise indicated. Alcohol is not allowed on Bowman's beach at any time. Alcoholic beverages are not allowed in any beach parking areas. Alcohol is not allowed on Captiva beaches.

Shelling: Sanibel is the most famous beach in the world for finding shells, but you cannot take live shells. That includes live sand dollars. If there is a living animal inside, look but don't take.

Lifeguards: Lee County, Florida does not employ lifeguards at its beaches. So you will not encounter lifeguards on any of the beaches on Sanibel or Captiva. Conduct yourself accordingly.

Camping: There is no camping directly on the beach, but the Periwinkle Park campground on Sanibel is within walking distance of the beach. Overnight parking at any of the beaches or parks is, of course, prohibited. www.sanibelcamping.com

To cross the bay to get to Sanibel you first have to pay a toll, which is now $6.00 for cars. You will then drive for about three miles across a causeway with three bridges which hopscotch across San Carlos Bay, and which were replaced by larger spans during 2004-2007. As you approach the toll plaza you may notice signs advising you that public beach access is limited on Sanibel. They aren't kidding. Still, if you arrive early enough, you can find some choice parking spots (it's worth it), or if you know where to go (that's why you bought this book!) you can find a spot without wasting your precious time driving around looking like a tourist.

On certain streets and in certain parking areas you will see signs referring to "A" parking permits, "B" permits, and "C" permits. "A" permits are for residents only. "B" and "C" permits can be purchased at the Sanibel Police Department by non-residents. A holder of a "B" permit can park at certain "permit only" beaches and can also park at some of the public pay lots without having to pay. A "C" permit allows you to park at Algiers Beach/Gulfside City Park, at the boat ramp on the south side of the causeway, or the lot on the north side of the causeway without paying the hourly fees. If you are going to be on Sanibel for a while, a permit might be worth considering. Roadside parking is not allowed on Sanibel or Captiva, except in designated parking areas. Overnight parking is prohibited in all residential or restricted parking areas. Oversized vehicles (RV's exceeding 20 feet in length) may park in designated areas at the Tarpon Bay Road beach and at Bowman's beach. Parking on Sanibel is clearly an issue and the police do enforce the parking rules. Parking on Captiva is even more difficult.

Sanibel and Captiva are among the most thoughtfully developed islands on the southwest coast of Florida. The extent of tropical lushness on these islands is unequaled on any other barrier island accessible by car. Sanibel is a large island--over 15 miles long. It's also rather wide, and its northeastern coastline facing Pine Island Sound and San Carlos Bay encompasses a vast area of mangrove forest and estuary known as Ding Darling National Wildlife Refuge. The refuge comprises nearly a third of the island.

Sanibel is world-famous for its shells. Why is it any better for finding shells than other Florida beaches? It has to do with Sanibel's physical orientation. Look at the map and notice that most barrier islands on Florida's Gulf Coast have a north-south alignment. Sanibel extends out into the Gulf with an east-west alignment and is the drop off point for shells carried northward by currents. Off the south-facing shore of Sanibel the Gulf floor slopes very gently for many miles out into deeper water, allowing the shells to roll gently onto the beaches, minimizing wear and tear on the shells. Sanibel's beaches have been subject to heavy erosion, so they are constantly monitored, and renourished with new sand when necessary.

Captiva Island, a truly enchanting place, is separated from Sanibel by Blind Pass, which has to be kept open by regular dredging. The two islands are connected by a bridge. You must drive the length of Sanibel to reach Captiva. Blind Pass is a particularly good shelling location, but you have to get there early. The best time to arrive is before sunrise. Bring your flashlight.

92: Sanibel Causeway Beaches

As you approach the toll bridge there is a beach on the south side of the road. You don't have to pay the toll to visit this beach and it has no facilities. But it, like all the beaches on the causeway, is a bay beach, not a Gulf beach. Bay beaches are usually narrower, lack the soft white sand, and the bottom feels a bit muddy and soft rather than firm and sandy. After going through the tollbooth, you are on the Sanibel Causeway, with beaches on both sides of the roadway. The causeway beaches are popular with sun-worshippers, windsurfers, fishermen, boaters, and families enjoying picnics and barbecues. There are two manmade islands on the causeway. Both have some shade from Australian pines and coconut palms. The first (east) island on the causeway has a rather wide white sand beach on the north side of the road. The second (west) island has covered picnic tables and

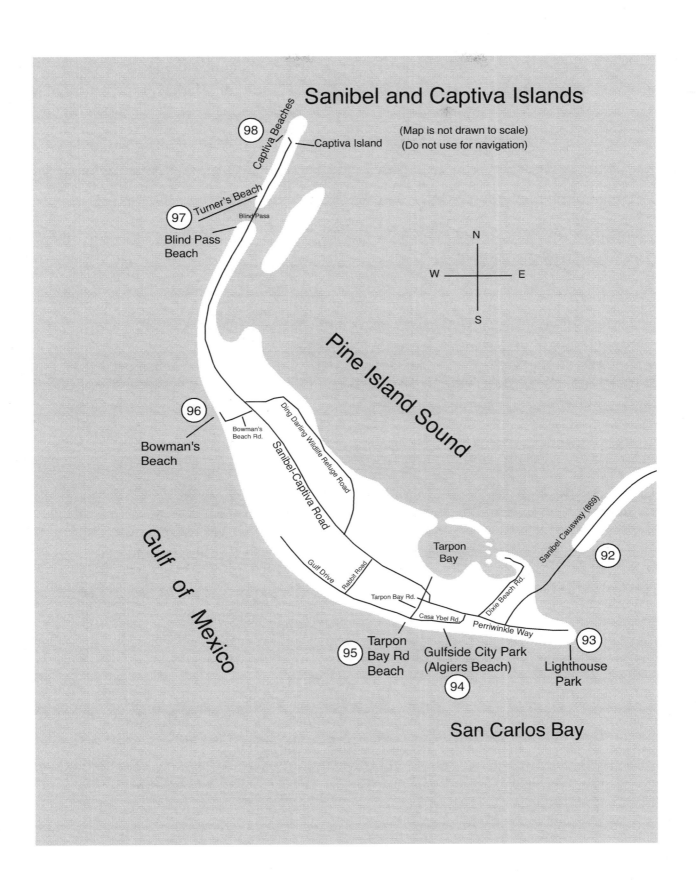

Sanibel and Captiva Islands

(Map is not drawn to scale)
(Do not use for navigation)

98 Captiva Beaches — Captiva Island

97 Turner's Beach
Blind Pass
Blind Pass Beach

96 Bowman's Beach
Bowman's Beach Rd.

Ding Darling Wildlife Refuge Road

Sanibel-Captiva Road

Pine Island Sound

Gulf of Mexico

Tarpon Bay

Sanibel Causway (869)

92

Gulf Drive
Rabbit Road
Tarpon Bay Rd.
Casa Ybel Rd.
Dixie Beach Rd.
Perriwinkle Way

95 Tarpon Bay Rd Beach

Gulfside City Park (Algiers Beach)

94

93 Lighthouse Park

San Carlos Bay

N
W E
S

restroom facilities, as well as more trees. Both islands are popular, I suspect, with people who don't want to spend another 15 or 20 minutes driving to the Gulf beaches and then pay to park. Parking is free on the causeway. Dogs are permitted on the causeway beaches but must remain on a leash. This is a very scenic picnic spot. There are no lifeguards or food and drink sales.

To the north you can see St. James City across the bay on Pine Island, and to the South is Ft. Myers Beach on Estero Island. Pine Island has no beaches; mangrove trees dominate its coastline. Pine Island is a trip in itself.

93: Lighthouse Park

(GPS: 26.45134, -82.01648) It's a short drive to Lighthouse Park after you drive onto Sanibel Island. Just turn left onto Periwinkle Way (the first stop sign you come to) and follow it a few minutes to the end. You'll pass a few shops, some residences, and some small resorts before you come to the beach access. If you continue straight, you'll be in a parking area that provides access to the Gulf beach. Parking fees are enforced 24 hours per day. The parking pay stations do not give change, but will generally accept coins, cash, and credit or debit cards. If you're going to be there all day feed the machine accordingly. This is the type of parking pay station you will find at all the beaches on the island, and most other islands as well.

The beach on San Carlos Bay is very flat. The sand is white and clean and speckled with shells that are generally in much better condition than those on most Florida beaches. The eastern tip of the island around the lighthouse is wooded, while a quarter mile or so further west the beachfront condos begin and extend west for miles. But don't let the word condo mislead you about the character of this beach, because they are not the tall blocky buildings found on Longboat, Siesta, Lido, Venice Beach, and Marco Island. The condos and resorts on Sanibel are quite pleasing to behold, are set back a considerable distance from the beach, and most are only 2 or 3 stories high. The landscaping near the beach is fabulous and makes the beach fairly private. You can walk west forever. This is also a very popular spot for pleasure boaters to drop anchor and wade ashore.

At the entrance to Lighthouse Park you can continue straight to the beach parking, or turn left on Periwinkle Way and drive around to a parking area on the bay side where there is a small wooden fishing pier, a narrow beach, some trails through the woods with boardwalks, and a dirt road that leads to the lighthouse. There are restroom facilities here. You cannot climb the lighthouse, but you can get close to it. Lighthouse Park does not have food or drink concessions or lifeguards. The park is under video surveillance.

Photo: Lighthouse Beach Park.

94: Algiers Beach / Gulfside City Park

(GPS: 26.425490, -82.065978) If you drive west on Periwinkle Way for a couple of miles and make a left on Casa Ybel Road (Casa Ybel Road later curves into Gulf Drive), then proceed to Algiers Lane and make a left, you will follow a winding shell road back to a wooded unpaved pay-and-park lot at Algiers Beach. There are boardwalks to the beach with ramps that are wheelchair friendly, and a picnic area with a few wooden tables and grills and limited shade. There's lots of beach vegetation on the dunes. The beach here has plenty of shells. Algiers is a very peaceful beach because the nearby resorts are well spaced and partially hidden by extremely lush landscaping. You can walk east or west as far as you want to. This is a first class beach. You won't be disappointed if you come here. Shelling is very good. If you visit early in the morning you can see the sun rise over Estero Island (Fort Myers Beach) on the southeastern horizon. The handicap accessible restrooms are open 7am to 6pm. Alcohol is not allowed on the beach after dark between December 15th and May 15th, and is not allowed in the parking lot at any time.

95: Tarpon Bay Road Access

This beach access is a short drive north of Algiers Beach on Gulf Drive. Tarpon Bay Road connects Sanibel-Captiva Road and Gulf Drive. There is a "pay and park" parking lot just east of the intersection of Gulf Drive and Tarpon Bay Road, (GPS: 26.424915, -82.079925). There is space for quite a few cars as well as several spaces for motor homes exceeding 20 feet in length. To get to the beach you must walk along a paved bicycle trail for about 5 minutes to reach the beach. It's about 1,000 feet from the parking lot to the beach. Parking for the handicapped is located close to the beach on the west side of Gulf Drive (GPS: 26.423195, -82.080019). Also, restroom facilities are located there as well. There is a long shaded boardwalk to the beach. This is an area where there are quite a few condominium/resorts on the beach. As on all of Sanibel/Captiva, they are somewhat hidden from the beach by amazingly lush landscaping, and do not spoil the natural beauty of the shore. This is a popular beach.

96: Bowman's Beach

(GPS: 26.461592, -82.154539) This is my favorite beach on Sanibel. If you want a remote, natural beach, this is it. To get here, take Periwinkle Way north to Sanibel-Captiva Road and continue north to Bowman's Beach Road. Bowman's Beach Road is past the entrance to Ding Darling wildlife sanctuary and is clearly marked with a sign. You can use the fire station as a landmark. The parking area is little more than an unpaved area in the middle of the woods cleared of trees, although it is now maintained very well and has the pay stations. It does offer a few spaces for larger RV's. There are beautiful trails to the beach and a small restroom facility maintained by the county. A wooden footbridge crosses a small backwater and puts you on a trail leading to the beach. The walk from the car to the beach is about 1,300 feet. There is an open air shower at the entrance to the footbridge and in front of the restrooms. Outdoor changing stalls are provided. The walk from the beach to the restrooms is about 1,000 feet.

There are quite a few shaded picnic tables with grills tucked off to the sides of the trail, which forks and leads to 2 separate boardwalks to the beach. There is a lot of interesting native vegetation here because the upper beach, the dune area, and the vegetation behind the dune are intact.

Bowman's Beach was formed from an emerged sand bar, so you have to cross a footbridge to get there. Obviously, the sandbar "emerged" a very long time ago since there are dunes covered with sea oats and acres of established vegetation. Bowman's beach gets my vote for the best beach on Sanibel. It's easily accessible, there are no houses or condos--making it very quiet and private, the shelling is great, the sand is clean and the water is fine for swimming. You can walk east or west on the beach as far as you like, but most of the undeveloped beach lies to the north of the Bowman's access. There are about 2.25 miles of completely undeveloped beach here.

Between the beach and the backwater (a distance of several hundred yards), there is a trail through an area forested with low native trees and natural undergrowth. The trail runs parallel to the beach for about a mile. Mangroves line the shore of the backwater. Every 500 feet or so along the trail, a sand trail leads over the low dunes toward the beach. Although there are signs prohibiting nudity on the beach, much of the beach is so remote that nude sunbathing is not all that uncommon. Be aware that there are some residents who consider it their duty to report nude sunbathers to the police.

Photo: Bowman's Beach.

Also, I must underscore that because this beach is remote and has woods above the beach, I do not recommend that women walk or sunbathe by themselves on the beach on the more remote areas of the beach, even during the daytime. Bowman's Beach gets very dark at night and the parking area is not lighted, so time your stay accordingly, depending on your personal circumstances. As the sun sets, the beach crowd disappears quickly and the parking lot empties. It could be scary to someone not used to being alone in a dark remote area. On the other hand, it might be just what you're looking for.

If you really want to come to a quiet beach, a beach where you don't hear car horns and motorcycles, trucks and jets, speedboats and jet skis, come to Bowman's Beach. Dogs are allowed on the beach here, but they must be on a leash and the owner's must clean up their mess. Alcoholic beverages are not allowed in the park or on the beach.

While it would be tempting to park your RV or truck camper here overnight, it is not legal to do so and it is certain that you would not get through the night without being told to leave. Better to get a spot at the Periwinkle Park campground up the street.

97: Turner's Beach and Blind Pass Beach

Past Bowman's Beach, about two-and-a-half miles further north on Sanibel-Captiva Road, you will find a small island village and its beach, Blind Pass Beach. It's located on the Sanibel side of Blind Pass (GPS: 26.482167, -82.181608). Across the bridge, on the north side of the pass, the beach is called Turners Beach (GPS: 26.483046, -82.183443), which is technically on Captiva Island, since Blind Pass is what separates the two islands. Although there is a pay-and-park lot on each side of the bridge, parking spaces are few in number. So get here very early or you will have to go back to Bowman's beach. The beach parking lots are too small for RV's. Public restrooms and a rinse-off shower are located in the parking lot on the Captiva side of the bridge.

The Blind Pass area, on the Sanibel side, has an eclectic arrangement of shops, restaurants, and colorful beach cottages. No matter where you are in this little village it feels like you're on the beach. Everything is bright and clean and the foliage is green and very tropical. I've heard that some years ago Conde Nast travel magazine rated this as one of the most romantic beaches. This is probably true if you are staying in one of the beach cottages. Otherwise, the inadequate parking arrangement could be a romance killer.

There is a rock jetty sticking out into the Gulf on the Captiva side of the pass. As long as the pass is open, it's an excellent fishing spot, especially at night on a strong tide. Blind Pass accumulates sand and shell quickly and will close itself off unless it is dredged every few years. The beaches on either side of the pass provide some of the best shelling in the world. If you're looking for the famed Junonia shell, Blind Pass would be an excellent place to focus your efforts.

Photo: Blind Pass, taken from the Captiva side.

98: Captiva Island

When you drive north across the bridge at Blind Pass (Turner's Beach) you enter Captiva Island. The entirety of Captiva is like a tropical jungle with homes secluded behind greenery. The road twists and turns and finally winds its way through the South Sea Islands Plantation, a private resort of considerable renown. Drive past the entrance to the South Seas Plantation and you will soon come to the end of the road. There you will find a small pay-and-park lot and a large beach at Alison Hagerup Beach Park (GPS: 26.526265, -82.193820). There isn't room for many cars here so you'd better get here very early. The lot is limited to vehicles no more than 20 feet in length. It's just a few feet to the beach. You can walk north or south as far as you care to. To the north you can see North Captiva Island across Redfish Pass, cloaked in greenery and not accessible by car. You can walk on the beach all the way to Redfish Pass, which was opened up by the great 1921 hurricane. From the Captiva Beach public parking lot it is nearly a four mile round trip walk to Redfish Pass and back. The only facilities at this small access are portable toilets and a parking pay station. There are no showers or drinking fountains. The parking lot is within walking distance of Captiva restaurants.

The best way to enjoy Captiva is on foot. You can easily spend the entire day enjoying Captiva, even though it is a small island. If you are not staying in one of the vacation homes here or at the South Seas resort, my advice is to arrive around 9 am and park at the Captiva Beach lot. Pay for the day and then head for the beach. When you're hungry, take a stroll through Captiva and take your pick of the many fine casual restaurants and café's here. Have a cool drink. Enjoy some ice cream and walk through all of the quirky shops that sell artsy crafts. Some of the restaurants and shops have a few parking spaces, but they fill up fast. Enjoy one of the most tropical and scenic islands in Florida, then head back to the beach for an afternoon swim. Perhaps try a different restaurant for dinner, then head back to the beach for the sunset before returning home. If you're looking for a restaurant right on the beach for a sunset dinner or drinks, The Mucky Duck has been an island landmark restaurant since 1976.

Neither pets nor alcoholic beverages are allowed on Captiva beaches.

Photo: A few minutes of shelling produces pleasing results at Blind Pass on Sanibel & Captiva.

Photo: Lynn Hall Memorial Park—view from Ft. Myers fishing pier.

Fort Myers Beach

(Estero Island)

Interstate 75 Exit: 131 (Daniel's Parkway)

Nearest mainland city: Fort Myers

Major access roads: Daniel's Parkway, Six-mile Cypress, Summerlin Road

Directions: Ft. Myers beach is on Estero Island, a highly developed and overpopulated barrier island to the west of Ft. Myers. To get there from Interstate 75, take exit 131 onto Daniel's Parkway. Follow the signs to Ft. Myers beach. From Daniels Parkway you will turn south on Six-Mile Cypress and follow that to Summerlin Road. Summerlin Road is also the way to Sanibel/Captiva. To get to Ft. Myers Beach on Estero Island, turn left on San Carlos Blvd. After a drive through a commercial area you will cross the Matanzas Bridge and enter Estero Island.

Pets: Dogs are allowed on most beaches but must be on a leash that is no longer than 6 feet. Dogs are not allowed at Lynn Hall Park, Bowditch Point Park, Crescent Family Park, or Newton Park.

Disabled Access: With valid handicapped permit you can park free for up to four hours in any city-owned metered space if a handicap space is unavailable. Ft. Myers Beach Parks (other than

Lover's Key) do not provide beach wheelchairs, but Fun Rental at 1901 Estero Blvd. on Ft. Myers Beach has them available for rent (239-463-8844).

Restrooms: Public restrooms can be found at all public beach parks.

Food and Drink: Bowditch Point Park offers a snack bar. Lynn Hall Memorial Park is located within steps of many restaurants and grilles. Lover's Key has a food concession.

Alcohol: Alcoholic beverages are not allowed on the beach except directly in front of the hotels which serve alcohol to their guests. It's best not to wander down the beach with a drink in your hand. The law is enforced.

Shelling: Ft. Myers beach is not the shelling hotspot that Sanibel is. Nevertheless, there are some shells to be found. Shelling on Lover's Key can be very good.

Lifeguards: Lee County, Florida does not employ lifeguards at its beaches. So you will not encounter lifeguards on any of Fort Myers beaches. Conduct yourself accordingly.

Camping: The Red Coconut RV park offers camping above the beach on what used to be a dune. Tents are allowed but most campers are in RV's. Everything is crammed in pretty tight, but it is on the beach. The park has 450 feet of beach front. There are 41 camp sites on the Gulf and more across the street. Don't expect a quiet camping experience. Sites are very small and close to the road which provides plenty of traffic noise. Some retirees come down and spend most of the winter at the Red Coconut. If you like to be very close to your neighbors and don't mind some noise, you might consider this park. www.redcoconut.com

An alternative way to visit Ft. Myers Beach and avoid all the traffic is to arrive by kayak. Park your vehicle at Bunche Beach at the end of John Morris Road (off Summerlin Road). Launch your kayak from the beach. You only have to paddle about 3,800 feet—about three-quarters of a mile-- across the shallow bay to arrive at Bowditch Point on Ft. Myers Beach. Slightly more than one additional mile of paddling will get you to the Pelican Pier and Lynn Hall Memorial Park.

Weddings: Fort Myers Beach is a popular destination for beach weddings. If you're looking for something off the beaten path, consider having a wedding on Lover's Key.

The Matanzas Bridge is the gateway to Estero Island and is very high to allow large boats to pass under without requiring a draw bridge. The view from the top of the bridge gives you a great opportunity to check out the lay of the land. There is a pedestrian lane on the south side of the bridge, and I highly recommend that you take a stroll to the highest point on the bridge and have a look around. It's a great place to take a photo of the island. Signs on the bridge warn drivers that they are entering a "congested area." They aren't kidding. This area at the foot of the Matanzas Bridge is known as the Times Square area and it is extremely congested with traffic. It is the heart of downtown Fort Myers Beach. People are everywhere; they are shopping, looking for something to eat or drink, going to the beach, or just seeing the sights. Parking is a big problem here. By 9 am on the weekend many of the beach parking lots are full. The overflow can park in various private lots that offer parking for a daily fee.

To ease the traffic congestion, Fort Myers provides a trolley that serves the beaches. They refer to the beach access trolley service as "Park and Ride." Most of us are used to driving our cars right up to the beach, but when faced with the difficulty in finding parking during a busy weekend, the trolley is an attractive option. There are two locations on the mainland near the beach where you can park for free and catch the trolley to the beach: First, Summerlin Square, at Summerlin Road and San Carlos Blvd is about 3 miles from the beach. Second, there is a free parking lot at Main Street and San Carlos Blvd just east of the Matanzas Bridge, which is less than a mile from the beach.

Public parking is available on the mainland side under the Matanzas Bridge, but you would have to walk a few blocks to Main Street to catch the trolley. Alternatively, you can park under the bridge and walk across the bridge to the beach. It isn't that far, perhaps three-quarters of a mile. If you like walking and don't have too much beach gear, I recommend walking over the bridge and maybe taking the trolley back. I can tell you from personal experience that unless you arrive very early on Fort Myers beach, you will definitely spend a lot of time looking for parking, and it probably won't be as close as you like to your intended beach destination. For Park and Ride options, follow the signs, or check the trolley web site for up-to-date scheduling and trip planning: www.rideleetran.com.

As of 2013, parking in any of the city lots, including beach parking and street parking is $2.00 per hour. Some metered street parking in the Times Square area has a two hour time limit. Most streets that dead-end at the beach have a few metered parking spaces with no time limit. Meters are enforced from 9 am to 6 pm, seven days per week. Most meters only take change, but pay stations at Palm Avenue, Connecticut, and Strandview Avenues will accept credit cards.

Once you are on the island, in the Times Square area, you can walk from the beach to any one of a number of restaurants, many with open air seating, in about one minute. Some of the restaurants near the pier have loud music and a mostly laid-back party atmosphere, particularly during the afternoon and evening. If you are in the party mood, this is the place. While alcohol is not normally allowed on most Florida beaches, on Estero Island alcoholic beverages are allowed on the beach in front of hotels that sell alcohol.

Further south, away from the pier and the Times Square district, the beach takes on a quieter personality. Fort Myers Beach is not the sterilized rarified air of an exclusive resort island for the rich and not-so-famous, nor is it undeveloped solitude. It is one of the most thoroughly used and enjoyed island I've seen. It is also one of the most affordable islands, and everyone is welcome. I always enjoy coming back here, even if it is a bit too busy and congested for my taste. Though the water is not always the clearest and prettiest, the sand is beautiful white quartz and the beaches are wide, flat and inviting. In fact, the sand is perfect for sand sculpting, which is why the International Sandsculpting Championship Festival is held each fall (usually late November) on Fort Myers Beach. It's a lot of fun. www.fmbsandsculpting.com.

Estero Island offers over 5 miles of sandy beaches, and you can walk from one end of the island to the other without obstruction under normal conditions.

About a half-mile south of the pier, Ft. Myers beach has some really beautiful stands of coconut palms. Most of the homes on the beach, until you get to the southern third of the island, are small, older beach cottages. Further south, the condominiums take over and beach access is very difficult unless you are staying in one of the condos. An interesting arrangement can be seen at the Red Coconut RV Resort. It is one of only two RV campgrounds in southwest Florida to be situated right on the beach. What a great way to spend your vacation at the beach!

Ft. Myers Beach is different than most Gulf beaches because it is sheltered from the deeper waters of the Gulf by Sanibel Island and by the shallow waters of San Carlos Bay. So, you won't be doing any surfing here. The water is too shallow and sheltered to admit swells from the gulf. Consequently, this is one of the safest beaches for swimming, though there are no lifeguards. The beach is very flat, and down near the water the sand is firm enough to ride a bike on. This is a great beach to go for a bike ride, especially at low tide when a large flat area of sand is exposed. You may find the water clarity to be better about mid-island than on the northern beaches near the pier. The outflow from the nearby Caloosahatchee River tends to reduce the water clarity on the northern beaches.

99: Lynn Hall Memorial Park and Pelican Pier

(GPS: 26.45401, -81.957110) After crossing the Matanzas Bridge onto Estero Island, turn right onto Estero Blvd. A block or so north there are several parking lots where you can pay to park all day, or you can park at the Lynn Hall Memorial Park located on the corner of Estero Blvd and San Carlos. The paid parking lot at Lynn Hall Park fills up early, sometimes as early as 9 am on weekends. It offers restrooms and outdoor showers and a few covered picnic tables with grills. The restrooms are ADA accessible and there are two sloped ramps down to the beach, at least one of which has a special beach access mat that makes it easier to get out onto the sand. This park is located next to the Ft. Myers fishing pier, called the Pelican Pier. Taking a stroll out onto the pier will give you a great view of the coast. You can also fish from the pier. The pier offers a bait and tackle shop, candy and snacks, cold drinks, souvenirs, beach toys, etc. Shark fishing is not allowed from the pier, nor is cast netting.

If you're hungry, you need only walk a few feet. Take your pick of restaurants, bars, and fast-food. There is a hamburger joint at the entrance to the fishing pier and an open-air restaurant with umbrella-covered tables overlooking the beach and pier. This is the center of activity on Fort Myers Beach.

Photo: Pelican Pier on Fort Myers Beach. Photo was taken from the end of the pier.

100: Crescent Beach Family Park

A few hundred feet south of the pier is this relatively new beach park with 400 feet of Gulf beach. It does not offer any parking spaces. It is mostly a large, open sandy area with volleyball nets, four covered picnic shelters with tables, portable restrooms, and four paths across the low dune to the beach.

101: Bowditch Point Park

(GPS: 26.463513, -81.966220) Bowditch Park is located on the north end of Estero Island about one mile north of the Times Square area. Bowditch Park has excellent restroom facilities, a wide boardwalk to the beach, sales of food and gifts, picnic tables shaded by coconut palms as well as covered shelters, and a short nature trail. Depending on where you stand in the park, you can have a good view of Sanibel Island to the west, or Ft. Myers to the north or east. You can also get a good view of the Matanzas Bridge to the south. You can easily walk a mile along the beach from Bowditch Park to the Pelican Pier in about 20 minutes, but it is not a particularly scenic section of beach because condominiums dominate the shore. The white quartz sand Gulf beach is very wide and flat, and the water is shallow and calm for swimming, though it is not particularly clear.

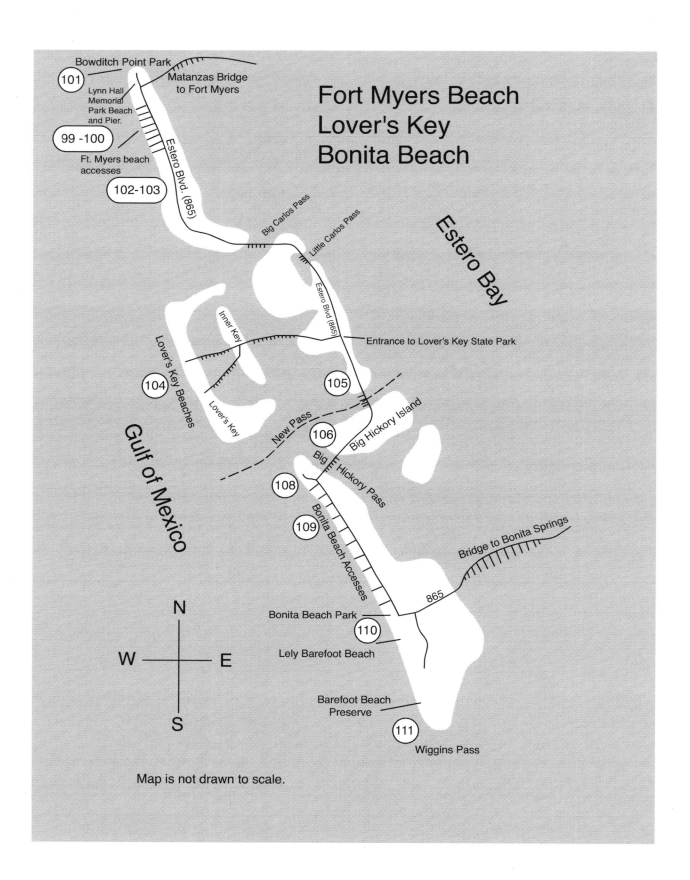

Fort Myers Beach
Lover's Key
Bonita Beach

Bowditch Point Park

101

Matanzas Bridge to Fort Myers

Lynn Hall Memorial Park Beach and Pier.

99 -100

Ft. Myers beach accesses

102-103

Estero Blvd. (865)

Big Carlos Pass

Little Carlos Pass

Estero Bay

Estero Blvd (865)

Inner Key

Entrance to Lover's Key State Park

Lover's Key Beaches

104

Lover's Key

105

New Pass

106

Big Hickory Island

Gulf of Mexico

Big Hickory Pass

108

Bonita Beach Accesses

109

Bridge to Bonita Springs

865

N

W   E

S

Bonita Beach Park

110

Lely Barefoot Beach

Barefoot Beach Preserve

111

Wiggins Pass

Map is not drawn to scale.

The parking area fills up quickly, even with the hefty parking fees charged on Ft. Myers Beach. Kayak, bike, paddleboard, and beach chair rentals are available from the park concession.

The restrooms, picnic tables and beach are wheelchair accessible. There is an access with special beach mats that make it easier to get a wheelchair out onto the sand, but it doesn't get you anywhere near the water. For that you'd need to bring a beach wheelchair.

Boat dock access is provided on the bay side of the park, which is a stopping point on the Great Calusa Blueway Paddling Trail. No pets, no alcohol, no lifeguard, and no taking of live shells.

102: Fort Myers Beach Accesses

You will see many signs up and down Estero Boulevard indicating beach access points. Most do not have parking areas, but are simply walkways to be used by residents and off-beach hotel guests. None of the access points north of the pier has parking. South of the pier, many of the access points do offer metered parking. The signs indicate whether parking is available at a particular access and also indicate if handicap parking spaces are available and whether a handicap beach access surface is in place on the sand. The signs are numbered from 1 to 45, with the numbers getting smaller as you drive south. Access points that do not indicate handicap access may have stairs to the beach.

As congested as this area is with restaurants, souvenir shops, bars, hotels, and people walking all over (reminds me of Key West), the beach is very laid-back. You won't find vendors out on the beach like you do in places like Daytona, though some of the hotels offer jet-ski or kayak rentals on the beach in front of the hotel. There's not much in the way of dunes along most of the shoreline, but most beachfront property owners plant coconut palms and other landscape plants that give the beach a tropical look.

Photo: Street-end access sign. "P" means parking is available.

The widest part of Ft. Myers Beach is at the southern end of the island, but alas, there are currently no beach accesses in this area (this could change in the future). Several of the larger resorts on the southern end of the island keep their beaches raked and prevent any dunes or vegetation from taking hold. This makes their white sand beach much wider. The beach is very flat, and is wide at low tide. The sand varies in color from white to light brown and is firm enough to ride a bike on. This is a very long beach and you can walk unrestricted as far as you like.

Photo: Looking south on Ft. Myers Beach from Newton Park. (Strandview Avenue).

103: Newton Park

This access is located on Strandview Avenue at the site of the historic home of Jim and Ellie Newton. The access has unpaved, metered parking, a small picnic shelter as well as a few uncovered picnic tables overlooking the Gulf, and restrooms open until 5 pm. A low sea wall separates the park from the beach. A wheelchair friendly ramp is provided for access to the beach. At the time of this writing, guided beach walks occur at this access every Wednesday at 9 am. Parking meters accept coins and credit/debit cards.

104: Lover's Key State Park

(GPS: 26.393006, -81.867752) Lover's Key is located just south of Estero Island, across Big Carlos Pass at 8700 Estero Blvd. It is one of several mangrove islands located between Ft. Myers Beach and Bonita Beach to the south. After crossing the bridge from Estero Island over Big Carlos Pass, you'll see a dirt parking area on the west side of the road and a narrow beach along the pass close to the bridge. This is the north park entrance. There is a reduced fee to use this beach. It offers picnic tables, grills, and portable restrooms. Open 8 am to sunset. No pets or alcohol allowed.

The main entrance to Lover's Key State Park is about a half mile further south. Turn right at the well-marked entrance and follow the road to the guard station and pay the state park entrance fee. Then follow the road back about a half-mile where you will find a parking lot, restroom facilities and outdoor rinse-off showers as well as a food concession and equipment rental vendor and, most importantly, you'll see the tram station. The park is open from 8 am until sunset.

Photo: Lover's Key State Park. Gazebo is visible. Distant buildings are on Ft. Myers Beach.

The trail to the beach splits, with one trail going about 1,000 feet straight to the beach and the other turning south for half a mile or so to a beach with a large gazebo, restrooms, and a food and drink concession, then turns east where it ends at a small pier extending into the backwater.

A tram makes continuous runs from the parking area to the beach, carrying beachgoers toting their gear. You never have to wait more than 10 or 15 minutes for the tram to come by. It's a nice walk from the parking lot to the beach on either trail if you are not carrying a lot of gear, but after you've baked in the sun for a while or worn yourself out playing on the beach it's nice to ride the tram back to the parking lot. The beaches are wooded and there are no buildings except for the gazebo, the concession and the restrooms. There are several picnic tables in the shade. Lover's Key offers nearly two miles of calm Gulf beach. You can walk north for about a mile to Big Carlos Pass and you can look across the pass and view the towering wall-to-wall condominiums on Estero Island to the north. Big Carlos Pass offers an additional 3,500 feet of sandy beach, facing north. Walking south for a mile (from the beach gazebo) will take you to New Pass. There is about 500 feet of south-facing beach on New Pass.

The park has a vendor that offers rentals of kayaks, canoes, bikes, beach chairs and umbrellas, a bait shop next to the public boat ramp on the bay side of the island, and a food concession on the beach with beach gear and a small gift shop. The vendor also helps coordinate events like beach weddings. They've got you covered. The gazebo was designed with weddings in mind.

The Friends of Lover's Key support organization has been holding a group Valentine's Day Vow Renewal Ceremony each year since 2010. More than 50 couples attend to renew their vows at the beach. If that sounds like fun to you, find out the details at www.FriendsOfLoversKey.org . The Friends of Lover's Key organization has helped make amazing improvements to the park since I first visited back in the mid 1990's.

Lover's Key State Park has regular guided nature walks and other activities to introduce visitors to the park's nature. Just a sampling of their current activities as of this writing includes: Beginning Birding, Lover's Key Fishing Clinic, Shoreline Exploration, Lover's Key Wading Trip, Black Island Kayak Tour, and Sea Turtles of Lover's Key Talk. In the park's future is a state-of-the-art visitor's center to welcome visitors and highlight what the park has to offer.

Lover's Key is a great place for an all day picnic, or to explore by canoe or kayak. If you want to launch a canoe or kayak you can do so at the foot of the New Pass Bridge, just south of the entrance to the park, or on the south side of the Big Carlos Pass bridge (the bridge connecting Lover's Key with Estero). For larger boats there is a public boat ramp (and bait shop) on the bay side of the road. The canoe/kayak launch inside the park is on the backwater and does not give direct access to the Gulf of Mexico.

Lover's Key State Park is actually four islands together: Lover's Key, Inner Key, Black Island, and Long Key. The park encompasses 1,616 acres and offers swimming, fishing, kayaking, bird-watching, hiking, or just laying around. Shelling is excellent on the Gulf beaches, but remember that you cannot take live shells.

You cannot bring alcoholic beverages to the park and pets are not allowed on the beach. Boats with motors are not allowed in the inland waterways within the park. The beach at New Pass is very popular with boaters, but remember my advice about swimming in inlets: don't.

105: Bonita Beach Dog Park (Lover's Key)

(GPS coordinates: 26.38041, -81.86213) This undeveloped beach is located on Lover's Key at the foot of the bridge over New Pass to Big Hickory Island. Parking is free. There is no lifeguard or other supervision. The only restroom facility is a portable toilet, but there is a doggie shower station to rinse the salt water and sand off your dog. The beach borders New Pass and is a narrow strip of sand in front of thick mangrove trees. The beach is a 300-400 foot long, 50 foot wide sand bar about 150 feet off the mangroves. You'll have to wade out to it. Plan to get wet. The crowd can be heavy on weekends, so plan to arrive early. Address is 8800 Estero Blvd. Fort Myers Beach, FL.

Photo: Bonita Beach Dog Park on Lover's Key.

106: Big Hickory Island Preserve

Between Lover's Key State Park and Bonita Beach is Big Hickory Island, which is a nature preserve owned by various government entities. The island does have white sandy beaches, but there is no access road to the beaches. Slogging through the mangroves is not an option, however the island's beaches are easily reached by kayak or power boat.

From the north, a kayak could be launched from Lover's Key's Dog Beach at the foot of the bridge over New Pass, however the best spot, in my opinion, to launch a kayak is at the north end of Big Hickory Island where Estero Blvd crosses New Pass. On the west side of the road there is a small unpaved parking area and a small beach that is suitable for a kayak launch (GPS 26.37619, 81.86040). A short paddle of about 1700 feet across the relatively sheltered backwater adjacent to the pass will get you to the northern tip of Big Hickory Island where you can beach your kayak and enjoy the beach overlooking New Pass and Lover's Key.

There is plenty of beach to enjoy, but a portion of the northern sand spit is owned by the Pelican Landing community located on the mainland and it is managed by the Pelican Landing Community Association. It is used as their private beach which is shared with the Hyatt Coconut Point Resort. Residents and guests are ferried back and forth between the Coconut Point Marina and the beach. They do have an elevated beach house with restrooms and a large deck and they provide beach equipment, but the facilities and equipment are only for resort guests. The beach house and restrooms are not open to the public. "Conservation rangers" are on the island to provide supervision of the facilities. From the north tip of Big Hickory, you are within a short paddle of the western beaches of the island.

The western (Gulf) side of Big Hickory Island offers slightly less than a mile of white sandy beaches. Because the island is a nature preserve, the beaches are secluded and undeveloped, but there are quite a few pleasure boaters that visit the beaches, especially on the weekends, so you are not likely to have the beach to yourself unless you visit on a weekday.

On the southern end of Big Hickory, a small unpaved parking area and sandy beach suitable for launching a kayak can be found at the base of the bridge that crosses from Big Hickory Island to Bonita Beach via Estero Blvd. over Big Hickory Pass. (GPS 26.36122, -81.85770). The paddling distance to the southernmost beaches of Big Hickory is roughly 2,500 feet. On a weekend this is most likely the route I'd choose because it would have less boat traffic than the northern end of the island.

On the Little Hickory Island side of the bridge over Big Hickory Pass—the Bonita Beach side—there is a small park called Bay Park North that has unpaved parking and an official boat ramp that would be fine for launching a kayak. (GPS 26.359015, -81.857919). Look for the Big Hickory Seafood Grille and Marina sign on the east side of Hickory Blvd. The turn-in for the park is not obvious but is marked with a small blue sign. It looks like part of the marina parking lot, but it does lead back to the boat ramp.

107: Bunche Beach

Note: This beach is not shown on any of the maps in this book.

Bunche Beach (GPS: 26.47636, -81.96738) is not actually on Estero Island. It is between Ft. Myers Beach and Sanibel Island and is part of a nature preserve. This bay beach is reached by taking Summerlin Road from Fort Myers toward Sanibel Island. Turn left at the traffic light at John Morris Road and drive south through San Carlos Bay / Bunche Beach Preserve. John Morris is a ruler-straight, mile long road through a mangrove preserve. The mangroves are tall and thick on each side of the road. Birds and other secretive critters lurk in the dark impenetrable mangle, safe from most of the dangers of development. John Morris abruptly dead-ends on the bay and provides access to about 3,900 feet of narrow sandy beach. This is a great beach for wade-fishing or shorebird watching or photographing nature, especially at sunrise when it is very quiet and there are few people. Sunset brings a small crowd each day and often attracts a few musicians who strum their guitars or play violin as the sun sets. You are lucky if that happens when you visit.

There is a fee for parking. There are a few unpaved parking spaces near the beach, but the majority of parking is either angle or parallel parking along roughly 900 feet of John Morris Road.

About 1,300 feet from the beach you'll find the Bunche Beach activities center with modern restrooms, additional paved parking with a pay station, boardwalks with overlooks and kayak launching ramps. Kayak Excursions, a local kayak rental and tour company, has a rental outlet at the activities center. Their hours vary according to the season. You can rent a kayak and explore on your own, or you can sign up for a guided tour. They rent beach chairs, umbrellas and fishing gear. Call them at 1-888-925-7496. They can hook you up with a kayak fishing guide.

Bunch Beach is part of the Great Calusa Blueway, Florida's first aquatic preserve. It is a 190 mile long marked kayak/canoe paddling trail through the mangrove islands and backwaters of Lee County. Visit the informational web site at www.CalusaBlueway.com .

The water at Bunch Beach is too shallow for serious swimming, but it is a great place to find live shells in the mud flats at low tide. This is a popular spot to launch kayaks. There are a few picnic tables but not much in the way of shade. The thick mangroves lining the shore behind the beach provide privacy to sunbathers and act as a windbreak on sunny winter days when lying out on a Gulf Beach might be a bit too cool for comfort. Bunche Beach provides a great vista of Bowditch Point at Ft. Myers Beach across the bay, and of the Matanzas Bridge far in the distance. Please note that none of the maps in this book cover Bunche Beach, however, the directions above will get you there should you decide to visit.

Handicap parking spaces are provided close to the beach and a special beach mat provides a wheelchair friendly surface to get to the nearest picnic table, as of this writing. In the past, portable restrooms were provided on the beach, but as of June 2013 they are no longer present. The nearest restrooms are about 1,300 feet away from the beach at the activities center. There is no parking allowed on the street after dark.

A cautionary note: Bunche Beach is rather isolated and has become known as a hangout where some gay men look for sex partners and engage in sex acts, sometimes in view of the public, according to media reports. Since I don't visit very often I have not personally witnessed this activity at Bunche Beach, but it is well-documented in the local media and I believe it is my responsibility to mention it. The authorities are clearly trying to combat this problem by removing the portable toilets and by not allowing parking after dark. This is not to discourage you from visiting this beach. It is enjoyed by many families with children every day without issue.

Photo: Bunche Beach.

Photo: Bonita Beach Park—a popular, attractive, and well-maintained public access.

Bonita Beach

(Little Hickory Island)

Interstate 75 Exit: 116 (Bonita Beach Road)

Nearest mainland city: Bonita Springs

Major access roads: Bonita Beach Road, CR 865 (Hickory Blvd)

Directions: Bonita Beach is located on Little Hickory Island, which you can reach either by following SR 865 south from Ft. Myers Beach, or by taking Interstate 75 exit 116 (Bonita Beach Road) and driving west to through the small town of Bonita Springs to Bonita Beach.

The island, from Big Hickory Pass to Wiggins Pass, offers 5.5 miles of sandy beaches. You can walk the entire length unobstructed if you wish. Hickory Blvd. (CR 865) is the main north-south route on Little Hickory Island.

Pets: Pets are not allowed on Bonita Beach, except for working service animals.

Disabled Access: Lover's Key State Park provides free beach wheelchairs for that location. Barefoot Beach Preserve County Park also provides a beach wheelchair. Other Lee County beaches do not currently provide beach wheelchairs.

Hours: Most Bonita Beach parks are open from 7 am until dusk.

Restrooms: Public restrooms can be found at Little Hickory Beach Park, Bonita Beach Park, and Barefoot Beach Preserve. The vendors in the county park Preserve have limited summer days and hours.

Food and Drink: Both Bonita Beach Park and Barefoot Beach Preserve Park have concessions that sell food and drink.

Alcohol: Alcoholic beverages are not allowed on the beach. Glass containers are not allowed on the beach.

Shelling: Bonita Beach is quite good for shelling, especially the northern reaches of Little Hickory Island Beach Park.

Camping: There are no beach camping facilities available on Bonita Beach.

Lifeguards: Lee County, Florida does not employ lifeguards at its beaches. So you will not encounter lifeguards on Bonita Beach. Conduct yourself accordingly.

Weddings: Bonita Beach is an excellent spot for a beach wedding, but there are no hotel facilities directly on the beach. Accommodations are condominiums and private homes. Picnic shelters and pavilions are first-come first-serve, so cannot be reserved. Local wedding vendors can help you plan your beach wedding.

108: Little Hickory Island Beach Park

(GPS 26.358434, -81.858911) Following highway 865 south from Lover's Key State Park takes you over New Pass, Big Hickory Island, and Big Hickory Pass. Now you have arrived at Bonita Beach. As you will see, the north part of the island is owned by the condominiums that block out the skyline here. Squeezed in-between two condominiums is Little Hickory Island Beach Park, which is a small but tidy beach access. There is a paved parking lot at the beach access as well as a small overflow lot across the road. There is an hourly fee for parking. This access also has restroom facilities, which the rest of the beach accesses don't have until you get to the main Bonita Beach Park public access.

Little Hickory Island Beach Park is a little difficult to find. If you are coming from Ft. Myers beach or Lover's Key, right after you cross Big Hickory Pass Bridge there is a sign that reads "Beach Access Right 300 feet." Slow down and make a right turn onto a side road that will take you a few hundred feet to the park. The parking lot doesn't hold many cars. If you are coming from the south, Little Hickory Island Beach Access is the last left turn before you round the curve and go over the bridge to Big Hickory.

If you like shelling, walk north for half-a-mile from the Little Hickory access to the north tip of the island. There you'll find two rock jetties that extend a short distance into the Gulf and act as "shell catchers." You can often collect some very nice shells there.

This little park provides restrooms, outdoor rinse-off showers, a drinking fountain, spaces for handicap parking and dune walkovers with wheelchair-friendly ramps to the beach. Vehicles over 20 feet in length are not allowed. The park is open from 7 am until dusk, when the park gates close.

109: Bonita Beach Accesses

If you continue south on County Road 865 (here named Hickory Blvd) you will start to see beach access signs between homes and condominiums. Most of them have several free parking spaces. They do not have restrooms, lifeguards, or food and drink. This area of Bonita Beach is residential and has plenty of greenery. The road is lined on both sides with beautiful coconut palms, and most homes are partially obscured by thick landscaping. Most of the beach access trails take you through thick shady foliage and over a boardwalk before you emerge on the beach. Certain access spots provide reserved handicap parking spaces, but this does not mean that ramped beach access is provided. You still may encounter several stair steps to get down to the beach. These accesses are open from 7 am to dusk.

Photo: Bonita Beach, residential beach.

The beach sand is white to a very light brown, is mixed with finely crushed shell, and is heavily littered with shells below the high tide line. There are no large dunes, but some sea oats have taken hold on the upper beach. The homes on the beach are mostly modern and well-cared-for. Some are quite palatial. When I'm on this section of beach, I feel like I'm in someone's neighborhood, not at a beach resort. This section of residential beach stretches for about 1.5 miles.

Note that you can also get to Bonita Beach from Interstate 75 without driving through congested Ft. Myers Beach by taking exit 116, Bonita Beach Road. This will reduce your driving time considerably. Bonita Beach Road will take you through the small town of Bonita Springs and then directly to Bonita Beach and Barefoot Beach Preserve.

110: Bonita Beach Park and Lely Barefoot Beach

(GPS: 26.331629, -81.845758) Just south of the public access points you will find Bonita Beach Park at 27954 Hickory Blvd. It is a public beach with modern, well-maintained facilities and paid parking. There is additional paid parking just north of Doc's Beach House Restaurant at beach access #1. Adjoining Bonita Beach Park to the south is Lely Barefoot Beach with its own pay-and-park lot (GPS: 26.33015, -81.84370). These beaches are located where 865 takes a sharp curve to the east and heads inland. If you follow the curve east for a hundred yards and turn south on Barefoot Beach Blvd, another sharp right takes you to paid parking at Lely Barefoot Beach. What's interesting is that the Barefoot Beach access is in Collier County with a parking fee of $8. Twenty feet away is the Bonita Beach Public access parking lot with a $2 per hour parking fee. The Barefoot Beach parking lot is mainly used by Collier County residents with a beach parking permit, or is used as overflow from the Bonita Beach lot. If you are staying all day, it would be cheaper to park in the Barefoot Beach lot.

Bonita Beach Park has excellent restroom facilities, an outdoor rinse-off shower, a drink vending machine, picnic tables with charcoal cooking grills, and a boardwalk overlook, all ADA accessible.

Photo: Bonita Beach Park, looking northwest over the Gulf of Mexico.

Bonita Beach Park's shoreline is the same as at the Bonita Beach accesses described above, but here there is some commercial activity on the beach—a restaurant and a few beach vendors, mainly. Between public access #1 and Bonita Beach Park you will find Doc's Beach House restaurant, a multi-story building that is packed with beachgoers in search of hamburgers, shrimp, and beer. On the beach you can rent kayaks and small sailboats.

Beginning at Lely Barefoot Beach and continuing south for two miles is a luxury housing development (I'm talking lifestyles of the rich and famous here). Boardwalks (private, keep-out) lead to the beach which is fairly well strewn with shells. Looking south, past the luxury home zone you can see the gentle greenery of Barefoot Beach Preserve in the distance. Way to the south on the skyline you can see the tall buildings of Naples.

111: Barefoot Beach Preserve (County Park)

(GPS: 26.304546, -81.834978) An unlikely entrance to a county park greets you as you turn south off 865 onto Barefoot Beach Blvd., just east of Bonita Beach Park. The sign at the entrance reassures you that you are in the right place, but what you see can cause doubts. A wide avenue leads you past the guard station of the Barefoot Preserve housing development with brick paver streets. Immense luxury homes stand ostentatiously against the open sky over the Gulf, quite incongruous with the idea of a preserve of any sort. You ask the guard: "Is this the way to the county park?" "Yes," she assures you, "two miles down this road." So you drive on south, down the winding road, cautiously negotiating the speed bumps, while heeding the signs warning you not to stop or turn down any side streets to gawk at the royal beach palaces, until finally the houses and condos end and nature takes over.

Photo: Barefoot Beach Preserve County Park, looking south toward Wiggins Pass.

There is an entrance fee to the preserve, which has restroom facilities, a snack bar, and beach accessory rentals, including canoes. The area above the sea oats covered dunes is wooded, and a lengthy wooden boardwalk connects the parking areas and leads to the beach. This is gopher tortoise territory. It is also one of the most attractive and well-maintained beach parks in Florida, thanks to the Friends of Barefoot Beach support organization.

Barefoot beach preserve is over 340 acres on the barrier island, separated from the mainland by mangrove swamps. There is over 8000 feet of beachfront here, accessible from three separate parking areas. The first is the main parking area with restrooms and a nature center. The second parking area is about 500 feet south of the main entrance, and the third is an unpaved loop which provides the southernmost access to both the Gulf beach and a backwater canoe/kayak launch.

A nature trail leads through the woods all the way to Wiggins Pass. Bicycles are not allowed on the trail. Since there are no homes or buildings on this thickly wooded part of the island it is not unusual to see wildlife, like raccoons and gopher tortoises, that you would not encounter on, say, Ft. Myers beach. There is a nature pavilion at the preserve, with exhibits by the Friends of Barefoot Beach Preserve organization. It is a great opportunity to learn about the shells, birds, wildlife (including sea turtles), and plants of the preserve. I learned that gopher tortoises and their burrows are an important part of the ecosystem here at the preserve. They are very slow moving creatures and are easily overlooked. They will occasionally venture out onto the beach in search of tender young plants to munch on, but they cannot swim.

I recommend walking the beach all the way to Wiggins Pass, then returning on the nature trail. Wiggins Pass is a narrow, beautiful and quiet outlet to the Gulf. On the other side of the pass is Delnor-Wiggins Pass State Park.

The park is open from 8 am till dusk. No alcohol, no glass containers, and no pets are allowed. A beach wheelchair is provided and the walkovers and restrooms are wheelchair accessible. There is no park food concession but there are beach vendors that sell food and rent beach equipment every day during the winter season, but only on weekends during the summer.

Photo: Naples beach as viewed from the pier at 12th Avenue South.

Naples

Interstate 75 Exit: 111 (CR 846 / Immokalee Rd), 107 (CR 896 / Pine Ridge Rd), 105 (Golden Gate Parkway).

Nearest mainland city: Naples.

Major access roads: Immokalee Rd, Pine Ridge Rd., Golden Gate Parkway.

Directions: For Delnor Wiggins Park and Vanderbilt Beach beaches, from Interstate 75, take exit #111 west on county road 846 (Immokalee Road / Bluebill Avenue), and drive west to the Gulf.

For Clam Pass and Park Shore beaches, from Interstate 75, take exit #107, Pine Ridge Road (CR 896) west all the way to the beaches. Pine Ridge Road becomes Seagate Drive on the west side of US 41.

For Lowdermilk Park, Naples Pier and southern Naples beaches, take exit #105, Golden Gate Parkway to US 41 (Tamiami Trail). Turn right (north) on US 41 and then left (west) on Mooring Line Drive and follow it to the beaches.

Pets: Pets are not allowed on Naples Beach.

Disabled Access: Most beach accesses provide designated handicap parking. Lowdermilk Park beach offers wheelchair-friendly ramps to the beach and a beach wheelchair is available.

Hours: Most Naples beach parks are open from 7 am until dusk.

Restrooms: Public restrooms can be found at Wiggins Pass State Park, the Bluebill Avenue County Access, Clam Pass County Park, and Lowdermilk Beach Park.

Food and Drink: Wiggins Pass State Park, Clam Pass County Park, and Lowdermilk Park have concessions that sell food and drink.

Alcohol: Alcoholic beverages are not allowed on the beach. Glass containers are not allowed on the beach.

Shelling: Naples beach is quite good for shelling.

Camping: There are no beach camping facilities available on Naples Beach.

Lifeguards: Lee County, Florida does not employ lifeguards at its beaches. So you will not encounter lifeguards on Naples. Conduct yourself accordingly.

Weddings: Naples is an excellent spot for a beach wedding. Delnor Wiggins State Park and Clam Pass County Park would be two locations to consider. Because of the wide variety of possibilities, contacting a local wedding vendor would be your best bet.

112: Vanderbilt Beach County Access on Bluebill Avenue

This small access is located right outside the entrance to Delnor Wiggins Pass State Park at 100 Bluebill Avenue (GPS: 26.27225, -81.82647). There is no parking at this spot, but there is circular driveway where you can drop off passengers or beach gear. At this access you'll find restrooms, a bike rack and a partially shaded trail to the beach. Parking for this access is located about 1,000 feet east on Bluebill Avenue at Connor Park (GPS: 26.272549, -81.821149). This is a pay-and-park lot. There is a sidewalk from the parking area to the beach, a distance of at least 2,000 feet. The better choice would be to use Delnor Wiggins State Park for beach access, but it often reaches capacity and closes to additional cars. Connor Park effectively serves as parking overflow for Delnor Wiggins. Please be aware that if you park at Connor Park and then enter Delnor Wiggins, you'll have to pay the fee at each park.

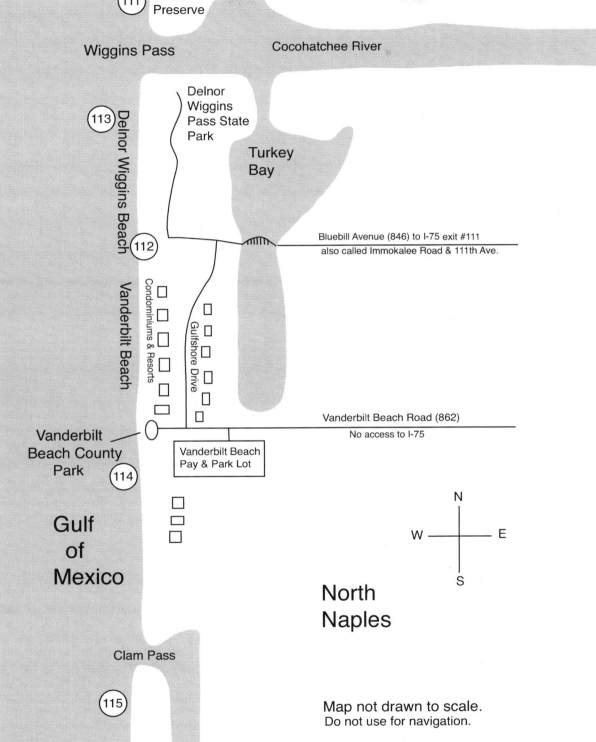

Vanderbilt Beach

Barefoot Beach Preserve (111)

Wiggins Pass

Cocohatchee River

Delnor Wiggins Pass State Park

(113) Delnor Wiggins Beach

Turkey Bay

Vanderbilt Beach

(112)

Bluebill Avenue (846) to I-75 exit #111
also called Immokalee Road & 111th Ave.

Condominiums & Resorts

Gulfshore Drive

Vanderbilt Beach Road (862)
No access to I-75

Vanderbilt Beach County Park

(114)

Vanderbilt Beach Pay & Park Lot

Gulf of Mexico

North Naples

N
W — E
S

Clam Pass

(115)

Map not drawn to scale.
Do not use for navigation.

113: Delnor Wiggins Pass State Park

(GPS: 26.273231, -81.827307) This park is located to the south of Wiggins Pass at the western end of Bluebill Avenue. The park is heavily used on the weekends, and even during the weekdays the park attracts plenty of visitors who take advantage of its quiet greenery. Florida State Park entrance fees apply. From Interstate 75, take exit #111 west on county road 846 (Immokalee Road / Bluebill Avenue), and drive west about six miles to the Gulf. The park is at the end of the road--you can't miss it. The paved entrance road follows the coast north for a mile or so with paved parking areas every few hundred yards, for a total of five separate parking areas. This park is heavily wooded with sea grapes, Australian pines, saw palmetto, cabbage palms, and a number of exotic species. Trails and boardwalks lead to the beach and to the well cared for restrooms and outdoor rinse-off showers.

Photo: Delnor Wiggins State Park beach, looking south toward Naples.

There is a vendor on site (at parking lot #4 as of June 2013) to sell food and drink and to offer beach gear rentals including chairs and umbrellas, canoes, kayaks and paddleboards.

Sea oats grow thickly above the beach on the low sand dunes. Tall Australian pines provide some shade for strategically placed wooden picnic tables and charcoal cooking grills, most of which are only a few steps from the beach. Across Wiggins Pass is Barefoot Beach Preserve, complementing the undeveloped character of the area. The condos near Bonita Beach stand out far to the north, and the condos of Vanderbilt Beach stand by the water's edge just south of the recreation area. Far to the south are the huge condos of Naples. This is a very scenic beach and is a great place to spend a day. On the north side of the northernmost parking area (#5) is a short trail leading to a lookout tower. The tower is just tall enough to clear the mangroves and allow a better look around. But it doesn't rise high enough above the trees to get more than a glimpse of the Gulf. This is a beautiful quiet beach with excellent facilities. You won't be disappointed. On busy days, the Park gates are closed when the park reaches maximum capacity.

Restrooms are wheelchair accessible and a beach wheelchair is available. If you need one, just tell the ranger at the guardhouse as you enter the park. Someone will meet you at either access #1 or #5 to assist you.

The park is open from 8 am to sunset and the usual state park rules apply: no pets on the beach, no alcoholic beverages, and no glass containers. No taking of live shells.

114: Vanderbilt Beach County Park

(GPS: 26.25382, -81.82321) If you turn south off of county highway 846 (Bluebill Ave) onto Gulf Shore Drive you will be in the Vanderbilt Beach area. This is condominium-land and you have to keep going south to get to the beach access at the county park. The park is located where Gulf Shore Drive makes a sharp turn to the east. If you turn right, toward the beach, there is a drop off area and several parking spaces designated for the disabled. To find parking you must turn east on 862 and drive about a block where there is metered parking along the north side of the street between Gulf Shore Ct., and Southbay Drive. There is also a large gated and partially covered public parking lot located on the south side of 862. This seems an unlikely place for a public beach access, and it would be easy to miss if you didn't know it was here. A boardwalk leads down to the beach. There are quite a few tall condos on the beach, but no public accesses nearby, so the beach is quiet once you get away from the public access point. If you are really ambitious, you could walk all the way south to Clam Pass, a distance of over 2 miles. This would take you to the Pelican Bay area which has a mostly undeveloped beach. Or you could walk north all the way to Wiggins Pass, about 2.5 miles away.

115: Clam Pass County Park and Boardwalk

(GPS: 26.21137, -81.81169) This beautiful and secluded beach park is located south of the Vanderbilt Beach area at the western end of Seagate Drive. From Interstate 75 exit #107, or from Highway 41, take county road 896 (Pine Ridge Road) west. Highway 896 is called Seagate Drive on the west side of highway 41. Follow it all the way to the park. The normal Collier County park entry fee is in effect. There is a pay station in the parking lot. The park is open from 8am till sunset. The Waldorf Astoria Naples is situated just north of the parking lot and operates the beach vending service. Many of the people on the beach are guests of the Waldorf.

On the northwest corner of the parking lot you will find the tram station. Since the beach is located a considerable distance from the parking lot, golf cart trams run continuously on the 3,000 foot long boardwalk between the parking lot and the beach. If you are carrying a lot of gear, have small children, or just don't feel like a 15-minute hike, take the tram. Quite a few people use the boardwalk as a jogging path, or just a place to go for a nice walk. It leads through a very dense and fairly tall mangrove forest. Some parts of the boardwalk are completely shaded by the mangroves, and on a hot summer day the temperature on the shaded parts of the boardwalk can feel 20 degrees cooler than the unshaded parts. When you are walking through a thick growth of mangroves like this, think about the Spanish conquistadores and the hell they must have endured to penetrate the endless miles of mangroves in their fruitless and barbaric quest for gold in Florida. To the tangle of mud and roots add the thick clouds of mosquitoes that plagued the coast in those days. The boardwalk doesn't seem so long now does it?

Photo: Clam Pass County Park, looking south toward Naples Park Shore area.

The tram ride ends at the concession building built on a raised deck, where you will find clean restrooms, water fountains, telephones, food, rentals of various types of beach equipment, and boardwalks down to the beach. The beach is white sand. A quarter mile walk to the north will take you to Clam Pass, a very narrow and shallow pass that links Outer Clam Bay with the Gulf of Mexico. This is a very scenic area. The beach on the south side of the pass is very wide with soft white sand. There are no buildings above the beach, just thick mangrove forest. The beach to the north of Clam Pass is undeveloped, but does have the beach facilities for the Pelican Bay community, which is private. Outer Clam Bay is bordered with thick green mangrove tangles, not seawalls and homes. There are, however, several tall condos about a mile or so to the east which reach high above the mangroves and can be seen from the beach. Clam Pass is a very natural and very popular place to visit. The beach to the south of the concession buildings stretches south for as far as you can see past the Park Shore beaches all the way to Doctor's Pass.

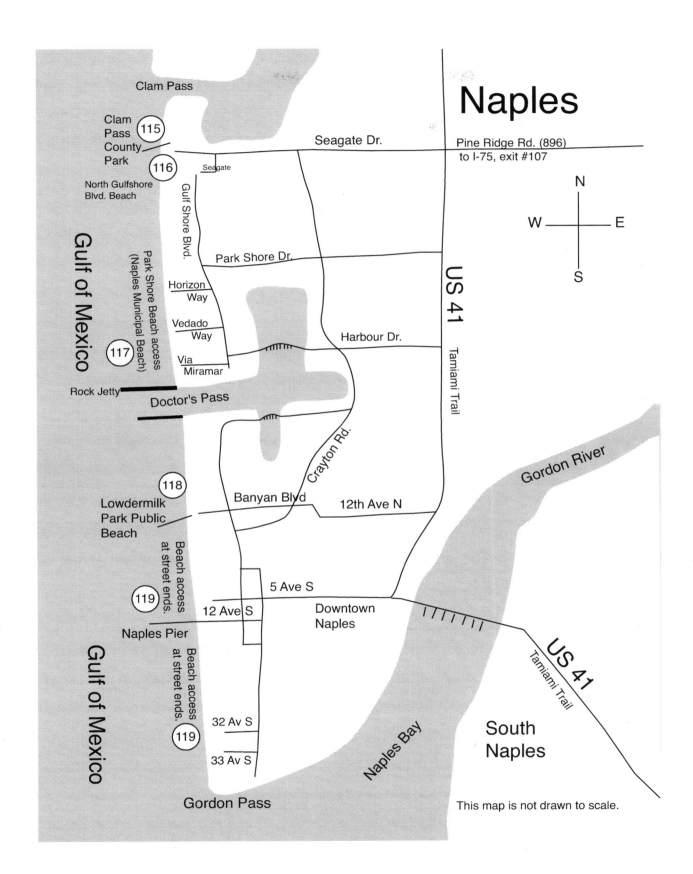

Naples

Clam Pass

Clam Pass County Park 115

116

North Gulfshore Blvd. Beach

Gulf of Mexico

Gulf Shore Blvd.

Seagate Dr.

Pine Ridge Rd. (896)
to I-75, exit #107

Seagate

N

W ———— E

S

Park Shore Dr.

Park Shore Beach access
(Naples Municipal Beach)

117

Horizon Way

Vedado Way

Via Miramar

Harbour Dr.

US 41

Tamiami Trail

Rock Jetty

Doctor's Pass

Crayton Rd.

118

Lowdermilk Park Public Beach

Banyan Blvd

12th Ave N

Gordon River

Beach access at street ends.

119

5 Ave S

12 Ave S

Naples Pier

Downtown Naples

Beach access at street ends.

Gulf of Mexico

119

32 Av S

33 Av S

Naples Bay

US 41

Tamiami Trail

South Naples

Gordon Pass

This map is not drawn to scale.

Clam Pass is the smallest inlet in the area covered by this book. Unless it has been recently dredged, the pass is normally shallow enough that you may be able to walk across it at low tide, during slack water. But be warned that when the tide starts to flow, the current moves very fast.

A kayak launch area is located at the west end of the parking area. It launches into Outer Clam Bay which gives direct access to Wiggins Pass, roughly a one mile paddle through a very sheltered backwater.

A beach wheelchair is available in the concession area. The park is open from 8 am until dusk. Pets and alcohol are not allowed on the beach. There is no picnic area at Clam Pass Park and you are not allowed to BBQ on the beach.

116: Gulfshore Boulevard Beach Access

(GPS: 26.207492, -81.814301) This has to be one of the most difficult to find beach accesses I know of. It's even hard to describe how to get to it. Located in a very upscale area, this beach access path is a luxuriously landscaped brick walkway between tall condominiums and is thickly landscaped with tropical foliage bursting with flowers. It ends at the beach with a small boardwalk depositing you gently on the sandy shore via a ramp. The walkway is located at the north end of Gulfshore Boulevard. There is a parking area across the street from the access on Gulfshore that appears to be used for beach parking. However, it is not marked as such and there is some question as to whether it is O.K. to park there. To get to the officially designated parking lot, you will need to approach via Seagate Drive. Go west on Seagate Drive (Pine Ridge Road) until you are at the entrance to Clam Pass County Park. Just after you pass the stop sign at Crayton Road, Seagate road actually turns south, parallel to Crayton Road, but the left turn is a bit hard to see. Follow Seagate through a very shady neighborhood about a half-mile or so. Seagate ends at the beach parking lot just past the Naples Cay condominium. The parking lot offers about 38 spaces with meters and is open from 8am till sunset. There are no restrooms or other facilities. From the parking lot, it is roughly an 800 foot walk to the beach over pavers. Though not marked as such, the path to the beach appears to be accessible to a wheelchair, including the ramp down to the beach.

There is something about Naples beaches that is so tranquil, and the quality of the light here is pleasing I think because of all the lush vegetation along the shore. Even though the shoreline is heavily dominated by condominiums it is still beautiful. The Gulf always seems so tranquil here, like a big lake. And the sunsets! Naples has some of the most beautiful sunsets I've ever seen. I remember staying on the beach in Naples with my family back in the mid 1970's for a week. My most vivid memory of that week is the sunsets that seemed to last forever. You won't find any crowds here since public parking is so limited.

117: Naples Municipal Beach (Park Shore area)

From US 41, turn west onto Park Shore Drive or Harbor Drive to get to these beaches. The condos along the Gulf in Park Shore (south of Clam Pass County Park) are quite tall and built very close to the water's edge. Although beach access is limited and tall condominiums line the beach, this is a very quiet, upscale area with a beautiful beach.

There are several street accesses to the beach off Gulf Shore Boulevard. Three streets, **Horizon Way**, **Vedado Way**, and **Via Miramar** each have attractively landscaped, paved, parking lots with easy access to the Gulf beach, open from 5 am to 11 pm. Parking fees are in effect and pay stations are provided. Via Miramar is the closest access to Doctor's Pass. Walking south along the beach from the Via Miramar access for about 20 minutes will take you to Doctor's Pass. There you will find a rock jetty extending into the Gulf along a narrow pass. Condominiums of various sizes dominate the shoreline here, and there are no restroom or concession facilities on the street accesses. Naples Municipal Beach continues on the south side of Doctor's Pass, but that section of beach can only be reached by walking north from Lowdermilk Park Public Beach.

Each of the street end accesses offers paid parking, a rinse-off shower and drinking fountain. The Horizon Way access has benches set up in a formation that would accommodate a small wedding ceremony. My personal preference is for the **Vedado Way** access because of the layout and the extra greenery and a bit of shade. No pets or alcohol.

118: Lowdermilk Park Public Beach

(GPS: 26.162446, -81.809985). From US 41 (also known as 9th Street N), turn west on Banyan Blvd (also known as 12th Avenue N). This extremely popular public beach is located at 1301 Gulf Shore Blvd North, at the intersection of Banyan Blvd (about 1 mile south of Doctor's Pass). This is a developed area right in the city of Naples and is the main public beach access for the area. The parking area is beautifully landscaped and carefully tended and there is a small pond surrounded by large tropical shade trees and picnic tables. Hourly parking fees are in effect from 5 am until dusk and pay stations are provided. The food concession, pavilion and the restroom facilities here are well maintained. Boardwalks lead to the beach, and there are shaded picnic tables with grills and a small children's playground. There is plenty of beautiful lush landscaping between the beach and the parking lot. It gets my vote for being one of the most attractive public beaches I've seen on the west coast of Florida.

The public beach offers 900 feet of beachfront covered with white or light golden colored sand. Condominiums line the shore both to the north and south of the public beach park. Lowdermilk Park is a first-class public beach in a beautiful setting. All facilities and dune walkovers are wheelchair accessible and beach wheelchairs are available at the concession.

Photo: Lowdermilk Park is the main beach facility near the town center.

119: Naples Municipal Beach (South of Lowdermilk Park)

My favorite area of Naples Beach begins south of Lowdermilk Park. The farther south you drive along Gulf Shore Blvd, the better the beach is, with my favorite part beginning south of the Naples Municipal Pier on 12th Avenue South. One of my favorite types of beach is the "neighborhood" beach, and that's what these beaches are. The neighborhood beach has heavily landscaped homes set back off the beach. It lacks the heavy crowds, and it has no tall condominiums or resorts. There is no highway close to the beach, so no traffic congestion (except a little by the pier), and there is no business district and no waterfront restaurants, just a quiet, peaceful, green neighborhood above a very relaxed beach. I love it. You will too.

In this area of Naples beach access is provided at the ends of streets intersecting Gulf Shore Blvd. The street ends have metered parking and short walkways to the beach, but no restrooms. Most have open-air rinse-off showers. Street parking begins at 8th Avenue North and is provided on nearly every street end for the next several miles (going south), all the way to 18th Avenue South.

Naples Municipal Pier is located at 12th Avenue South and offers public restrooms and rinse-off showers. The pier is a popular access point and the metered parking availability can be very tight. There are lots of young people and teens that frequent the pier beach, especially after dark. The pier has a bait shop and sells drinks and snacks. It's a very busy pier and is especially popular with sunset-watchers and people who come to fish. The view is outstanding.

Parking is generously allowed from 5 am until 11pm on most streets. The homes above the beach are very attractive and extremely lushly landscaped with coconut palms and other tropical foliage. The trees and foliage are so thick along the beach that when looking down the beach it appears wild and undeveloped even though there are actually homes here.

Photo: Naples beach near 33rd Avenue South.

Just past 18th Avenue South, Gulf Shore Blvd curves east and merges with Gordon Drive, which continues south along the coast. The most southern beach accesses in Naples are off Gordon Drive at 32nd and 33rd Avenue South. These streets also have metered parking, and are in a very quiet, upscale residential neighborhood with enormous homes, tall tropical trees and beautiful coconut palms. Like all the beaches in this area, once you park and get your gear out to the beach you can walk north or south as far as your legs will carry you. There aren't any restrooms, concession stands, or lifeguards at these street-end beach accesses.

Photo: The historic Naples Pier.

Photo: Marco Island, looking south from Tigertail Park.

Marco Island

Interstate 75 Exit: 101 (Collier Blvd / CR 951)

Nearest mainland city: Naples is the closest significant city, about 30 minutes north of Marco.

Major access roads: Collier Blvd.

Directions: Marco Island, located in Collier County about 30 minutes south of Naples, is the southernmost island on the southwest coast of Florida that has beaches accessible by car. Beyond Marco Island, to the south, are Cape Romano, the Ten Thousand Islands, Everglades National Park, and the Florida Keys. To get to Marco Island from Interstate 75, take Collier Blvd. exit #101 (County Road 951) and follow the signs to Marco. You will drive through an area where there is not yet much development, but more condos, shopping centers, and generic fast food restaurants are quickly being constructed. This is a beautiful part of the state, so come and enjoy it while you can, because it won't stay this way long.

Pets: Pets are not allowed on Marco's beaches.

Disabled Access: Both South Marco and Tigertail Park provide ADA access. Tigertail Park has a beach wheelchair available.

Hours: Marco Island beach parks are open from 8 am until dusk.

Restrooms: Public restrooms can be found at both South Marco beach and Tigertail Park.

Food and Drink: Tigertail Park has a food concession.

Alcohol: Alcoholic beverages are not allowed on the beach. Glass containers are not allowed on the beach.

Shelling: Marco Island beach is very good for shelling.

Camping: There are no beach camping facilities available on Marco Island.

Lifeguards: Collier County, Florida does not employ lifeguards at its beaches. So you will not encounter lifeguards on Marco Island. Conduct yourself accordingly.

Weddings: Marco Island is an excellent spot for a beach wedding. Excellent beach front resorts offer excellent wedding venues. Because of the wide variety of possibilities, contacting a local wedding vendor would be your best bet.

Marco Island is very overdeveloped. It was once covered with mangroves and Native American middens (mounds of discarded shells and other refuse); but most of the mangroves were bulldozed, finger canals were carved into the coast so everyone could have a boat dock, and the land was filled in so homes and condos could be built. So here it is, out almost in the middle of nowhere, a retirement/vacation paradise with all the comforts of any city. There is a lot of money on Marco; that's obvious. You won't see any run down areas or low rent districts. It's high class and modern construction all the way. Everything looks as if it were just built. The landscaping on Marco is absolutely gorgeous. Beautiful coconut palms are everywhere, along with a great variety of tropical trees and flowering plants. Even the condominiums have plenty of greenery. You really feel you are on a tropical island when you arrive on Marco. Going over the high Jolley Bridge to Marco you get a great bird's-eye view of the island. The tall buildings you see in the distance are not the downtown business district; they are the beachfront condominiums, of which Marco has too many. Marco Island is the opposite of Sanibel Island. Everything on Marco is overbuilt and exclusive.

If you are staying in one of the beach front resorts, beach access is no problem. But if you are exploring by car, you only have two beach choices on Marco: Tigertail County Park, or South Marco Beach. The best sand and water are on Sand Dollar Island at Tigertail County Park.

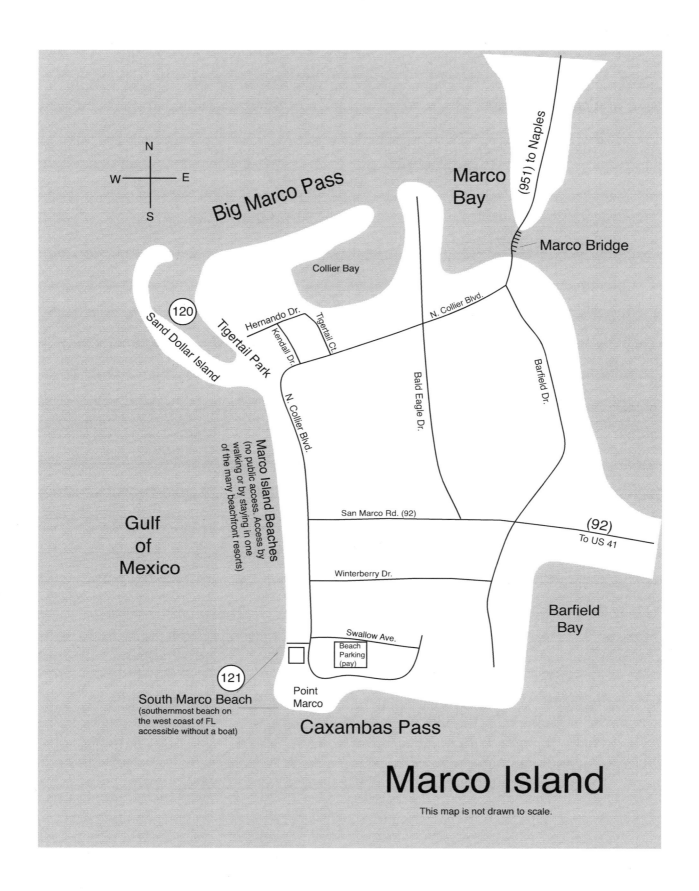

N
W   E
S

Big Marco Pass

Marco Bay

(951) to Naples

Marco Bridge

Collier Bay

120

Sand Dollar Island

Tigertail Park

Hernando Dr.

Tigertail Ct.

Kendall Dr.

N. Collier Blvd.

N. Collier Blvd.

Bald Eagle Dr.

Barfield Dr.

Gulf
of
Mexico

Marco Island Beaches
(no public access. Access by
walking or by staying in one
of the many beachfront resorts)

San Marco Rd. (92)

(92)
To US 41

Winterberry Dr.

Barfield Bay

Swallow Ave.

Beach Parking (pay)

121

Point Marco

South Marco Beach
(southernmost beach on
the west coast of FL
accessible without a boat)

Caxambas Pass

Marco Island

This map is not drawn to scale.

120: Tigertail Park

(GPS: 25.94930, -81.74270) After crossing the bridge onto Marco Island you will be on Collier Blvd. Follow Collier Blvd. to Kendall Road and turn right. A sign at Kendall Road directs you toward Tigertail Park. You will follow Kendall to Hernando Drive, then turn left on Hernando and it will lead you directly to Tigertail Park.

The Collier County park fee (currently $8.00) must be paid to enter the park. There are several parking lots, a concession/cafe with indoor and outdoor seating, restroom facilities, and beach equipment rentals (kayaks, water-bikes, covered beach chairs, etc.). Boardwalks take you from the parking areas to the beach. The park is open from 8am to dusk. There are no lifeguards on duty.

Photo: Sand Dollar Island is a long walk from the parking lot, but well worth the trip.

Tigertail Beach is the widest and most expansive beach on the lower Gulf coast of Florida. The designated public beach is nearly a half-mile long, although as with most beaches, there are no visible boundaries. If you are accustomed to visiting other beaches in this part of the state you will be amazed at how much beach there is here. As soon as you step off the boardwalk there is a wide, white, sandy beach. In front of the beach is a murky tidal lagoon several hundred feet across, then there is another wide beach before you finally reach the Gulf shore. The farther beach is called Sand Dollar Island and is partly roped off during spring and summer to protect nesting birds. One reaches the Gulf beach on Sand Dollar Island either by wading across the shallow lagoon or by walking around it. Sand Dollar Island is connected at its south end to Tigertail Beach. So you can walk to the Gulf Beach without crossing the lagoon. If you choose to walk around the lagoon, it's nearly half a mile to the Gulf Beach. If you cross the lagoon and walk across Sand Dollar island, it's about 1,400 feet to the Gulf Beach, or a bit more than half the distance required to walk around the lagoon. It is well worth the walk. Depending on the tides, Sand Dollar Island offers nearly three miles of completely undeveloped beach. This is one of the quietest beaches in central and southwest Florida.

251

Looking toward the south from the park, you have a sweeping view of all the condos on Marco, as well as of the continuous wide beach which runs the entire length of Marco Island. You can walk from one end of Marco to the other in about an hour or so at a brisk pace. At Tigertail Beach, and to the north, there are no condos or homes on the shore, only thick beach grasses and woods. As for the rest of the Marco shoreline, the only place where there are no condominiums is at the Resident's Beach, a private beach access only for Marco residents.

The Gulf waters here on Marco are shallow, calm, and clean. Marco Island is a long way from any significant source of pollution, and is adjacent to a very large expanse of mangrove forests and estuaries which act as natural pollution filters. Also, since the waters remain fairly shallow for a long way off shore, there is less wave activity here than on beaches further north. On the west coast of Florida there generally isn't much wave activity anyway, to which the frustrated surfers will attest. Since the water is relatively shallow, the really large boats stay far enough out not to pollute with their engine noise. The loudest sound out here is the sound of screeching birds guarding their nests in the sand. If you want the true castaway feeling, I would suggest coming here on a weekday when there are fewer people. Walk out to Sand Dollar Island and go for a long walk up the beach. Take your towel and something to drink, and perhaps a beach umbrella. Now you can really relax.

Tigertail Beach itself curves around the north end of Marco and gradually turns into mud flats and mangroves. Sand Dollar Island is just a stone's throw across the lagoon.

121: South Marco Beach (Point Marco)

Follow Collier Blvd to the south end of Marco near Caxambas Pass. Parking for this beach is located on Swallow Avenue, which is directly across from The Apollo Tides condominium and the Cape Marco condominium. Turn east on Swallow and you will find two parking lots, one for the residents of Marco (Sarazen Park), the other for visitors (South Marco Beach Parking). This pay-and-park lot (GPS: 25.91220, -81.72568) requires the payment of the standard Collier County park entry fee. The lot is paved, fenced, and landscaped and has restrooms that are handicap accessible. Follow the sidewalk to the beach. You have to cross the wide Collier Boulevard and walk down a path leading between two towering condos to get to the beach. (Beach GPS: 25.912512, -81.728631).

The beach is very wide, but is not the soft white quartz sand that you might expect. It is rather an odd mix of white sand and dredged-up shell, regularly groomed by the mechanical rake to keep it from packing hard. You'll want to wear shoes until you get down to the water's edge. The entire beach on this part of the island is dominated by condos, but the beach is wide enough to distance yourself from them. There are lots of nice shells on the beach and the sand is packed firm, which makes for easy walking. There are no public restrooms or changing facilities out on the beach.

The water here on Marco is excellent for swimming. The white sandy beach slopes very gently into the Gulf, creating a shallow swimming area that extends a considerable distance from shore. The large expanse of gleaming white sand you see in the distance at the north end of Marco is Tigertail Public Beach.

Photo: South Marco Beach, looking north. Note the patterns in the sand from the beach rake.

If you look to the south along the shore you will see a rock jetty extending into the Gulf at the southern end of Marco. This is the southernmost beach on the west coast of Florida. The Cape Marco condominiums are built at the southern tip of the island but are much too large and seem out-of-place, even for Marco. Some developers just don't have a sense of scale, except as it relates to their bank account. Indeed, such monstrosities also raise questions about local government oversight. Standing near the rock jetty will give you a great view of several large mangrove islands. One of them has a beach, but you need a boat or jet-ski to get to it. As you are standing here on the southern tip of Marco Island, realize that you are at the very edge of development on the lower west coast of Florida. From here south to the Keys there is little more than water, mangrove tangles, mosquitoes, and wild critters. If you are a fisherman with a boat, you're in heaven.

Beach Survival Tips

(Sharks, jellyfish, stingrays and other scary things)

Although this book focuses on the joys of going to the beach and exploring the islands, there are some things everyone should be aware of before stepping onto the sand or into the water. Some of the following things are only a minor threat to your comfort, while others pose a threat to your health or life. Being aware of them is the best way to avoid problems.

The safest beach to swim at is one with lifeguards on duty. Florida beaches have a uniform system of flags to warn you of any known dangers. These flags may be flown on the lifeguard tower or on some other beach structure. A green flag means "low hazard," and is flown when conditions are generally known to be safe for swimming. A yellow flag means "medium hazard," and to exercise caution, usually because the surf is up and there may be strong currents. A red flag means "high hazard" because of high surf or strong currents. Two red flags means the water is closed to the public. A purple flag means that dangerous marine animals have been seen in the water. This could mean jellyfish, stingrays, sharks, or something else.

It is not unusual to see more than one flag flying from the lifeguard tower. For instance, a yellow and a purple flag flying at the same time mean that you should exercise caution because of moderate surf and currents and because hazardous marine life has been seen in the area. If you see a purple flag, I always recommend asking the lifeguard why it is flying. Usually it is because of jellyfish.

Red Tide

Red tide is a condition found in the water that causes fish to die and pile up on the beach, and causes humans to experience respiratory irritation and discomfort. It comes and goes. Sometimes we don't have it for several years. Sometimes it tends to linger for months. It is usually somewhat localized, meaning there may be a bad outbreak in Sarasota, while the beaches of Fort Myers are completely unaffected. How does it affect you? Well, sometimes the dead fish can pile up pretty deep on the beach. I don't have to tell you how bad that stinks. Also there is something in the air that causes mild respiratory irritation or worse if you are particularly sensitive. If you have asthma or some other respiratory condition, stay away from the beach during red tide outbreaks. Don't take your pets onto any beach that has dead fish from a red tide kill.

Red tide is caused by a huge bloom of tiny, single celled algae called Karenia brevis. This algae bloom is made up of microscopic plant-like cells called dinoflagellates that produce potent chemical neurotoxins. These toxins kill fish, contaminate shellfish and create severe respiratory irritation to humans near affected waters. The water can take on a reddish tint, but it is very difficult to see it unless you are up in the air except when the concentration is extremely high. To find out if red tide might be affecting a beach you are planning to visit, go to www.myfwc.com and under the "Research" menu item, click on "Red Tide." Then choose the "Red Tide Current Status" link. If the web site has changed, just use your favorite search engine and search for "red tide current status."

Water Quality

Florida does monitor the health aspects of its coastal waters. On most beaches you'll see signs advertising Florida's Healthy Beaches water monitoring program. The coastal beach water samples collected by the county health departments are analyzed for enterococci and fecal coliform bacteria. High concentrations of these bacteria may indicate the presence of microorganisms that could cause disease, infections, or rashes. County health departments will issue health advisories or warnings when these conditions are confirmed. For reports on water testing near the beach you plan to visit, go to www.myflorida.com and click on "Floridian," then click on "Nature and Environment," then "Beach Water Quality."

On some beaches you'll see signs indicating that it is a "Blue Wave Beach." The organization that created this voluntary self-certification campaign has been defunct for many years. The signs mean nothing.

Strong Currents

There are several situations that cause strong water currents. First, high surf will cause strong currents. The breaking surf washes up on the beach and has to find its way back to the Gulf or Atlantic. This may cause what is known as a "rip" current, a fast moving stream of water moving from the shore out past the breakers. If you get caught in it, don't try to fight it, it won't take you to Mexico. Just swim out of it by swimming parallel to shore. Then let the waves carry you back in. I've been swimming and surfing on the Gulf coast all my life and I've never felt threatened, even though I've been knocked down and pulled off my feet numerous times in high surf.

High winds will also cause a strong current. This type of current is usually a longshore current and is very common, even in very small surf. It can carry you down the beach quite a distance before you realize you've drifted so far. It is more of a nuisance than anything else. You go in the water at point A and get out at point B and realize you don't recognize your beach towel anywhere.

A large volume of water moving through a narrow channel will also cause a very strong current. This happens daily in most of the passes. A pass is the narrow channel between islands where water flows between the bay and the Gulf. As you can imagine, the current is strongest when the tide is moving either in or out. I do not recommend swimming in or near any of the passes at any time.

Ninety-eight percent of the time there is no surf on the Gulf coast and strong currents usually only occur in or within a few hundred yards of the passes. If you swim in relatively calm waters on the Gulf beach it is highly unlikely you will ever encounter any strong currents.

Strong surf

Don't underestimate the power of the surf on either coast. If you are experienced with surf and are a strong swimmer that's one thing, but so many people come to Florida and swim in surf for the first time and are caught by surprise at the strength of the water. It is especially dangerous for small children. If you are not an experienced surfer, stay out of the surf so you can live to swim another day. The best way to learn how to handle surf is the way the locals do. You start out in very small waves, and gradually, over months or years, move up to larger waves as your experience grows, and you never go in alone.

Lightning

Every summer I find myself looking out toward the beach from the safety of my car, saying "are these people crazy?" while I watch people going about their normal activities as lightning strikes violently a short distance up the beach in a rapidly approaching storm. Every summer I read about some of them in the newspaper as victims of deadly lightning strikes. If you can see lightning striking, even in the distance, it's time to get off the beach, get off the fishing pier, beach your sailboat/kayak/fishing boat, and find shelter. Get into your car or into a building. Wait a while and the storm will pass. Florida is often referred to as the lightning capital of the world. During the summer months, from June through September, we normally have lightning daily. Often it is quite ferocious. You don't have to let it freak you out, just respect it.

Sting Rays

There are many types of rays in Florida waters. Most of them will cause you no harm. The sting ray can cause a painful wound. They lay on the sandy bottom partially covered with sand. Sometimes only their eyes are poking out of the sand. Sting rays have a sharp bony barb at the base of their tails. If you step on the animal, it reacts by whipping its tail at your foot or leg. The barb does have venom and it causes a very painful wound which can easily produce a nasty infection. The best way to avoid sting rays is to shuffle your feet when you are walking in the water. During some months the rays are particularly common and it is not unusual to see a dozen or more swimming away if you are the first person in the water. They are not terribly shy and will allow you to approach quite closely before fleeing. Yes, I have been speared by a sting ray. It was a very small one and it stuck me in the toe. I lived. Actually I am amazed that in all the years I spent surfing as a kid, paying no attention whatsoever to where I was stepping, I only got stuck once. Sting ray season is generally May through October.

If you are injured by a sting ray, wash the area with salt water. Remove any foreign material from the wound. Alert the lifeguard if there is one. Lifeguards know how to handle sting ray wounds. Soaking the wound in water as hot as the injured person can stand it for 30 - 90 minutes helps relieve the pain. Deep wounds from large sting rays and wounds to the abdomen or chest are very serious and the person should be taken to the hospital right away. Most injuries are to the feet and legs. If you are fishing and catch a sting ray, be very careful because even if it is out of the water it can stab you by flipping its tail violently. Never step on a stingray to remove a fishhook.

Public beaches have signs warning about the presence of sting rays in the water. But hotels and resorts may overlook their unwritten obligation to inform their guests of dangerous marine animals. So don't think that just because there are no warning signs, there are no stingrays. Shuffle those feet!

Sharks

Sharks: everyone's favorite fear. First you should know that there are LOTS of sharks in the Gulf of Mexico and in the bay waters. There always have been. In fact, there are so many sharks that if they really wanted to eat people, you would never be able to swim in the water. Sharks avoid people. I've watched large hammerhead sharks patrolling the beach in the morning. When they come upon a person swimming in the water, they make a large detour around the human. But sharks make mistakes. Sometimes the water is murky. Sometimes there are lots of fish around and the sharks are feeding recklessly. Sometimes people get chomped on. Usually the shark realizes its mistake and lets go with minor damage. But usually a few times a year, for some unknown reason, a large shark decides it wants an easy meal and attacks a person. I think it is aberrant behavior, but it does happen. The best ways to minimize your chances of being bitten by a shark are published all over:

- Never swim if you are bleeding (this includes menstrual blood).

- Don't swim very early in the morning or late in the evening. Definitely don't swim after dark.

- Don't swim in large schools of bait fish or mullet.

- If you are fishing while wading in the water, don't tie a stringer of fish to your waist. Duh!

- Don't jump off a pier, dock, seawall, or boat into dark murky water. In fact avoid swimming in dark murky water. If you jump on a shark, it may think it's being attacked and bite you. It happened in St. Petersburg not long ago. Man walks out on dock to go for daily swim in murky bay water. Man jumps in water, lands on big shark. Shark bites man once. Man dies. Shark escapes. A very sad story, but true.

- Don't wear shiny objects while swimming. This will avoid attracting Barracudas as well. WHAT! Barracudas? Yep. They might think your shiny gold watch is something to eat.

- Avoid swimming in or near passes. Passes have swift currents and deep water. Lots of fish move through the passes with the tides. Sharks know this. Hungry sharks come to the passes to eat. Get the picture?

- And of course, if you see sharks in the water, don't be paddling your surfboard out just to catch "one more wave, dude." Don't laugh, they do it.

- After writing all that cautionary stuff, I must say I've been swimming in the Gulf since I was a kid and I've never been bitten. In fact for several years as a teenager I spent a lot of time on a surfboard splashing around like a wounded seal before sunrise, long after sunset, in murky water, in the Atlantic Ocean and the Gulf of Mexico. So just follow common sense rules and there's a 99.9999999% chance you won't have any problem. Yes, I know, it's that .00000001% chance that you just can't get off your mind.

Sunburn and dehydration

This topic is probably the most important one to pay attention to. Sunburn and dehydration can quickly lead to heat exhaustion and/or heatstroke. Heatstroke can be fatal. If you've never been out on the beach in Florida in the spring and summer, I have to tell you, the heat is BLISTERING. If you do not have a fairly dark complexion, it only takes about 15 to 20 minutes to get a nasty sunburn. On the beach not only do you have the sun coming down from above, but you also have fierce reflection off the water and off the white sand all around you. It's like being in a reflector oven. Wear maximum sunscreen. Sorry, "baby oil" won't help you.

Most importantly, when you are out on the beach or on the water, carry lots of cool water and drink frequently. The water doesn't help you if it is sitting in the cooler. You have to drink it. Note: Beer is not water. Gatorade is good. Coconut water is my favorite. Also, take frequent breaks from the sun to go in the water and cool off. Take an umbrella, at least for the most intensely hot part of the day, between 11am and 3pm.

For all you snowbirds who think that since you are only going to be here for a week and don't have time for a proper tan, that you'll just get a good sunburn to prove you've had so much fun on the beach; Forget about it! For one thing it is very painful, increases your risk for skin cancer, and shows all the locals that you're just another foolish tourist. If you have very light skin you need to be using a sunscreen with a protection factor (SPF) of at least 45. Don't forget your children. Their tender skin burns much more easily and they also become dehydrated more quickly than adults. Make sure they drink a lot of water. A bad sunburn can ruin your vacation on the first day. It can take a week to get over it.

Insects

Bugs are not usually a problem at the beach because of the constant sea breeze. On very still days, some beaches can have bothersome insects, especially during the early morning hours and around sunset Mosquitoes are common on all but the most overdeveloped islands after dark. This is because most of the islands have wet mangrove forests and marshes that breed mosquitoes. During some months of the year, usually during the heat of summer, the no-see-um gnats (also called sand gnats) come out at night with a vengeance. You can barely see them, but they sure see you. And their bite really stings. It can happen on any beach if conditions are right, but I think it is more common on beaches that are not regularly raked. Sand gnats lay their eggs in the sand and I think the raking probably buries them too deep to hatch. That's my theory. Usually, if there is even a slight breeze, insects are not a problem. There is almost always a breeze on the beach because of the different rates at which land and water heat up or cool off. Rare are the times I've been bothered by insects at the beach.

Alcohol

Many beaches do not allow the consumption of alcoholic beverages because it makes some people get into fights, and because drunk swimmers tend to drown. Generally if alcohol is not allowed there will be signs stating this. If the warning signs do not prohibit alcohol, it's probably legal. They don't post signs that say "alcohol encouraged." I once spoke to a sheriff on the beach and asked him if alcohol was allowed on that beach (there were no signs). He said "yes, but we try not to advertise it." Regardless, glass containers of any kind (including beer and wine bottles) are not allowed on ANY beach.

Crime and personal safety

Overall, I have always felt very safe on all the islands and beaches. I think nothing of walking alone at midnight on most of the beaches. I would not recommend that women ever walk alone on the beaches after the sun goes down. Don't take this lightly. You may be in that "I'm on vacation in paradise" mood, but don't put yourself in a position here that you wouldn't put yourself in back home. Not everyone here is on vacation.

Most crime at the beach involves property theft and car break-ins. Never leave anything on your beach towel that would cause you to be terribly upset or inconvenienced if it were stolen. There are sneak thieves who watch and wait till someone goes for a walk or for a swim, then steal their valuables off their beach towel. It is very easy to do without being caught. Also, thieves know that tourists have valuable items like cameras, jewelry, cash, etc. in their car in some far off corner of the parking lot. Lock your valuables in the trunk.

Here's a tip: If you know you will be out on the beach until late at night, park your car near a lighted area. If those spots are all taken, remember to come back and move your car to a lighted area when most of the crowd has gone home, and before it gets late. Many public beaches are quite busy until late at night, so there are always people nearby. For example, Clearwater Beach, Manatee Public Beach, Lido Beach, and Siesta Beach, just to name a few.

Jellyfish

Just stay away from jellyfish, OK? Many are harmless, some give a mild skin irritation, and others can really ruin your vacation or send you to the hospital. Do not touch dead jellyfish lying on the beach. If you see them floating in the water, don't get near them. Some of them have stinging tentacles that trail many yards behind. If you are familiar with jellyfish and know how to identify them that's a different story, but the general rule is: Leave them alone. The very small clear ones you may see around you in the water are quite harmless, in my experience. Any that has tentacles and/or purple coloring I would keep my distance from. OceanCareSolutions.com makes a vinegar-based gel spray that works great on jellyfish stings. It will fit right in your beach bag so you can always have it with you in case you need it. It works great on mosquito bites too.

Falling Coconuts (I swear I'm NOT making this up!)

If you do a little research on the internet you will find various claims about how many people are killed each year by falling coconuts. While the accuracy of the numbers is debatable, it does happen too frequently. (Once is too often, don't you think?)

Here are the facts: Coconuts grow high up on the palm tree. Coconuts are very hard and quite heavy. Coconuts fall to the ground when they are ready. Coconuts do not announce when they are ready to fall. How do I know these things? Walk around under some coconut palms that are growing somewhere that the lawn maintenance people don't tend. You will see old coconuts lying around on the ground. They fell. Bonk! Don't be directly underneath coconuts.

Many hotels and other places that have deep pockets to be sued keep all the coconuts trimmed off the trees to avoid problems.

Sea Lice

I've been swimming in Florida waters for decades and had never encountered sea lice until I swam in the Atlantic at Miami Beach one May. I only swam for about half-an-hour, but I remember feeling a biting or stinging feeling later and seeing red bumps where my bathing suit was. A friend who had been swimming with me felt the same thing. The next day, while walking on the boardwalk, I saw a sign on a lifeguard tower warning of sea lice in the water.

I searched around on the internet and found out more about sea lice, which scientists think are jellyfish larvae. It seems they like to hide in your bathing suit. Your suit rubs them the wrong way which makes them angry so they sting you. After a few hours you start to feel the irritation, which may last for several days or more. Hydrocortisone cream and Calamine lotion help relieve the itching, and some sources suggest that wearing a smaller bathing suit helps, since the organisms don't have as much fabric to hide in. Hey, now there's an argument in support of nude beaches! Beaches that have occasional sea lice problems often post warning signs on days when they are present. Sea lice mainly affect the lower Atlantic coast, not the Gulf coast (however they can occur on the Gulf coast). Minimize problems with sea lice by not wearing a t-shirt in the water. Ladies should wear a 2 piece suit. Bathing suits should be removed soon after leaving the water and you should rinse with fresh water as soon as possible. Don't shower while wearing your "contaminated" suit as this will cause more stings. I recommend applying vinegar as soon as you notice any stinging feeling. I would try the jellyfish sting relief spray from www.OceanCareSolutions.com .

After removing a contaminated swim suit, it must be washed in hot soapy water and dried, preferably in a hot dryer, before wearing it again. Personally, I'd throw in a bit of chlorine bleach as well. Use the same treatment for any towels you used to dry yourself off.

For more information on being safe at the beach, download my **Beach Survival Guide** which is available free in pdf file format on my websites, BeachHunter.net and BlogTheBeach.com .

Quick Reference Guide

If you are searching for a particular type of beach and don't have the time or patience to wade through the whole book right now, I've compiled this list of beaches to make your search easier. I've classified the beaches into groups ranging from "very remote" to "resort beaches." Some beaches don't clearly fall into one category or the other, so be sure to read the description in the book before you make a decision. This list does not include every beach listed in the book, but includes the main beach accesses that fit fairly easily into a category. Here's the list:

Very Quiet Beaches

These beaches have no homes or buildings above the beach. The land above the dunes is mostly forested with Australian pines, mangroves, palmettos, and native or exotic vegetation. The following locations have beaches that fall into the "very quiet" category, though this does not mean that you will have the beach to yourself, especially on weekends and holidays:

- Anclote Key State Park (Dunedin)

- Honeymoon Island (Dunedin)

- Caladesi Island (Dunedin)

- Shell Key Preserve (St. Petersburg)

- Fort Desoto Park (St. Petersburg)

- Egmont Key (St. Petersburg)

- Palmer Point Park (Siesta Key)

- Caspersen Beach Park (Venice)

- Stump Pass State Park (Manasota Key)

- Palm Island group (Placida)

- Cayo Costa Island State Park (La Costa Island)

- Bowman's Beach (Sanibel Island)

- Lover's Key State Recreation Area (Lover's Key, Ft. Myers Beach)

- Big Hickory Island (Bonita Beach)

- Barefoot Beach Preserve (Bonita Beach)

- Tigertail Public Beach (Marco Island)

Quiet Beaches

These beaches have a few widely spaced homes or buildings on or near the beach. There are generally lots of trees and plenty of vegetation above the beach. Although they are not usually crowded, there are usually people walking the beach who come from nearby public beaches that may have crowds. The following beaches fall into the "quiet" category:

- North Clearwater Beach

- Beer Can Island (Longboat Key)

- North Lido Beach (Lido Key)

- South Lido Park (Lido Key)

- Service Club Park (Venice)

- Venice Fishing Pier (Venice)

- Blind Pass Beach (Manasota Key)

- Lighthouse Beach Park at Boca Grande (Gasparilla Island)

- Lighthouse Park at Sanibel (Sanibel Island)

- Algiers Beach/Gulfside City Park (Sanibel Island)

- Tarpon Bay Road Access (Sanibel Island)

- Turner's Beach (Captiva Island)

- Blind Pass Beach (Sanibel Island)

- Delnor Wiggins Pass State Park (Naples)

- Clam Pass County Park (Naples)

Residential Beaches

These beaches are located in mostly residential areas. The local people use these beaches frequently, so you will find walkers, joggers, bike riders, surfers, fishermen, sunbathers, kids, teenagers, etc. Of course some of the residences are available for rent, so there are some visitors on the beach too. These beaches are rarely crowded. Residential beaches often present a parking problem because parking is on the streets that dead-end at the beach. Some neighborhoods make their streets available for parking, others do not. Most street-ends that end at the beach will have a beach access trail. The following beaches fall into the "residential" category:

- Indian Rocks Beaches (St. Petersburg)

- Anna Maria Beach (Anna Maria Island)

- Holmes Beach (Anna Maria Island)

- Bayfront Park (Anna Maria Island)

- North Shell Road Access (Siesta Key)

- Siesta Accesses north of the public beach (Siesta Key)

- Point of Rocks (Siesta Key)

- Casey Key (all beaches are residential except for Nokomis Beach)

- Manasota Beach Park (Manasota Key)

- Boca Grande Beach Accesses (Gasparilla Island)

- Sanibel Street Accesses [(Parking Permit required) Sanibel Island]

- Bonita Beach Accesses (Bonita Beach)

- Naples beaches south of Lowdermilk Park (Naples)

Congested / Public / Developed

These beaches are subject to dense crowds. They generally have food concessions, playgrounds, picnic tables, restroom and changing facilities, outdoor showers, and they have parking lots that may fill up early on holidays and weekends and that may charge an hourly or daily fee. Many public beaches have lifeguards during certain hours. The following beaches fall into the "congested" category:

- Clearwater Beach (Clearwater)

- Sand Key Park (Sand Key)

- Archibald Memorial Beach Park (Madeira Beach)

- St. Pete Municipal Beach at Treasure Island (112th Ave)

- Treasure Island Beach Access (104th Ave)

- Treasure Island Beach Center (Sunset Beach, Treasure Island)

- Upham Beach (St. Pete Beach)

- St. Pete Municipal Beach (St. Pete Beach)

- Pass-A-Grille Beach (St. Pete Beach)

- Manatee County Public Beach (Anna Maria Island)

- Cortez Beach (Anna Maria Island)

- Coquina Beach (Anna Maria Island)

- Lido Public Beach (Lido Key, Sarasota)

- Siesta Key Public Beach (Siesta Key, Sarasota)

- Nokomis Beach/North Jetty Park (Casey Key, Sarasota/Nokomis)

- Venice Municipal Beach (Venice)

- Englewood Beach / Chadwick Park (Manasota Key, Englewood)

- Sanibel Causeway Beaches (Sanibel Island Causeway)

- Ft. Myers Beach (Ft. Myers / Estero Island)

- Bonita Beach Park (Bonita Beach)

- Lowdermilk Park (Naples)

Resort / Condominium Areas

These beaches have a landscape heavily dominated by beachfront resorts and condominiums. While many beachgoers don't like the condo landscape and the parking hassles, there are certain positive attributes to these beaches: They are usually very clean and are located in very upscale areas. They typically lack public restrooms (it is assumed that you have a bathroom in your hotel/resort/condo). Also they do not generally have lifeguards, water, or food vendors. Some of the resorts offer a "grille" type restaurant on the beach that is open to the public. Oh, and one more thing is usually missing—crowds. You can count on finding either towering condominiums or some type of resort at the following beaches:

- Tiki Gardens Accesses (Indian Shores)

- Redington Shores Accesses

- North Redington Beach Accesses

- Madeira Beaches

- Treasure Island Beaches

- Upham Beach (St. Pete Beach)

- 51st Ave Access (St. Pete Beach)

- Longboat Key beaches (except for Beer Can Island) (Sarasota/Manatee)

- Crescent Beach (Siesta Key, Sarasota)

- Vanderbilt Beach (Naples)

- Naples Municipal Beach in the Park Shore area

- South Marco Beach (Marco Island)

Dog Beaches

- Honeymoon Island

- North Clearwater Beach

- Fort Desoto County Park

- Paws Park, Brohard Park, Venice

- Little Gasparilla Island and Don Pedro Island (outside the state park).

- Gasparilla Island (outside the state park)

- Sanibel Island

- Bonita Beach Dog Park, Lover's Key

- Fort Myers Beach

The Author & the Book

I was born and raised on the Florida Gulf Coast, in Bradenton. The beach has always been a part of my life. I've always lived within a 30 minute drive of the beach, and currently live in Saint Petersburg, Florida. I am frequently referred to as "Beachhunter" after the name of one of my web sites.

I first published this book in 2005, but much has changed since then. From 2007 through 2009 I had the opportunity to work with Miles Media to provide multimedia content for VisitFlorida.com. I explored the beaches all over Florida, wrote articles, took photographs, helped produce videos, and answered questions on the VisitFlorida.com web site about Florida beaches.

Since publishing the first edition of this book in 2005, I've met and learned from many people, from fellow writers to park rangers, biologists, sea turtle volunteers, shorebird stewards, professional birders, real estate developers, surfers, photographers, shelling enthusiasts, sea beaners, beachcombers and so many more. Through my contacts, I've been to many places that I did not have access to when I first started writing and have included a lot of new information in this edition.

You can find me on the web at:

- BlogTheBeach.com
- Beachhunter.net
- Facebook.com/FloridaBeachhunter
- Twitter.com/Beachhunter
- YouTube.com/FloridaBeachHunter

Works Cited

Clayton. (2012). *How to Read a Florida Gulf Coast Beach*. Chapel Hill: University of North Carolina Press.

Goff, B. (2012, September 25). *Redington Long Pier Celebrates Milestone*. Retrieved from tbnweekly.com:
http://www.tbnweekly.com/pubs/beach_beacon/content_articles/092512_bhb-01.txt

Hurley, F. T. (1989). *Surf, Sand, & Post Card Sunsets: A History of Pass-A-Grille and the Gulf Beaches*. Frank T. Hurley, Jr.

LighthouseFriends.com. (n.d.). Retrieved from LighthouseFriends.com:
http://www.lighthousefriends.com/light.asp?ID=368

Merry Pier web site. (n.d.). Retrieved from Merry Pier web site: merrypier.com

Norwood, C. (2004). *The Early Days 1893 - 1940*. Anna Maria, Florida: Anna Maria Island Historical Society.

INDEX

ADA Access, 16

Alcohol, 259

Algiers Beach, 211

Anclote Key, 27

Anna Maria City Pier, 122

Anna Maria Island, 118, 264, 265

Archibald Memorial Beach Park, 265

Banyan Street, Boca Grande, 194

Barefoot Beach, 234, 263

Barefoot Beach Preserve, 235

Beach Camping, 10, 202

Bean Point, 118, 121

Beer Can Island (Greer Island Park), 132, 263, 267

Belleair Beach, 62

Belleair Shore, 62

Best beaches, 8

Big Hickory Island Preserve, 227

Birding, 10

Blind Pass Beach (Manasota), 177, 263

Blind Pass Beach (Sanibel), 214, 264

Boca Grande, 191, 263, 264

Boca Grande Village, 194

Bonita Beach, 231, 263, 265, 266

Bonita Beach Dog Park, 227

Bonita Beach Park, 234

Bonita Beach Road, 231

Bonita Springs, 231

Bowditch Point Park, 221

Bowman's Beach, 212

Bradenton, 117, 130

Bradenton Beach, 118

Bugs, 259

Bunche Beach, 229

Burnt Store Road, 200

Caladesi Island, 9, 10, 44, 262

Camping, 10, 202

Cape Haze, 182, 191

Captiva Island, 206, 215, 264

Casey Key, 155, 156, 264, 266

Caspersen Beach Park, 8, 168, 262

Caxambas Pass, 252

Cayo Costa Island State Park, 10, 200, 262

Chadwick Park/Englewood Beach, 178, 266

Clam Pass County Park, 241, 264

Clearwater, 10, 48, 56, 263, 265

Clearwater Beach, 10, 48, 263, 265

Clearwater Beach Pier 60, 48, 51

Clearwater Marine Aquarium, 55

Coconuts, 260

Coquina Beach, 127, 265

Cortez Beach, 125, 265

Cortez Road, 117

Crescent Beach, 9, 151, 267

Crescent Beach Ft. Myers, 221

Crime and Personal Safety, 259

Daniel's Parkway, 206, 217

Delnor Wiggins Pass State Park, 237, 264

Ding Darling National Wildlife Refuge, 208

Dog beach, 105, 227

Dog beach list, 267

Dolphins, 21

Don Pedro Island, 186

Don Pedro Island State Park, 181

Drum circle, 89

Dunedin, 9, 39, 44, 262

Egmont Key, 110, 262

Englewood, 172, 262, 266

Englewood Beach, 178, 266

Englewood Road, 172

Erosion, 18

Estero Island, 217, 266

Fort Desoto County Park, 8, 10, 103, 262

Fort Myers Beach, 10, 217, 263, 266

Fred Howard Park, 32

Gasparilla Island, 191, 263, 264

Gay beach, 92, 141, 171

Great Calusa Blueway, 229

Gulfshore Boulevard (Naples), 244

Gulfside City Park, 211, 263

Holmes Beach, 118

Honeymoon Island, 9, 10, 39, 262

Hurricane Restaurant, 96

Hurricane season, 6

Indian Rocks Beach, 8, 64, 264

Indian Shores, 68, 266

Insects, 259

Jacaranda Blvd, 161, 172

Jellyfish, 260

Knight Island, 184

La Costa Island, 200, 262

Largo, 56, 61, 63

Leffis Key, 128

Lely Barefoot Beach, 234, 263

Lido Beach, 138, 263, 266

Lighthouse, 28, 210, 263

Lightning, 256

Little Gasparilla Island, 189

Little Hickory Island, 231, 263, 265, 266

Little Hickory Island Beach, 232

Longboat Key, 130, 131, 263, 267

Longboat Pass, 128, 134

Lover's Key, 225

Lover's Key State Park, 227

Lowdermilk Park, 245

Lowdermilk Park Public Beach, 245, 265, 266

Lynn Hall Memorial Park, 220

Madeira Beach, 78, 265, 266

Manasota Key, 172, 262, 263, 264, 266

Manatee Avenue, 117

Manatee County Public Beach, 265

Manatees, 21

Mandalay Park, 53

Marco Island, 8, 10, 248, 263, 267

Matanzas Bridge (Estero Island), 217, 221

Midnight Pass, 154

Mosquitoes, 259

Naples Beaches, 8, 10, 237, 246, 264, 265, 266, 267

Naples Pier, 246

Newton Park, 225

Nokomis, 155, 158, 264, 266

Nokomis Beach, 155, 158, 264, 266

North Gulfshore Boulevard, 244

North Jetty Park, 155, 159, 266

North Redington Beach, 75, 266

Nude Beaches, 10

Palm Harbor, 39, 44

Palm Island, 182, 184

Palm Island Resort, 184

Palma Sola Causeway Beaches, 124

Park Shore Beaches (Naples), 237, 245, 267

Passage Key, 119

Pass-A-Grille Beaches, 8, 96, 97, 265

Pier 60, 51

Pine Island Road, 200

Point Marco, 252

Red Coconut RV Resort, 220

Red Tide, 254

Redington Beach, 77

Redington Long Pier, 73

Redington Shores, 71, 266

Rip currents, 255

Sand flies (gnats), 259
Sand Key, 57, 265
Sand Key Park, 56, 57, 265
Sand, black, 4
Sand, brown, 4
Sanibel Island, 8, 9, 10, 162, 206, 263, 264, 265, 266
Sarasota, 8, 130, 138, 144, 155, 266, 267
Sea lice, 261
Sea turtles, 21
Seminole, 68, 71, 75, 77, 78
Service Club Park, 165, 166, 263
Shark's teeth, 9
Sharks, 9, 257
Sharky's Restaurant, 166
Shell Key Preserve, 100, 262
Shells, 9
Shore birds, 22
Siesta Key, 8, 9, 10, 144, 262, 264, 266, 267
Snorkeling, 9
South Jetty (Venice), 164
South Marco Beach, 252, 267
St. Pete Beach, 93, 94, 96, 265, 267
Sting ray, 256
Stump Pass Beach State Park, 180, 262
Summerlin Road, 206, 217
Sunburn, 258
Suncoast Seabird Sanctuary, 70
Sunset Beach, 90, 265

Sunset Beach Park, 35
Sunshine Skyway Bridge, 112
Surf Hazards, 256
Surfer's Guide to Florida, 13
Surfing, 13

Tarpon Bay Road, 211, 263
Temperature, Air, 5
Temperature, Water, 5
Ten Thousand Islands, 248
Thornton Key, 184, 186
Three Rooker Island, 43
Tigertail Park Beach, 8, 251, 263
Tom and Kitty Stuart Park, 80
Treasure Island, 83, 84, 87, 88, 90, 265, 266
Turtle Beach, 152, 153

Upham Beach, 94, 265, 267

Vanderbilt Beach, 237, 267
Vanderbilt Beach County Park, 241
Venice, 8, 9, 161, 162, 172, 262, 263, 266
Venice Avenue, 161
Venice Fishing Pier, 9, 165, 263
Venice Inlet, 159

Water quality, 255
Weather, 5
Whitney Beach, 132
Wiggins Pass, 236, 240

To order additional copies of this book, please visit me on the web at www.BeachHunter.net or www.blogthebeach.com

Or

Send an email to beachhunter@beachhunter.net

Made in the USA
Columbia, SC
11 April 2018